# A reader in library management

# A reader in library management

edited by

## ROSS SHIMMON

*and with linking commentaries by*

## JOHN ALLRED, K H JONES, PETER JORDAN

CLIVE BINGLEY      **&**      LINNET BOOKS
LONDON                          HAMDEN · CONN

FIRST PUBLISHED 1976 BY CLIVE BINGLEY LTD
16 PEMBRIDGE ROAD  LONDON W11
SIMULTANEOUSLY PUBLISHED IN THE USA BY
LINNET BOOKS AN IMPRINT OF THE SHOE STRING PRESS INC
995 SHERMAN AVENUE  HAMDEN  CONNECTICUT 06514
SET IN 10 ON 12 POINT PRESS ROMAN AND
PRINTED AND BOUND IN THE UK
BY REDWOOD BURN LTD  TROWBRIDGE AND ESHER

BINGLEY ISBN: 0-85157-194-8
LINNET ISBN: 0-208-01378-4

Library of Congress Cataloging in Publication Data
Main entry under title:

A Reader in library management.

    Bibliography:  p.
    1.  Library administration—Addresses, essays,
lectures.  I.  Shimmon, Ross.  II.  Title.
Z678.R4  1976      025.1      76-10382
ISBN 0-208-01378-4

# Contents

5

# Acknowledgements

The following acknowledgements are due for permission to reprint the articles contained in this volume.

'The need for administrative know-how in libraries' by Beatrice V Simon first appeared in the *Bulletin of the Medical Library Association* 57 (2) April 1969.

'All very well in practice! But how does it work out in theory?' by Paul V Gordon is reprinted by permission of the author from the March 1968 issue of the *Wilson library bulletin*, copyright © 1968 by the H W Wilson Company.

'Creative library management' by K H Jones first appeared in *The assistant librarian* 66 (10) and 66 (11) October and November 1973, and is reprinted by permission of the editor.

'The development of library services: the basis of their planning and assessment' by P H Sewell first appeared in the *Journal of librarianship* 2 (1) January 1970, and is reprinted by permission of the Library Association.

'Goal determination' by John R Haak is reprinted by permission of the author from *Library journal* May 1 1971, published by R R Bowker Co (a Xerox company), copyright © 1971 by Xerox Corporation.

'A systems concept of organization and control of large university libraries' by G C Burgis first appeared in *Canadian library journal* Jan-Feb 1971, and is reprinted by permission of the Canadian Library Association.

'The administration of diffuse collections' by Wilfred Ashworth first appeared in *Aslib proceedings* 24 (5) May 1972, and is reprinted by permission of Aslib.

'Staff management and staff participation' by B G Dutton first appeared in *Aslib proceedings* 25 (3) March 1973, and is reprinted by permission of Aslib.

'Factors affecting librarians' job satisfaction' by Kenneth H Plate and Elizabeth W Stone first appeared in *Library quarterly* 44 (2) April 1974, and is reprinted by permission of the authors and the University of Chicago Press.

'Review of criteria used to measure library effectiveness' by Edward Evans, Harold Borko and Patricia Ferguson first appeared in the *Bulletin of the Medical Library Association* 60 (1) January 1972.

'Management techniques applied to the operation of information services' by D Mason first appeared in *Aslib proceedings* 25 (11) November 1973, and is reprinted by permission of Aslib.

'Bibliotheconomics: or library science revisited' by A Graham Mackenzie first appeared in *An leabharlann* 28 (3) September 1970, and is reprinted by permission of the author and the Library Association of Ireland.

# Introduction

It is strange, is it not, that although many people now seem to accept that every kind of organisation — multi-national conglomerates, nationalised industries, charities, hospitals etc — all have to be 'managed' and, therefore, need staff with management expertise, so many people concerned with libraries deny, or accord low priority, to the study of library management?

Of course, some people tend to be attracted to librarianship as a career by the desire to work in a bookish environment or by the ideal of serving other people; more rarely by an interest in managing a library or an information centre. Yet it is a truism to say that libraries and their parent bodies increasingly are complex and expensive organisations (both in terms of 'straight' finance and in their use of human and physical resources). If they are to be managed efficiently on behalf of the parent body (and the taxpayer) and effectively for the benefit of the user-community, then some understanding of current concepts, as well as considerable skills, are required by those responsible.

Management is no longer, even if it ever was, something that is practised only by senior staff. Many young librarians manage considerable human and financial resources at relatively early stages in their careers, and need a sound educational base from which to develop their managerial skills. In any case, they are themselves being managed, more or less effectively, and it is as well for them to know something of current thinking if only in their own self-interest!

While attempting to teach in the field of library management at the College of Librarianship Wales, I became acutely aware of the inadequacy of the range of appropriate learning materials in this area, compared to, say, bibliography. One of a number of items which would have proved very useful was a library management reader. It became apparent at a meeting of the Association of British Library and Information Studies Schools (ABLISS), held at Brighton Polytechnic Library School in the spring of 1974, that the need for such a reader had also been identified by a number of lecturers at other schools. One of the outcomes of that meeting was that I was asked to prepare this reader for publication.

The purpose is to present, in an accessible and convenient form, a group of articles which have been found to be of more than average usefulness by several lecturers concerned with courses in library management. The number of monographs in this field is surprisingly small compared with the other 'core' areas in librarianship curricula – bibliography and information storage and retrieval. However, there are a few, and it is the intention behind the present volume to complement, rather than to compete with: Paul Wasserman and Mary Lee Bundy: *Reader in library administration* (Washington: Microcard Editions 1968), the *Studies in library management* series edited by Brian Redfern (volume 1) and Gileon Holroyd (volume 2) (Bingley, 1972 and 1974; Hamden, Conn, Archon); and, of course, in the field of stock provision A W McClellan's *The reader, the library and the book* (Bingley, 1974; Hamden, Conn, Archon). This may help to explain the otherwise apparent idiosyncrasies in the choice of articles, which is also partly accounted for by the relative scarcity of good articles in certain specific areas; surprisingly, for example, in the area of objectives. A further consideration was the availability, in other form, of suitable materials (eg, Thomas and V A Ward (eds): *The corporate approach to library management* (Aslib, 1974) ).

A further constraint which must be mentioned is the willingness or otherwise, of a copyright holder to allow a reprint at a reasonable fee: One question that may well arise is why have I not selected items from outside the narrow scope of the literature of librarianship? There are a number of reasons for this:

1 Many seminal management texts are in monograph form already – eg A Etzioni, *Modern organizations* (Englewood Cliffs, NJ: Prentice Hall, 1964) and D McGregor, *The human side of enterprise* (McGraw-Hill, 1960) – and it was felt preferable to refer students to the original rather than to derivative articles.

2 Librarianship students, in my experience at least, tend, perhaps unfortunately, to be resistant to material which derives directly from industrial and commercial contexts.

3 The final selection, chosen from a large number of candidates in both the librarianship and the management literature, comes nearest, I think, to achieving the objectives set by the ABLISS meeting.

This reader is primarily intended for students of library management; the problem is that it is currently studied in a wide variety of situations and at a number of different levels in the English-speaking world. Periodical articles are, in any case, not usually written with students in mind, and the present selection exhibits a number of different levels of treatment. The North American origin of many of the articles may well be questioned. Increasingly, library management, like many other studies, is becoming international, both in the nature of the problems confronted and in the solutions attempted, despite the differences in social cultural and administrative contexts. Perhaps even more significant is the fact that whilst the output of American articles on library management issues is so great, many areas have not been adequately treated in British journals.

The commentaries which preface each section have a number of important purposes: (a) to offer the reader a 'map' of the subject, which will both locate the different contributions within the field and indicate the extent of that field; (b) to indicate areas of controversy, and the need for the reader to adopt a constructively critical stance in the face of a prescriptive literature in which doubt is so rare; (c) to make links with management studies in other fields where especially appropriate; (d) to indicate select additional readings, shown in parentheses and cited in full in the bibliography on page 210.

It is hoped that this volume will go some way in achieving the objectives set for it and also prove of some use to practising librarians confronting management problems.

# 1
# Why
# library management?

We will leave the writers of the three papers which follow to answer the above question. Our concern in this commentary is to assist the reader to identify the animal, since the twelve papers do in themselves offer only a shadowy delineation. They are confined to the core of library management—its theory and methodology—comprising the process of establishing aims and objectives, planning, organising, controlling and evaluating, together with personnel management.

The older kinds of library administration programmes in first professional courses at librarianship schools distinguish between this management theory on the one hand and, on the other, a large body of descriptive material (sound current practice) relating to such subjects as library services, staff establishments, buildings, budgets and estimates, and so on. However, a curriculum development is under way in the schools in which this descriptive material is being systematised and reshaped by management theory, thus creating a more homogeneous body of professional knowledge. In time understanding and explanation should replace pure description, which, being a static concept, implied a conservative approach to librarianship. It is hoped also that librarians will gain sufficient understanding of libraries through education and experience to recognise that a good deal of industrial management literature, rooted in concepts like profit, competition and production, cannot be translated into library terms without careful thought.

In the same way that a dichotomy has been emphasised between theory and practice, so many writers distinguish between management and administration, frequently employing different terminology. Beatrice Simon, in our first reading, refers to 'administration' and 'operating' whilst Green (1964) makes similar observations substituting 'management' for 'administration' and 'administration' for 'operating'. Whilst the observations are worth making, good management, particularly where innovation is given high priority, needs to emphasise the relationship between management and administration as much as the difference.

Space has limited the selections in this reader to the core of management theory, but it is important to remember that library management is in fact concerned with the purposive *managing* of all areas of library provision and service, in contrast to *running* a library in accordance with time-honoured and unexamined procedures. It is with the management of specific services and sub-systems that the junior and middle manager is most concerned, yet, apart from important beginnings in the management of library materials, there is very little literature which attempts to apply management theory to the management of, say, a public library reference and information service or an academic library student instruction programme (Hunter, 1974). A breed of library managers has emerged, but their achievements are limited by the absence of enough middle and junior grade librarians-who-manage.

Following the example of some of the schools of librarianship, we may stake out the concerns of library management as follows:

1  Information about the community served by the library; library and information needs; means of discovering these.

2  Parent bodies of libraries (such as local authority, university, private company), and the government and finance of libraries. The corporate management of libraries. Relations with central government.

3  The library as a system. Systems theory. Purpose and planning of library services. Framing library objectives and their implementation. The management cycle completed: feedback, control, evaluation.

4  Organisation theory. The organisation of libraries. Principles of organisational division and structuring.

5  Staff. The claims of behavioural science. Patterns of staff deployment. The cycle of manpower planning, recruitment, appraisal, development.

6  Management systems and techniques (including financial management) and mechanisation of library operations.

7  The management of library materials and their accessibility.

8  The management of the different library services, eg circulation systems, information systems.

9  Library accommodation and equipment: planning, design, selection.

10  Access to wider resources, eg cooperative schemes, and use of central agencies.

Many of the above topics have other (and more important) dimensions than that of management; nevertheless, the management dimension *is* pervasive. The development and operation of information retrieval systems, for example, has to be managed, if only because they operate within a managed environment.

The reader is invited to construct an alternative taxonomy to that offered above. As always, it is the *relationship* between 'things' that defines our understanding, as much as a knowledge of the different topics themselves.

Part of the rationale behind the above model is that it provides a progressive learning sequence, with earlier subjects supporting those introduced later in the list. It could however, be rearranged to illustrate the systems approach on which it is founded. This is to say, the library manager

15

assesses the restraints, the resources, and other opportunities conferred upon him by the library's parent organisation and its wider environment; he pictures and measures the community which his library serves; he aims his service in certain directions, he determines the line of route, as it were, balancing costs against effectiveness, and marking out successive objectives to be achieved. He deploys his resources for the achievement of these objectives—finance, people, materials, equipment, accommodation. He monitors the operation of this system, and evaluates each stage of achievement against the objectives he has set. This systems approach to library management pervades several of the papers selected for this reader, and further accounts will be found in those by Mackenzie, Dutton and Mason. In addition, we would particularly recommend D J Simpson's simple introduction to systems theory and analysis, and their relationship to library mechanisation (Simpson, 1968).

Of course, with the Olympian library manager of the above abstraction we are only the the genesis of library management theory, and we must leave the reader with a firmer sense of reality. Far from being God, the library manager, if he be a good manager, is one of 'Us'; if he is not such a good manager, he is one of 'Them'. Moreover, he cannot escape from history, which tends to be overlooked by systems makers, but which lies so heavily on librarianship. Certainly history will help to explain the attitudes of many of his staff, and the expectations of his readers. Library history is the library manager's starting point; he neglects it at his peril.

The formal theories and techniques of library management come to life—or are denied—in a real world of conflicting perceptions, and attitudes, imperfect communication, conflicting individual and institutional powers and a whole complex of interpersonal relationships. This is the world studied by the behavioural sciences, from which management theory draws its validity. (That it has sought to prostitute the social sciences for its own narrow purposes is not a cheap gibe, but a half-truth worth arguing.) Sociology and communication studies provide one of the intellectual contexts within which librarianship (and library management) is evolving as a sophisticated professional activity in place of a time-honoured craft. In one form or other, and more or less, they provide a foundation for most first professional courses in UK schools of librarianship. This important intellectual basis for the practice of library management still has to be developed; its content has been discussed at length by Shera (1972).

Perhaps it is too late in the day to ask *why* library management? The real choice is, what *kind* of library management?

# THE NEED FOR
## ADMINISTRATIVE KNOW-HOW IN LIBRARIES

*Beatrice V Simon*

In the topics proposed for discussion at conferences, and in articles appearing currently in library journals, there is ample evidence that librarians are already aware of a need to acquire additional administrative know-how. What I think we wish to know more about is how to make use of at least some of what has been and what is still being discovered in other fields where administrative expertise is an all-important element in the survival of administrators.

*What is administration?*

It is making decisions that facilitate the decisions of others.

It is searching the environment for ways and means of improving performance in achieving the objectives of the organization.

It is looking ahead to anticipate increased demands or new directions for development.

It is studying all possible means of achieving these improvements and promoting new developments.

It is choosing from among alternate ways and means those which seem most likely to accomplish the desired objective or improvement.

It is drawing up plans of action.

It is establishing sure and certain communication between the head and shoulders of the organization and thus creating a climate wherein everyone wants to work as a member of a team.

It is a way of thinking—*not* of doing.

*What is not administration?*

It is not sending out orders for books.

It is not cataloguing books.

It is not circulating books.

It is not selecting books.

17

It is not answering reference questions.
*That* is operating.

And right there we have one of the chief sources of administrative problems that arises in libraries—the difficulty that so many people in management positions experience in differentiating between the activities of operating and those of management. This is especially true in smaller libraries where the lines between the two sets of activities often become blurred. In the one-man library, where the administrator must do everything himself, it is essential that he be able to identify and keep separate in his own mind the activities of each function—to know at any given point whether he is acting in his capacity of manager or operator. Failure to do this is very often the reason that administrators of such libraries have difficulty in achieving proper recognition of the professional side of their work. It is sometimes much easier to get the point across to people who can only see the librarian as a glorified clerk by describing one's position as that of *manager* of the library's activities. The professional element can always be stressed by the superior quality of the information service given.

In larger libraries this same mental block can create very great difficulties. For example, when the staff of the reference department consists of one solitary librarian, he must, perforce, not only plan and organize the work of the department, but he must also carry it out. If he is too busy operating to do any planning, he should do it outside office hours, for planning *must* be done. But, when there are five or six librarians and several clerical assistants, the head of the department becomes almost a full-time administrator, and the amount of time he is free to spend working on interesting reference questions diminishes, while the time he must allot to organizing the work of the department, and solving the problems that arise, increases to and often exceeds 50 percent.

Should a supervising librarian insist upon being a reference librarian first and a manager second, the service will come apart at the seams. The answer is *not* to slough off distasteful administrative duties onto a bright and willing assistant. Anyone who prefers to be out on the floor answering reference questions, or behind the scenes compiling bibliographies, instead of creating the environment in which excellent work can be done by a team, should never be tempted to accept a supervisory position, no matter what the financial inducement might be. To do so is not only unfair to the staff, it is unfair to the organization, and it is unfair to himself. No matter how democratic a group activity is, whenever two or more people are brought together to achieve a predetermined objective, *one* must be given and *accept* full responsibility for planning, decision-making, and reporting

18

results within the specified area of his command. When properly done, this consumes a considerable amount of his time.

As the size of an operation increases, the amount of time that must be spent on management activities also increases. It has been suggested that top executives in large business organizations should be able to spend at least 90 percent of their time on purely administrative activities (1). The administration of a large university has become so complex and time-consuming that its president can no longer take an active part in the teaching program without endangering his efficiency in both roles. It is obvious that the chief administrator of a large library system, or even a medium-sized library, must also devote the greater part of his time to management, that is, if he wishes to conduct the total operation efficiently towards achievement of the library's goals.

## The problems of library administration

I have not found that the problems of library administration differ in any significant way from those found in other types of organizations, and they are much more readily solved if looked upon as management problems rather than as library problems. Conventional librarianship, however, does not offer solutions to such problems, but study of the lessons learned and the skills and techniques used in the practice of professional management does provide the insight necessary for their analysis and an understanding of how they should be handled.

The observations of discerning administrators, the results of scholarly analysis of the methods and techniques employed in successfully managed business enterprises, and research in other disciplines—notably the behavioral sciences—have provided a body of tested information in three areas which should not be overlooked by librarians in their search for ways and means of solving management problems in the environment of the library. These are:

1 The concept of the administrative process which identifies and defines the activities and responsibilities of management.

2 An understanding of how essential management skills may be learned and improved.

3 The technique of operations analysis, which provides an invaluable tool for performance measuring and control and an aid to planning and decision-making.

## The activities of management

The activities of management as distinct from those of operating were first identified and described by the brilliant French industrialist, Henri Fayol. In his famous report *Administration générale et industrielle,* first

19

published in 1916, Fayol maintained that, regardless of the size or complexity of an undertaking, six groups of activities or essential functions were always present. These he described as:

1 Technical activities (production, manufacture, adaptation).

2 Commercial activities (buying, selling, exchange).

3 Financial activities (search for and optimum use of capital).

4 Security activities (protection of property and persons).

5 Accounting activities (stocktaking, balance sheet, costs, statistics).

6 Managerial activities (planning, organization, command, coordination, and control) (2).

Counterparts of the five groups of operating activities can easily be found in the work carried on in a library. The five managerial activities are the basis of what, in recent years, has become known as the 'administrative', or 'management' process.

### The administrative process

In one of the best discussions of the modern concept of management that I have discovered to date, Professor John Mee describes the administrative process as a 'flow-process for setting and achieving predetermined objectives in an environment by the intelligent use of human effort and facilitating resources' (3). The elements of this definition he sees as: 1, an established and accepted objective for achievement by group effort, 2, a process based on logical and effective thinking for guidance to achieve the objective, and 3, human effort, facilitated by other resources, to be utilized in the process to achieve the objective which has been established (4).

In the carrying out of this 'flow-process', Professor Mee identifies seven essential steps: 1, the decision-making process, 2, the policy-making process, 3, the planning process, 4, the organizing process, 5, the motivating or directing process, 6, the controlling or measuring process, and 7, the innovating process.

Most people include decision-making and policy formulation in the planning process, but as Professor Mee points out, it is quite possible to make a decision without planning, but it is impossible to plan without reaching a decision to do so. Hence, he places decision-making as the very first step in the 'flow-process', and the first decision is that which sets the aims and objectives to be achieved.

The second step in the management process is to *formulate the general policies* that are to serve as guides in planning. Policies, it should be remembered, are not rules or procedures. Policy decides to have rules and establish procedures. The third step in these preliminary steps is the *planning process,* 'to develop courses of action to achieve the predetermined goals in accordance with the general policies formulated'.

The organizing process then provides 'the vehicle to release and channel human effort with technological aids in effecting the plans to achieve the goals established'. This is followed by the *motivating or directing process* to get the project off the ground and into operation by hiring staff and generating and maintaining the desire of everyone to 'effect the plans to arrive at the goals set within the policy framework'.

The *controlling* or *measuring process* is next put into operation 'to enable the actual performance to motivated and directed people in the organization to accomplish the desired goals in conformance with predetermined plans and policies'.

Finally, Professor Mee suggests the *innovating process* 'to improve performance, reduce costs, and achieve greater human satisfaction' (5). This process involves research and development, and generates new proposals for future action from which management again reaches the point where choices from among alternate courses of action must be made, and the whole flow-process is set in motion once more (Fig 1). In a dynamic organization, business or library, this flow-process never ceases—at every level of management.

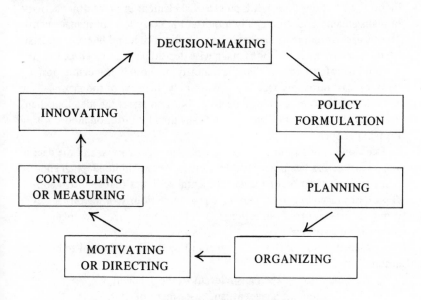

Fig 1—The administrative process

21

This concept of management as a process has enabled scholars to think about business management 'in terms of objectives, of functional processes, and of guiding principles instead of descriptions of procedures and events' (6). Librarians, if they are ever to develop a real philosophy of librarianship and become a true profession, must also stop thinking about library administration in terms of operational procedures and clerical routines.

### The problem-solving skills

Another important result of research into the functional processes of administration is to be found in our increasing understanding of the mental activities involved in problem-solving. It has been said that since an administrator spends the greater part of his time in solving problems, the most important skill for him to develop is that of problem-solving. I believe that it is even more important for him to acquire those management skills which, when properly applied, can *prevent* many problems from ever arising. Perhaps the most necessary skills are those involved in carrying on the decision-making, planning and communication processes.

*Decision-making*

Of all the sub-processes of the management process, decision-making is by far the most important; it is an essential element in every other activity of management; and it is equally important at every level of management. The success or failure of leaders in every walk of life, and in every era, have been judged by their ability to make wise decisions. Nevertheless, I think it would be safe to assume that the majority of those in leadership positions, at least until very recently, are not only unaware of the mental activities involved in reaching a decision, but also reject the idea that their decisions are arrived at by any other means than by intuition alone, arising from experience.

Decision-making is, in fact, a somewhat lengthy process, and the decision when reached has been described by Louis Allen as 'an intellectual endpoint—the culmination of a series of mental activities that lead to a conclusion or judgement. This may take place consciously or unconsciously; it may or may not result in action' (7). These mental activities might be summarized as follows:

1 Identification of the *real* problem to be faced, or the end to be accomplished.

2 Accumulation of the facts relevant to the problem.

3 Classification, arrangement, and assessment of these facts.

4 Formulation of alternate courses of action.

22

5 Choice from among the alternatives of what appears to be the best, or most workable, solution in the particular circumstances.

It is not possible to make wise decisions unless the relevant facts of the situation to be decided upon have been assembled and assessed. Able administrators maintain that there is not always time to gather much more than 75 percent of the facts, but experience does make it possible to recognize at once where *vital* information is missing. Experience is also the basis for those apparently 'snap' decisions that executives sometimes make, but no experienced executive ever does make a *really* snap decision. However, the speed at which such an executive's mind can work is often so great that he may be forgiven for believing that he reaches these decisions intuitively.

I am sure that everyone has heard someone, at one time or another, say that a bad decision is better than no decision. This is one of the worst assumptions ever made. One may make an interim decision, a negative decision, or frankly postpone a decision; but a bad decision, arrived at in haste and based on insufficient information, can only lead to further problems. There is, of course, such a thing as a genuine mistake, and there is only one proper way in which to deal with this situation. As Ordway Tead remarks:

'One proper aspect of decisiveness is to know when a wrong decision has been reached and decide to change. How that new decision is to be conveyed to followers is a point to be carefully thought through in each particular situation. But, done in the right way it does not lessen the confidence of the led, but reinforces their respect for the honesty, integrity, and insight of the leader (8).'

Generally speaking, decisions may be classified as either positive—that is, decisions to take, cease or prevent action; or they may be negative—decisions not to decide. In that classic of management literature, *The functions of the executive,* written by the late Chester Barnard, I recently came across a delightful definition of the negative, or nondecision. It contains so much homely wisdom that I cannot resist passing it on to you:

'The fine art of executive decision consists in not deciding questions that are not now pertinent, in not deciding prematurely, in not making decisions that others should make. Not to decide questions that are not pertinent at the time is uncommon good sense, though to raise them may be uncommon perspicacity. Not to decide questions prematurely is to refuse commitment of attitude or development of prejudice. Not to make decisions that others should make is to preserve morale, to develop competence, to fix responsibility, and to preserve authority (9).'

The consequences of decisions must not be overlooked in any discussion of decision-making skill. It is well to remember that a decision which appears to benefit one department greatly may, inadvertently, bring about problems in another department which far outweigh any beneficial results in the first department. Therefore, before making a decision to change an established procedure, one must consider the possible effects of that decision on the organization as a whole. This is very true in the library situation where decisions made, arbitrarily, in the cataloguing department have often created unfortunate difficulties in the service departments. One of the most important factors in creating a well-motivated organization is to make sure that one's decisions will be accepted. The way to accomplish this is to invite participation in the decision-making process. And that is the very essence of decision-making skill.

This stages by which the mind approaches the solution of a problem were first described by John Dewey in 1910 (10), and since then the subject of decision-making has been explored endlessly throughout the literature of management. However, it has been only since the 1950's, when the possibilities of the computer began to be recognized, and more sophisticated mathematical processes became available for research, that investigation of the human decision-making process began to leap ahead. One of the foremost researchers in this area is Dr Herbert Simon. In a short treatise based on a series of lectures given at New York University, he records some of his conclusions concerning computerized and human decision-making and assures us that the skills necessary to good human decision-making are 'as learnable and trainable as the skills involved in driving, recovering, and putting a golf ball' (11). Apparently, while the workings of the mind in reaching decisions are quite easy to simulate in the computer, the really fascinating research is in connection with the way the mind works in entirely new situations. A by-product of the results of research in this area will be improved methods of training in personal problem-solving skill.

A better understanding of how the mind works when faced with a novel situation, and recognition of the mental steps that must be taken in order to reach an acceptable solution of the problem will not eliminate all mistakes, but would go a long way toward reducing the number of unwise decisions—decisions that can at times paralyze an undertaking. And practice in this, as in all else, improves performance.

*Planning*

It is possible to make decisions all day long and nothing whatsoever will happen. If decisions are to be implemented, action must be taken, and as

24

Louis Allen points out, 'there are two basic ways of getting things done. The first is to plunge ahead, doing the things that appear to be necessary, handling problems as they come up, and taking advantage of opportunities as they occur' (12). In other words, making decisions on the spur of the moment. This is improvisation, and nobody can deny that there have been and always will be brilliant improvisers. But, sooner or later, as the project or enterprise grows, it will become too complicated to be handled in this way, and the improviser will be forced to resort to the second way of taking action, that is, planning ahead, if he hopes to remain in operation.

Planning is concerned with developing courses of action to achieve predetermined aims and objectives. The planning process involves the establishment of procedures, programming of the work to be done, and includes budgeting for present needs and future developments. It forms an essential preliminary process in the *structure* of any organized effort, and it makes tremendous demands on the planner's decision-making capability. However, sound planning *will* result in good organization.

There are three types of planning: organization planning, management planning, and development planning. Organizational planning is the kind of planning that initiates a new enterprise or a new project. It is concerned with setting the primary goals or aims and objectives of the enterprise as a whole, and with formulating the major policies which determine the form and structure of the organization into departments or divisions. Management planning, on the other hand, is concerned with developing the policies which determine the organization of work in these departments or divisions in order to carry out the major policies of the organization and so to achieve the predetermined objectives. Development planning looks to the future and seeks ways and means of improving performance and of increasing the effectiveness of the organization.

Although the need for planning had long been recognized by military leaders, architects, and engineers as essential to the sucess of their undertakings, it was not until 1945, when the entire world went temporarily mad about social and economic planning, that the subfunction of management planning began to attract the attention of scholars as a field for study and research, and the first book on management planning was published (13). Sixteen years were to elapse before a second study in this field appeared (14). And then, in 1965, one of the coauthors of the latter study reported the results of his analysis of what he calls the 'planning and implementation process', and outlined the steps he believes should be taken if a good and workable plan is to be constructed (15). If one analyzes a really good plan that has been put into successful operation, it will be found that LeBreton's steps will have been taken without realizing it. I suggest that anyone who has had trouble drawing up action plans might find this book very helpful in developing planning skill.

*Planning and the library*

Along with every other type of organization, libraries, if they expect to keep pace with currect social and economic development, must engage in all three types of planning: organizational, management, and developmental. Planning is not only essential to the organization and administration of large library undertakings, it is even more necessary in small libraries. It is equally essential to the successful operation of a department and to the carrying out of an individual's allotted responsibilities. In the case of a small library, it is often possible by skillful planning of the work for the librarian not only to keep his head above water but also to develop the library into a much more effective role in the parent organization. Lack of planning, insufficient planning, or faulty planning are very frequent sources of problems in the administration of every size and type of library.

In an interesting article describing the organization of Dupont de Nemours and Company, the Vice President, Robert L Hershey, made some general remarks about organizational planning which bear repeating at this point:

'All human organizations have three essential features. First, they have an objective—a result to be achieved. Second, there are people, the implements by which the organization gets its work done and produces the results which are the reason for its existence. Third, there is the structure, the way the people are placed in working relationship with each other. For greatest effectiveness, both people and the structure of an organization must be well tuned to its objectives. The people will need to have whatever special skills are required, and the structure must bring the people together in a way which stimulates maximum use of those skills on the essentials of the job to be done. Proper structure provides for doing those things necessary to attain the objective, and at the same time, firmly excludes the doing of those things which are unnecessary. . . . While some kinds of organizations find it unnecessary to adjust their structural arrangements from time to time, and may for years have unaltered objectives, business organizations will neglect the matter of re-examining objectives and altering structures only at great peril (16).'

Could it be that the reason why some libraries find themselves in a somewhat perilous position today is that *they* have neglected these matters?

In the early years of the twentieth century, when the standard techniques and practices of library science were being worked out, the chief objective of libraries was simply that of building a scholarly collection without much thought for the people who might be interested in using it. But today, and especially on this continent, the predetermined objective is, or should be, to provide the user with the *information* he needs, not merely by calling upon the resources of the library where the request is made, but by tapping all the other resources that may be available elsewhere. This change in emphasis in the purpose of libraries, their growing size and diversification of activities, and their increasing involvement with new technical methods and equipment—an involvement often requiring the addition of staff with specialized skills and knowledge—pose the question of a possible need for a new look at the organizational structure of libraries. Are we, in fact, grouping library activities in the best way in which to get the work done, or are we still blinded by our inability to distinguish between what is truly professional in our work and what is not?

Special libraries in business and industry have always been much more user-oriented than any other type of library, and their total disregard, at times, for traditional library organization and practice has resulted in some of the most highly developed information services in existence today. Since World War II, the physical structure of university and college libraries, with their open stacks and easy access to the materials of information, has reflected a dynamic change in library architecture from the 'storehouse' to the 'user' point of view. But the possible need for an equally dynamic change in the work structure of libraries seems not to have been recognized generally.

Examined from the point of view that information service is the chief product of the library, could we not borrow the concept of line and staff from industry and divide the work-to-be-done in a library by placing all the activities concerned with the production of information, ie, reference and bibliographic services, subject analysis, and collection-building, in the position of line authority, and all supporting services such as purchasing, processing, reprography, and research and development (operations research) in the staff relationship along with personnel and financial management and other administrative services? Heads of these departments would report to the chief librarian or a deputy, and would have no line authority whatso-ever, but their services would be available to everyone (Fig 2).

Mary Lee Bundy, in a recent article, 'Conflict in libraries', proposes something very similar as a means of resolving the conflict that all too often exists in libraries between professional and nonprofessional staff (17). I suggest that librarians by studying some of the modern writing on

27

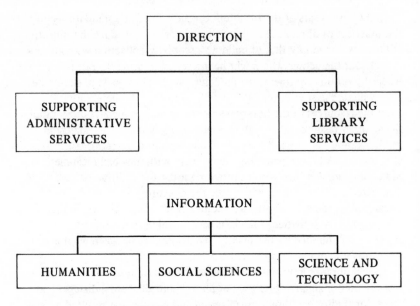

Fig 2—Organization chart of a
hypothetical information-service-oriented library

organization structure—possibly Litterer's *Analysis of organizations* (18)—
might find the answer to some of those administrative problems which
develop as a direct result of blindly following traditional patterns of library
organization.

Before we leave the subject of organization structure, I would like to say
a few words about organization charts. I believe in charts no matter how
small the library. They serve a very useful purpose as the visual and symbolic
representation of all the decisions that have been made concerning the
division of work, the assignment of responsibility, and the delegation of
authority. While most large libraries today have organization charts, I doubt
if many small libraries or departments in a library use them. May I point
out that the act of plotting a library's existing organization structure is a
very useful method of detecting faulty organizational planning.

*Communication*

The problems facing administrators in two areas of their functional responsibility are receiving intense study today. These are *motivating* and
*innovating.* The management function of motivating is concerned with
selection and development of staff, coordination of activities, and that

28

intangible essence called leadership. The objective of motivating is to create and maintain in all persons working in an organization the desire to achieve the objectives of that organization.

The intelligent use of human effort did not receive very much attention until after World War II, when the results of the famous experiments conducted at the Hawthorne Works of the General Electric Company were made more generally known (19). In the early days of management thinking, the belief was held that employees worked *only* for economic gain. Incentive methods of all sorts were devised—piece rates, company shares at reduced prices, etc, but the Hawthorne studies soon began to reveal that some other factor was involved: they called it 'motivation'. Today, lack of motivation is one of the most serious problems of management in industry—it has also become evident in libraries.

Of all the many human relations problems which develop in group undertakings, those which arise as a direct result of the introduction of new techniques are among the most difficult to handle. The ways and means of achieving group acceptance of the innovations has always been an important responsibility of managers in industry, but the technological explosion of the past fifteen years has served to bring the problem into even sharper focus. Library administrators will face this problem, increasingly, as they try to take advantage of the new technology which is creating a revolution in our traditional approach to the practice of librarianship. The key to the solution of both problems—motivation and innovation—is *effective* communication.

The ability to communicate effectively is, therefore, a vitally necessary skill for administrators at all levels to develop. We can make sound and forward-looking plans based on wise and discerning decisions, but if we are unable to communicate these decisions in such a way that they will be understood and, what is even more important, accepted, there will be no action. 'Communication', as one writer has pointed out, 'is the most important tool we have for getting things done. It is the basis for understanding, for cooperation, and for action' (20).

In 1945, Alvin Dodd, then president of the American Management Association, described communication as the number one problem of management (21). Twenty years later Louis Allen finds that it is still a major problem:

'A great deal of information is conveyed about communication without much real understanding taking place as to what is meant. Many a book has been written on the subject with never an attempt to define the term (22).'

With his customary care for precise definition, Allen then proceeds to describe management communication as 'the work a manager performs to create understanding'. What could be more simple than that? Developing his thought further, he says:

'From the standpoint of the professional manager, it must result in comprehension, *the sharing of the same meaning,* or it is not true communication. Communicating is what a manager does to understand other people and their motives, to get others to understand him. . . . For true communication to take place, the manager must understand other people as they understand themselves; he must get them to understand him as he sees himself (23).'

Research into the processes of effective communication shows that it is far from being a two-way process of telling and being listened to. Rather, it is a four-way process which involves asking, telling, listening and understanding. *Listening* is one of the most difficult skills to learn. It requires great self-discipline because the general tendency is to want to talk, but mastery of this skill will ensure that there will be understanding. A good administrator trains himself to ask, to listen, and in doing so, he encourages that feedback which is so very necessary to him in building up a store of information on which he can base future decisions.

I have not found that librarians, with some notable exceptions, are any more skillful in communicating than any other category of administrator. In common with business executives, I suspect that we have a tendency to pay too much attention to the 'devices' and 'techniques' of communication, and too little to its purpose. In the October issue for 1966 of *Special libraries,* the authors of seven articles explore various aspects of communication in libraries, all of which seem to indicate that librarians are not communicating as well as they should. Norma Shosid puts it thus, quite bluntly:

'Everybody today worries about communicating—businessmen with customers, government with the public, teenagers with parents. Librarians, too, are in the communication business. They talk, write, and create problems in a futile attempt to communicate something to somebody (24).'

Communication in libraries is carried on in four directions—up, down, across, and out—up to a superior authority, down to subordinates, across to librarians in peer positions, and out to the library's clientele. The chief librarian often finds that he has to communicate in all directions, using a different approach in each case. He may have to interpret the library's needs to a governing body that has little understanding of, or even interest in, the operations of the library. His task then is to create understanding

30

by translating the needs of the library into terms that will have meaning for his listeners. In dealing with his supervisory staff it might be presumed that, with a common vocabulary of librarianship, comprehension would be automatic, but here again, even with professional staff, a bridge of understanding may need to be built, especially when the purpose of communication is concerned with administrative duties and responsibilities. Nor is it uncommon to find that librarians operating in a supervisory capacity on the same management level are not communicating as well as they should. If they were, we might have fewer instances of conflict of interest between department heads.

Communication in the library system is not limited to internal communication. In common with all other service organizations, there is for libraries that most important problem of all—direct communication with the public. I think that we must not only be understanding in our communications with the library user but also especially careful about understanding exactly what it is he needs to know. The ability to interrogate a library user in order to help him find the information he needs, or find it for him, and to do this without annoying him, is a skill that borders on being an art.

Communications in the context of the library might then be defined as the work of a library administrator performs to create understanding between himself and the organization of which his library is a part, between himself and his staff, and between the individual members of the staff. It is also the work he and the library staff together perform in order to create understanding between the library and the user.

The consequences of miscommunication are beyond measure. I am certain that all of us have had the experience of being confronted with statements we are supposed to have made and that have become completely unrecognizable. The results, in many cases may have been wellnigh disastrous. The remedy, of course, is for everyone to improve his personal skill in communicating and receiving communications. This *can* be done. The results of research into the reasons why so many executives have failed to make themselves understood, the analysis of the process of communication, and the tested methods for improving one's ability to communicate are being reported regularly in management literature. We need only to become aware of our need to develop this administrative skill, to seek the relevant information, and to apply ourselves to its study.

### Operations analysis
The systematic study of the process of setting and achieving objectives by group effort began at the turn of the century with Frederick Winslow

Taylor's careful analysis of operations at the shop management level, and his theories concerning efficient shop management started the so-called 'scientific management' movement (25). During and after World War II, many of us became familiar with the time and study techniques used by Taylor, and later the Gilbreths, in setting performance standards. It was called 'job analysis'. Today this basic technique is still with us in the much more sophisticated form of 'operations analysis'.

Operations analysis is now used in business and industry as a basis for decision-making and planning. It is the key to performance measuring and control of operations. It is already being used extensively in libraries to analyze all aspects of library work in order to make better use of both professional and supporting staff. The professional systems analyst is no longer an unusual figure on the planning team of the large library.

However, it should be pointed out that there is nothing new about the basic concept of 'systems' or 'operations analysis'; there is merely a new terminology borrowed from the computer trade and the use of symbolic representation. Librarians, whether they realize it or not, have been playing around with a similar idea for years when trying to establish time-saving routines and set them down in somewhat unsatisfactory 'routine manuals'. Surely it is time that a more systematic approach be made to the organization of work at the operating level in all sizes and shapes of libraries. As Dougherty and Heinritz remark in their recently published manual, *Scientific management of library operations,* even though a librarian is never called upon to make a management study himself 'he may find it necessary to decide when and if a study is appropriate, who should carry it out, and how to make the best use of the results' (26). Now that there is this 'how-to-do-it' book, specifically addressed to librarians, there is not longer any excuse for not profiting from the use of one of the most valuable management tools ever devised.

## Conclusion

The need for administrative know-how has never been greater, and that need is increasing every day. In business and industry, libraries have become increasingly important as information departments; in academic institutions, they are acknowledged to be an indispensable part of the teaching and research program; in a growing number of hospitals, the immense potential of the library as an adjunct to their expanding role in the training of health practitioners and research scientists is becoming more and more evident. It follows that anyone called upon to develop the library service of such organizations must know and understand how they are structured; he must know, and identify with, the aims and objectives of the organization of which the library is a part; and, in order to have his views on library matters listened to with respect, he must be able to communicate with members of the governing body, and with the heads of other departments in the organization, in the language of administration rather than that of librarianship.

The concepts on which modern management theory is based may have been worked out and tested in the environment of business, but they are equally valid in every situation where the objective is that of 'getting things done through people'. The very simple mental exercise of applying the steps in the administrative process to an analysis of the management activities in our own libraries will bring illumination into hitherto dark corners. Adoption of the techniques of operations analysis and the systems approach to planning will result in a better organizational structure and better performance at the operating level.

*References*
1  Allen, Louis A: The management profession. New York, McGraw-Hill, 1964, p 80.
2  Fayol, Henri: Administration industrielle et générale. Paris, 1916. Second English translation by Constance Storrs. London, Pitman, 1949, p 3.
3  Mee, John F: Management thought in a dynamic economy. New York, New York University Press, 1964, p XIX.
4  Ibid, p 11.
5  This explanation of the management process is based on Professor Mee's discussion of the flow of subprocesses as given on p 54-55 of his Management thought in a dynamic economy.
6  Ibid, p 53.
7  Allen, op cit, p 247.
8  Tead, Ordway: The art of leadership. New York, McGraw-Hill, 1935, 1963, p 125.
9  Barnard, Chester I: The functions of the executive. Cambridge, Mass, Harvard University Press, 1950, p 194.
10  Dewey, John: How we think. New York, Heath, 1910.
11  Simon, Herbert A: The new science of management decision. New York, Harper & Row, 1960, p 4.
12  Allen, op cit, p 98.
13  Hempel, Edward Henry: Top management planning; New York, Harper, 1945.
14  LeBreton, Preston P, and Henning, D A: Planning Theory. Englewood Cliffs, NJ, Prentice-Hall, 1961.

15  LeBreton, Preston P: General administration: planning and implementation. New York, Holt, 1965.

16  Hershey, Robert L: Organizational planning. Business topics 10: 29-40, Winter, 1962.

17  Bundy, Mary Lee: Conflict in libraries. Coll Res Libr 27: 253-262, July, 1966.

18  Litterer, Joseph A: Analysis of organizations. New York, Wiley, 1965.

19  Roethlisberger, F J, and Dickson, W J: Management and the worker. Cambridge, Mass, Harvard University Press, 1939.

20  Fischer, Frank E: A new look at management communication. Personnel 31: 487-497, May, 1955.

21  Ibid.

22  Allen, op cit, p 272.

23  Ibid, p 273.

24  Shosid, Norma: Freud, frug, and feedback. Special libraries 57: 561-563, Oct, 1966.

25  Taylor, Frederick Winslow: Scientific management; comprising shop management, the principles of scientific management, testament before the special house committee, with a foreword by Harlow S Person. New York, Harper, 1947.

26  Dougherty, Richard M, and Heinritz, F J: Scientific management of library operations. New York, Scarecrow Press, 1966, p 21.

# ALL VERY WELL IN PRACTICE!
## BUT HOW DOES IT WORK OUT IN THEORY?

*P J Gordon*

'This is all very well in practice! But how does it work out in theory?'
The foregoing was the response of a senior executive to a presentation at
the Irish Management Institute in the spring of 1967. The remark serves
well to open this article because it points up at least three considerations
that are important for what follows.

The first is that experienced administrators will have developed their
own criteria for judging the credibility and usefulness of what follows.
One way or another, some of these ideas will have been heard before. The
key contribution, therefore, is likely to be that of inviting reappraisal of
perspective rather than original contribution to ability or knowledge. If
a short statement does no more than induce reappraisal of perspective
(confirm some views as reasonable and generate alternatives for others),
then much will have been accomplished.

The second is that people concerned *to be* administrators of complex
organizations and people committed to building knowledge *about* the
administration of complex organizations may share more common cause
than appears on the surface. Both must proceed without any widely
accepted, well-established, well-organized, well-verified, readily accessible,
and up-to-date treasury of knowledge. This means, in both instances,
that people are taking bets. This they share in common; and, in common,
they share a stake in improving the payoff on the bets they take. In plain
though loaded talk, much of modern theory concerning decision, organization, and administration is based on notions of behaviour and probability
in a world assumed to be characterized by uncertainty, complexity, and
change. Such a world, all but the most protected administrators (where-
ever they may be) will recognize as their own.

This leads to the third point, one of four major ones (indicated by the
subheads). That is, the concern of the practicing administrator with

theory, his understanding of what theory is supposed to be and to do, and his questions about the present state of theory and how it squares with the practice that he knows. Put summarily, much of what is posed as theory is neither good administration, by any measure, nor good theory. Without getting metaphysical about theories *per se,* we can recognize two issues that trouble many administrators and then proceed to say something about them. One has to do with the flood of literature, which is enough to make one quit altogether. This is not likely to stop. The other is the question of discernment—knowing what may be valid and what may be relevant. The key to speed reading, in the last analysis may be to read less! But isn't this easier when one has a preliminary fix on a field and knows what he can afford to skip, at what risk, and where he must slow down?

### Consumers' guide to contemporary theories

With regard to theories of organization and their administration, there are two sports in which a number of academic people have been engaged for the last ten years. One has been that of commenting on the 'jungle' of theories extant, suggesting luxuriant growth, as opposed to claiming that the condition more resembles a 'desert' with no theory worthy of the name. The other is that of categorizing and labelling—with or without regard to whether alternative perspectives help either in advancing human knowledge or in improving organizational practice. This means, as a minimum, that many of the perspectives are partial; that the yardsticks for judgement are frequently at odds; that bits and pieces do not add up to any widely accepted unified theory today; that dilemmas for practising administrators are posed; and that any attempt to pull things together (including this one) must be viewed with scepticism. Yet practising administrators are not always concerned with all the detailed niceties of the academics and may be helped with a kind of consumers' guide to the present state of the field.

As a kind of offbeat note, not to be one-up on colleagues, but because much insight can be telescoped in a short span of time, I want to note that Ljubljana University in Northern Yugoslavia held its first executive development program for administrators of state enterprises in the summer of 1967. Asked about theories of administering and notions brought to mind by terms such as 'organization' and 'administration', the responses were somewhat surprising to a North American who was not inclined to bend all responses to fit his own cultural map.

The Yugoslav executives spoke first of the production problem. That is, making internal *operations* more efficient to meet the requirements set by Belgrade. That was before the rejection of the more highly centralized Russian planning schemes. Subsequently, they referred to the problem of improving productivity and *performance* through workers' councils. New kinds of incentives and new kinds of attention to measuring and distributing profits are being tried. They said that efforts to decentralize on a countryside basis were bogging. A number of factory managers who were successful in working for goals set elsewhere were not able to cope with *decision* strategy for a total enterprise under now economic and marketing conditions. Further, they were concerned about the development and use of *information* for administrative decisions at the top policy level. The limits of traditional accounting and the need for better information were discussed. Of immediate and practical concern to these men was the correct reading of the political and economic *environment.* The changing social condition, the purchasing capacity of people in Yugoslavia and elsewhere, and the market for their products and services are now of more interest than previously. Further, if industrial development is to continue, problems of *resources*, capital, and foreign exchange will become more important. So joint ventures with industrialists and financiers beyond Yugoslav borders will have to be considered.

In a nutshell, yet with no assertion of simpleminded one-two-three relationship, the foregoing is intended to suggest: some relationship between the kinds of problems that are to be faced and the theories that may be sought, developed, or espoused; not just a time-sequence development in theories but a continuous opening of new emphases without total rejection of the old; the change of theoretical orientation especially in relation to to such factors as technology, environment, and the greater importance and wider dissemination of knowledge; and the possible implications of this kind of thinking better to understand what has happened and what may continue to happen in organizations such as libraries and information centers.

For brevity, the consumers' guide to contemporary theories will be classified arbitrarily in six categories. A later diagram is intended to capsulize what will have been said and to suggest a relationship among the categories already implied in the Yugoslav story.

The oldest in time perhaps is that category concerned with the work to be done, the division of labor, spelling out authority, matters of hierarchy, and so on. We will call this *operations.* For the manufacturing company, this is the production problem in all of its internal dimensions, the problem of efficiency, procedure, controls, and all the rest. For banks, in many instances, the preoccupation was with safeguarding the cash rather than making a profit. For libraries, the preoccupation was probably safeguarding the books and documents rather than evaluating the service. Out of this focus were developed a number of ideas about organizations that emphasized especially their anatomical attributes and a number of ideas about administration that emphasized especially controls necessary to achieve predetermined objectives.

More recently subject to systematic attention has been the matter of individual and group behavior in the work situation and this in the context of a larger social, cultural, and political system. Attention has been directed both to the behavior of individuals and groups *within* organizations and to the behavior *of* organizations as social-cultural-political systems interacting in many ways with environment. For practising administrators looking at developments in the many streams of literature and research, the potential confusions are many. There is considerable variation among the works classified as 'human relations'. Some tell how people should or should not be treated, along with criteria, stated or implied, that might be regarded as controversial. There is also great disparity among works called 'behavioral'. Some represent no more than a quick renaming of older 'human relations' material. Some represent more preoccupation with scientific aspects than social aspects of social science, and many fine works represent nevertheless the perspective of a particular social science discipline rather than meeting the administrative hope that a book or two might provide the bare essentials. Regardless of internal disparities, however, theories in this category (in contrast to the previous one) start with a different focus and honor a different type of evidence. Out of this focus are developed a number of ideas: first, minimizing the efficacy of organizational structure and control, and, second, building a body of knowledge based on observation and experimentation with actual behavior. This category is *performance,* meaning that work does not get done unless people perform.

To the foregoing, let us add a *decision* category. As a minimum, we are concerned with sorting out what really important decisions have to be taken, seeing that they are taken, and seeing that solutions are implemented. As suggested earlier, we assume conditions of uncertainty, complexity and change. These lead to complicating the decision problem. The generation of alternatives and models to aid in the decision process, the recognition that some problems are well defined and others poorly defined, and the fact that people with quantitative capabilities receive education in quite different university departments also make the pursuit of knowledge in this area sometimes complicated for the practising administrator. Yet the decision-maker cannot but be helped by notions of probability, variables and variations, and calculations on the direction, rate, and impact of change. Out of this focus are emerging a number of theories and techniques related to the design of organizations and their administration.

In 1968 there can be little question that most readers of a journal of this sort have been overwhelmed with *information* of one kind or another, including the current large emphasis on 'information' and the pressure on some libraries to be modish in describing themselves as 'information systems'. Traditionally for executives, and even recently, most references to something called 'information' dealt with feedback on the internal operation of the interprise and through this the performance of its people and the wisdom of its decisions. And surely one needs information if he is to scan the horizon to see what decisions need making and if he is to get 'the right things done' (according to Drucker) in some reasonable way. Out of this focus as well, theories and data are being developed related to the design of organizations in order to assure the better flow of information and improved administrative decision.

Add to the foregoing, concern for the *environment* in which we operate and from whence our demand derives. It is the environment which has much to do with setting and resetting our objectives, organizationally and personally. This includes not only the market or customer base with its rapidly changing concepts and demands (without which there would be no problem of production or finance because there would be no reason for being) but also includes, directly or indirectly: a legislative and financial context; an economic and social base; rapid changes in technology; and the continuous nagging question of what business we are in, what to be, what to do, and what niche to create and occupy in a rapidly changing context so as to avoid obsolescence or being subsumed as part of other activities. Out of this focus, too, there have developed theories which in the aggregate suggest that traditional theories of organizations and their administration have had the telescope turned the wrong way around. Pursued far enough, the implication would be that organizations still tied to internal problems of resources, means, and efficiency (which may be largely whipped), while ignoring external problems having to do with purpose, constituency, and future, may have something less than a brilliant outlook to contemplate!

And finally, for this half dozen, let us add one more category called *resources,* not because it is completely apart from the others, but because it is important enough to receive special attention. Constantly, administrators and their associates, in one way or another, are negotiating for a continuous flow of human and material resources as well as markets for the products and services that the organization has been established to create. Complicating the picture are the facts that the resources must be secured from ever-changing sources and parties and that the products and services must continuously be reassessed, reconceptualized, and psychologically and physically repackaged. All this effectively redefines the mission of the organization in relation to its environment and the constituencies on which it depends for support.

## A preliminary systems model

Now, with regard to this type of categorizing, three points are important. The first is to relate the half dozen items, each in themselves a complicated set of variables, to each other through introducing one possible view of an enterprise as a system. The second is to call to attention that the boundaries of this system are intentionally not well defined. And the third is to suggest the relevance and the likely impact of these ideas for administrators in libraries as elsewhere.

On the first point, what counts is *relationships*. It is relationships rather than facts that administrators (generically) can change. The administrator is an agent for change no matter how well he avoids or conceals it. The most crucial decisions the administrator can make or ignore are with regard to the relationships of the system itself and the role, or roles, he will take in relation to them. That is, for example, with regard to its purpose, its design, its flexibility, its relationship to constituencies, its gathering and processing of intelligence, and its allocation of resources. Add as well, its spirit, its climate, and its attitude toward cooperation, dissent, experiment, innovation, and change. And consider that only through influencing the direction and rate of change can the administrator add improvement—which in the United States' twentieth-century culture is his job (and his joy?). And how does one decide which are the more desirable improvements and the more appropriate directions and rates of change? (High motivation, endurance, timing, and strategic hedges also count.)

All these things, of course, are easier to say than to do or to map out or to prove. Any effort to suggest in a schematic way some possible relationship among the categories superficially sketched might be misleading to the innocent. If we assume, however, that few experienced administrators are quite so innocent (at least in administrative matters), then oversimplification in chart form may be useful. There can be no question that the effort may invite the hostility of those who harbor animus to

40

schematics in all forms. It may raise false hopes and, later, backlash from those who see computerization potential in any set of boxes joined by suggestive arrows. And one major omission will make this less than organizational charts generally, which at least show administrators even if they show no one else! But chart we will!

Incorporating in crude fashion the idea of open and closed systems and the possibility of comparing quite varied kinds of organizations, Figure 1 illustrates one way in which these incipient theories of organizations and their administrations may be related. (Figure 1 and these few closely related paragraphs have appeared in 'Administrative strategy for a graduate school of administration', *Academy of management journal* (December 1967). The foregoing incorporates not only discussion of a school and the diagram presented here but also a statement on objectives for education in administration that some readers will find of interest.)

Fig 1—A preliminary systems model for an enterprise

| *Inputs* | *Processes* | *Outputs* |
|---|---|---|
| Environment eg<br>Economic<br>Political<br>Technological<br>Social<br>Marketing | Choice of value criteria<br>Generating basic intelligence<br>Design of systems framework<br>Problem solving strategies<br>Creating/appraising alternatives<br>Setting and revising goals | Performance eg<br>Individual behavior<br>Individuals & groups<br>Social organization<br>Power-influence<br>Cultural factors |
| Resources eg<br>Human<br>Capital<br>Power<br>Material | Forming plans and programs<br>Building formal structure<br>Allocation and assignment<br>Inducements and contributions | |
| Information eg<br>Accounting<br>Financial<br>Mathematical<br>Statistical<br>Evaluative | Facilitating communication<br>Development and improvement<br>Coordinating operations<br>Feedback and control<br>Innovations and change<br>Evaluating corporate effort | Operations eg<br>Research/development<br>Create goods/services<br>Distrib goods/services<br>Strengthen resources<br>Finance operations |

*As suggested in the accompanying text, inputs and outputs and their relationships can be varied; the semantics can be altered for different enterprises; the organizational 'boundaries' may encompass all, more or less than the above; and the real interaction cannot be pictured in a two dimensional diagram.*

41

The *environment* category (Figure 1) immediately departs from some of the more traditionally and more internally preoccupied materials on administration. The concern is not only to study the economic, political, technological, social, and marketing variations at different times in different environments but also to relate these factors to the study of complex organizations and their administration.

The *resources* category is an old one among economists and others, yet one of renewed interest in terms of investment, income, development, and human urgencies about the world and one of renewed interest in terms of relationships with which organizations and their administrators must be concerned.

The *information* category here represents feedback from operations withou the introduction of new information about environment and resources. Since the ways of processing raw data on operations and relating them to the activities of the enterprise are better established, there is a somewhat conventional, though in no way a necessary, division between outside and inside (open and closed) categories.

The *operations* category is to encompass the most basic activities that the organization has been established to perform. Subdivisions will, of course, vary in nature and designation with the purpose and type of effort in question. Increasingly, however, most organizations of sufficient complexity to warrant this discussion will have to see to: strengthening the research and development base for future operations; creating goods and/or services or both; distributing goods and/or services or both; strengthening human and capital resources currently and for the future; and financing these and other activities with attention to costs, benefits, return-on-investment, and appropriate plans for achieving and distributing any loss or surplus.

The *performance* category set forth is related more to behavior within organizations in contrast to behavior of organizations; the latter is no less important and not intended to be absent in contemplating the possible utilities of this diagram. This is simply to comment on meaning in this part of the diagram in contrast to fuller coverage earlier.

The notion of processes, whatever they may be, and interdependent subsystems is far from new. The way of conceiving and labelling them, however, is a matter of importance. Traditional terms include 'planning', 'organization', 'control', and so on. For this exercise the terms were chosen in part inductively and in part as dependent variables. That is, their exact framing was taken as dependent on the availability of some ongoing and developing stream of theory and research, in each instance insofar as possible, in order to enrich the meaning of the terms and the potential in this way for adding to knowledge in the field. The hope is that of relating process and system to larger substantive and human considerations. The arrows in the diagram really point in only one direction. Most people should be concerned with more than one box. The boxes, the boundaries, and the arrows, in the final analysis, are more in the mind than elsewhere. And these can be adapted so long as the mind can be adapted as well!

*Happenings that change boundaries*
Earlier, it was pointed out that the boundaries of the foregoing 'system' are intentionally not well defined. Definitions, on the one hand, are imposed by the way that administrators perceive their problems. On the other, they change in ways not always subject to the rationale of administrators. The boundaries may be thought of as 'permeable' (a word now popular in the literature) and 'escalatable' (a word now popular in political and military affairs). In brief, for your purpose, the schematic may be related to the world as perceived from the cataloguing section of the library interacting with other units within and beyond the library; or to the whole library; or to a whole system of libraries; or to some other universe. Clearly, the variables that are important and the ways in which they may be related may differ from one situation to another over time and may be subject to change. Equally clear, what is independent and what is dependent, what is cause and what is effect, are frequently difficult, at the least, to pin down.

For students and practitioners of *administrology* generally, there have been four major happenings in organization theory of sufficient importance and potential impact to require comment, that is, in this context quite arbitrarily, even at the risk of omitting ten points that others might consider more significant. For these and many others, it might be said that events may have gotten ahead of theoretical and research efforts to explain and predict them. Yet, if one is to reappraise the world that is, and the way that one perceives the world, these relatively unsupported comments may be useful to share.

Not necessarily in the correct sequence, nevertheless, the first major happening was that of turning the telescope about at least long enough to recognize environment as an important reference in planning purpose, survival, growth and change. So long as goals were taken as predetermined, environment counted less. Traditional concepts for organizations were developed when production was perceived to be a major problem and the rationalization of central authority a major issue. The impact of environment and later technology and affluence may be put down by historians of the future as important forces in softening traditional views. The

43

growing importance, wider availability, and greater dissemination of knowledge offer the potential of further diffusing the older power base.

The second major happening was the growing realization of the impact of technology on organizations and their administration. Not only is work arranged and accomplished differently, not only has the meaning of work and the emotional relation to work undergone change but new kinds of problems have to be solved, frequently by methods not yet invented or validated. Information has to be moved and can be moved differently. Times and space dimensions have been radically altered. Venerable activities have been made obsolescent and new combinations have been created. Even more important, however, than these observations which have become hackneyed by now, are the implications for the design of organizations and their administration for the future. Architecture developed for job-shop and mass-production activities, even the organizational arrangement developed for universities, medical centers, and research enterprises, may not do for the high-technology activies of the future. Research into technology as a variable or set of variables related to organization has just begun. One can cite a few studies at home and abroad, and there have been some preliminary investigations of new forms of organization in space, defense, electronics, and other industrial, public, and institutional sectors. Technology here implies not only new ways of having work done; it implies tremendous impact on communication and social arrangement that add up to a whole new culture. The implications, library administrators are beginning to witness even at this date.

The third major happening was that of breaking out of the closed-systems approach as the main option and the open-systems approach as the only sort of black-or-white alternative. In Figure 1, the closed-systems approach would incorporate the world as pictured but without the environment and resource categories. One might be running the library more and more efficiently by some measure without regard to environment, resources, changing purpose, concept, and market. The opposite would be preoccupation with the environment and resources categories as holding the solution to all problems while omitting everything implied in the other four. One might have all his outside bases covered without knowing anything about a library or about the state of affairs in his own.

Thinking in terms of systems—decision, social, adaptive, open, and closed, and interacting on many levels, sometimes with imposed rationality and sometimes without—adds a flexibility and a potential reality to the study of complex organizations and their administration as well as to the armament of the administrator, which augurs more promise for the future than many of the incantations that many of us have inherited but never fully believed. The breakthrough helps in unfreezing that which was confining if seriously held, so permitting rearrangements in the mix, yet providing some kind of a flexible, even if more tentative, platform from which to proceed.

The fourth major happening had to do with the greater importance and wider dissemination of knowledge; that is, not only as this relates to technology and environment, not only as it relates to patterns of specialization and profession, not only as it affects the aspirations of people on and off the job, but also as it relates to undermining the traditional power base on which many organizations have been built, and as it effectively de-emphasizes decision power growing solely out of formal position in the hierarchy and reinforces the potential power base of those who own the knowledge. (The reference here is primarily to persons and groups whose principal mission is that of creating new knowledge, whose professional differentiation is high, and whose capacities and views are inextricably tied to the potential and direction of the enterprise or one of its major segments.)

Totally unsupported as posited, nevertheless change in some dimension one may anticipate. Knowledge-based industries are generally growth industries and knowledge-based organizations and segments of organizations are generally on the increase. One may expect increased technology, increased emphasis on cross-cultural and intercultural communication, some lag in the design and functioning of organizations accommodated to new demands, and perhaps further lag (though one hopes not) in the development and explanation of theories of administration suited to these new conditions.

*Implications for library administrators*
Meantime, what is the present relevance and what will be the future impact for library administrators? Much, of course, has been suggested through example and inference already. You will have made and you will continue to cogitate more relevant interpretations. A few closing encouragements, however, may be appropriate.

With regard to libraries as institutions engaged in rendering services which are only deceptively tangible in their counting of cataloguing and inventory transactions, comparison with health care and university systems might prove insightful and productive of thought on at least three fronts:

1 These kinds of institutions along with many others in our society are engaged in providing services that are more and more in demand, no matter how diverse the motives and no matter how slight the serious consumption

45

and resulting behavioral change. Libraries, along with health and education, are 'a good thing', and the arsenal of offerings for an affluent society is ever greater. It matters not whether producers demand greater markets, or increased markets demand more products. The effect is that libraries and librarians are now no longer any more sure or secure in their stance before a knowledgeable, critical, and demanding world than university and health-care systems and their respective administrators. All are under pressure and will be more so in the future. There is no question about change but only from what base, in what direction, and at what rate, by whom, with what outcome. There is no need to assume that top-flight library administrators will fare less well than their confreres in other professional fields.

2 Assuming that problems of economics and technology present imperatives that cannot be ignored, that preoccupations with these will readily permit the substitution of motion for the horror of lonely introspective thought, the quiet crisis will be that of purpose. What will be the unifying core that will hold together the clusterings of what intellectual and professional talents in order to provide what services and to solve what problems? This is not so much to suggest any lack of work on this point in the profession. Even less does it suggest originality on the part of an itinerant who can move from one professional group to another. The significant item is that capacity to raise questions about this point suggests that many other professional associations are facing similar needs for reassessment. With library administrators as with others, choice of posture for the future will entail relating gaps and demands in the market-place for public services to known strengths, which are so already well established, and constantly upgrading.

3 And, briefly, because so much has been said on the point, solutions will probably need to be viable in a larger systems context, in order to assure institutionally both the talent and resource concentration of largeness and the flexibility and service advantages of smallness for the future.

With regard to library administrators, the analogies suggested probably hold equally well:
1 Pressures, not alone derived from environmental change but arising out of internal anxieties shared widely with other professionals in like situations, will be experienced. Comfort can be taken from seeing that one is not alone either institutionally or personally. That accomplished, however, a case can be argued that library administrators, more than some other groups, may experience difficulty in breaking the mold into

which schooling and personal considerations have helped to cast them, and, out of which, society may not be ready for them to rebound. Personal change can be difficult when all of the former alliances and constituencies insist on their out-of-date expectations being met. And one cannot always run about shouting that he is not what people think he is, especially when the perceived role is taken to be honorable, and when one has not precisely figured out the new role.

2  This leads to solving anew the question of what is a library administrator, or better still, which aspects of the work may be administrative and how these change over time. The tug-of-war between the purely technical aspects of the work and the purely administrative aspects of the work has been rather well covered in supervisory publications in many related fields. And if the distinctions are pure, the advices are probably of little use. More taxing for administrators at higher levels, however, (and this may vary with size and deputies) is working out a rolling balance between emphasis on the internals of the closed systems as outlined and externals of the open systems as suggested in this statement. Again, the question of a unifying core is at stake. What purpose most represents that for which the administrative office has been established, and, for its occupants if there be more than one, what purposes of the institution will you make your own?

3  Finally, as you join your efforts with others to those of a larger system, questions of integrity and constitutional fiber may be involved. In the more severe tests in the most critical situations, from where does one draw the power to engage and disengage intellectually and emotionally and the spiritual strength to go it alone without the consolation of widespread understanding? This, too, may be an important question for those who aspire truly to lead.

# CREATIVE LIBRARY MANAGEMENT

*K H Jones*

**Part one—the limiting factors**

'Scientism' has been defined in the sense of a 'tool-box' borrowed from the physical sciences and inappropriately applied to human affairs (1). We define it here as the use of reductionist (2), mathematised methodologies, derived from the technologies, in areas, for purposes and with implications which result in inadequate, simplistic and distorted perceptions of problems and opportunities. It affects disciplines as varied as education, psychology, and environmental planning.

This article first, characterises scientism in the organisation and management of libraries; secondly, it argues the limits to be set upon reductionist methods in libraries; thirdly, it examines the other, complementary, mode of perception in library management, and, fourthly, it discusses the implications of the latter in various areas of library activity.

The paper is concerned with scientism as a *tendency* which detracts from, and limits, the effective application to library problems of scientific method and general systems theory (both of which are sometimes confused with scientism). Our Polemic is not directed at particular groups or interests, but is concerned rather to define and to criticise certain tendencies in the thinking of perhaps all of us in librarianship today.

*The effects of scientism*

Scientism brings to librarianship the 'value free' knowledge which some social scientists claim to have inherited from the physical sciences.

The determination of values, of the library's aims and major policies, is ostensibly not within the province of scientism. In an academic library, for example, it is for the governing body, advised by the librarian, to decide what weight should be given to library stock and services supportive of research needs, as opposed to the needs of teaching and learning, or, in a public library system, the support of specialised central library service departments as opposed to neighbourhood branch libraries. How, then, does scientism affect a library's aims and purposes?

48

First, a word on systems analysis is necessary. This is a valuable library management technique, and, founded upon the scientific method, can be argued as a fundamental approach to problem solving. Although its value is by no means limited to its employment in a highly structured, mathematised mode, it is in this latter form that it becomes a reductionist methodology which is particularly liable to scientistic misuse. It is concerned with very specific quantitative objectives to be achieved by measured outputs from a system comprising various dynamically inter-related elements. Parameters of the system are defined, major constraints upon its successful operation are identified, and, ideally, quantified inputs into variant systems are compared with the resultant outputs (possibly by mathematical modelling).

To return to library purpose and policy, there is, in the first place, an *inherent conservatism* in scientism. Ends in librarianship are inherently difficult to define, and there is a tendency to improve upon means the better to serve ends which remain largely unexamined. In the final analysis, scientism tends to reinforce this traditional limitation.

*Traditional preoccupations*
Librarianship is traditionally means-centred or techniques-centred, or, at best, materials-centred, as opposed to being user-centred or aims-centred. Much library history could be written around this theme. There is, for example, the traditional public library preoccupation with 'lending' and 'reference' as a first principle of departmentalisation, which has introduced an element of confusion into at least one attempt to formulate public library aims (3). There is the university library distinction between 'technical processes' and 'reader services' as a major principle of organisation. (In both cases the introduction of the 'subject' principle (subject librarians, subject departments) marks a welcome shift away from the paramountcy of techniques and materials towards more effective reader service.) Similarly, there is the traditional library school preoccupation with bibliographic organisation and classification and the relative neglect until recently of user studies (communication studies, culture, sociology). Whether this tendency is historically conditioned or somehow inherent in librarianship is difficult to say. The fact remains that the library manager is constantly faced with the problem of goal displacement, that is, the tendency to lose sight of aims and purposes and to see means as ends in themselves (4).

For example, how is a college librarian to *know* when his diligent stock building policies, his library instruction programmes, and his tireless liaison with teaching staff, are really beginning to have beneficial effect upon those learning and teaching achievements which are the raison d'être

49

of the college and its library? Increased issues of library material will tell him something, as well as more 'subjective' evidence. However, the periodic achievement of systematic stock revision schemes or the completion of a programme of library instruction are more likely to be accepted by the library staff as meaningful objectives—and not unreasonably—though these are in fact measures of *provision* rather than *impact*.

## Conservative goals

It will be argued that some mathematised systems analyses do attempt to measure overall 'library effectiveness' (as well as improving a library's housekeeping efficiency). The point is that effectiveness can only be gauged in terms of achievement of certain aims and objectives, whereas a systems analyst will only be concerned with quantifiable outputs and impacts. Emphasis is thus placed upon goals which are reductionist and limited in perspective, and, since also these goals are commonly derived from an analysis of the library's current major activities and preoccupations, they tend to be conservative goals. Fundamentally, the library is enabled to do better what it was doing before, and our argument is that scientistic modes of thought tend to close off perspectives of what the library *might* be doing. These limitations will be less, at one extreme, in certain technological information bureaux, where user needs and the purposes of the library can be defined with considerable precision. They will be greatest in the public library, where the range of possible user needs and interests, and of possible literature, will be extensive and ill-defined, and where the library's potentiality for actively conditioning the use which is made of it is very great. All this is not to deny the great value of such systems analysis and the useful measures which it provides, provided always it is subordinated to a wider perspective of library aims and activities.

An example will illustrate the above argument. *Measures of effectiveness of a university library* is a sophisticated American study by Rzasa and Baker (5) in which the 'primary goals of the (university) library are defined as follows:

1 Maximize user satisfaction;
2 Minimize the time loss (opportunity cost) to the user . . .

The criteria established for (these) primary goals were 1, the number of material items utilized; 2, the number of actual users; 3, the number of informational items sought; 4, the number of satisfactory informational items received; and 5, the amount of study space utilized.' Mathematical formulae are constructed to enable the librarian to measure the library's achievements in terms of each of these criteria.

This is a valuable analysis, not least because of the several different criteria established for measuring achievement of the library's goals. The goals themselves, however, are both limited and misleading. The aims of the parent body—the university—are nowhere mentioned in this article, and the university library is presented as a kind of autonomous processing mechanism. Let us assume that the aim and purpose of the university library is to support *and stimulate* the education and research activities of the university. If, with regard to education, this means no more than that the university library's purpose is to secure a satisfactory level of student access to the books on tutors' reading lists, then this is a relatively mechanistic task and a very necessary one—admirably suited to the mathematical constructs of Operational Research, though it leaves little scope for librarianship. However, if methods of learning and study are such that the student is required to exercise his knowledge of a subject literature, and his abilities in bibliographic and library exploitation, towards successful completion of projects and programmes on his courses, then the library is required to do much more. Positive results may be achieved in respect of all Rzasa and Baker's five criteria—and it *is* we repeat extremely useful to have measures for them—but they would still not afford adequate and conclusive evidence of the extent to which the library is helping to achieve the university's goals (as compared with its own). Indeed, it is possible to stimulate a great deal of formal activity in the library of an educational institution which may rather resemble teaching performing animals a variety of tricks than signify a meaningful educational experience. The assessment of library effectiveness can only be completed by reference to the estimates of tutors, students, researchers (for the above applies even more forcibly to the quality of research) and the subject librarians with whom they work. Did the library adequately support—and perhaps even stimulate—the work on courses X and Y or research projects A and B? Perhaps the last word on the conclusiveness of the kind of reductionist analysis criticised here rests with an anonymous but frank behavioural scientist:

'Shannon and Wiener and I
Have found it confusing to try
To measure sagacity
And channel capacity
By Sigma pi log pi.' (6)

We have noted that analyses like the above example direct thinking towards a 'closed', library-centred system, in contrast to an 'open', community-centred one. The overall effect of several such papers is to make the librarian feel that some vast, mechanistic 'open prison' has been built around him

51

which is invincible *on its own terms,* and in which he is 'free' to make only a limited range and kind of choice. This, of course, is not true, though the ingrained habits of reductionist thinking (the 'binary mentality' as it has been called) may perhaps have this limiting effect on some people. It is here in librarianship's mathematised backyard that the librarian will find seductive predictability, and the problems which have answers—problems so 'simple' that even a computer can answer them, and answers, moreover, which can be readily expressed in pounds and pence and will really mean something to senior executives who will not be persuaded by anything else.

Scientism introduces technology and then thrives on it. The computer, in particular, carries prestige and, incredibly, its utilisation is perceived as success *per se.* Sometimes librarians even spell this out. For example, among the reasons given for introducing a computer generated union cataglogue into a London public library system was that 'the image of the library as a modern service, employing the latest techniques, is also being fostered.' (7) Yet the computer-centred library follows in the same negative tradition as the catalogue-centred library.

To conclude, quantitative management techniques and their supportive technology are essential for the continued development of librarianship. What is feared is that they may create a mentality (scientism) which is reductionist, conservative, restrictive, and techniques-orientated, and which may stultify a different, though complementary, kind of mentality which is held to be more relevant to the central concerns of librarianship. Ultimately, as a profession, we may hope to achieve that fusion of the two mentalities which at present may be discerned in only a few gifted individuals. (8)


*The limits of reductionism*
In essence, librarianship is about the dynamic interaction of the thought processes of library users and library staffs, and the thought content of library materials, with a piece of original writing as one possible end product. This is a creative synergy (9) far removed from the mathematised reductionism of the technologies.

Consider first the 'documents' which constitute the library's stock, each of which is a more or less complex unit of thought. (In very few libraries can this 'thought' be entirely broken down into retrievable pieces of information.)

It is practicable and desirable to develop a quantitative stock provision system which, for example, will advise the book selector of the age of a particular section of the stock, or how many titles, at what level of sophistication, in what subjects, should be added to achieve an acceptable sophistication, in what subjects, should be added to achieve an acceptable shelf stock. However, it remains for the book selector to choose from the range of available titles presented to him by the (machine readable) bibliography, and to decide whether to replace existing copies, to duplicate or to buy new titles. The point is that mathematical microstructuring tends to become insufficiently flexible and subtle (as well as progressively uneconomical) as attention focuses down to a complexity of 'soft' variables. Mathematised machine-based systems are desirable for high speed manipulation of large quantities of 'hard-edged' data. It is a question of knowing at what point to turn the job over entirely to the human brain. That this is not generally understood is evidenced by the more ambitious hopes which are sometimes voiced for highly sophisticated machine information retrieval systems.

*Decision making*
These limits upon reductionist information processing for decision-making apply in other areas of librarianship. Writing of managerial decision making, D I Colley (10) observes that 'there are two kinds of information beating on any point of decision: the subjective group—the expression of emotion, opinion, feeling, rumour; and the objective group—the hard fact. Management is decision-making and the desire of any manager in a situation requiring a decision is to attempt to transfer as much as possible from the SUBJECTIVE group to the OBJECTIVE group.' Colley claims that the law of diminishing returns operates as information is maximised and costs escalate. 'There is not necessarily a correlation between the amount of information and the validity of a decision . . . moreover, if the right decision is made, is it of any consequence in what proportion it was based on fact or flair? If the wrong decision, would information of greater quantity and quality have affected the issue; was there time to assemble it?'

Actual and potential users constitute the second major element in librarianship, in synergic relationship with the library's stock of materials.

The characteristic reductionist model is one in which users present themselves at the library with a specific need, either a specific document or a specific 'piece' of information. If this can be 'satisfactorily' matched against a document in the library then addition can be made to record the 'number of satisfactory informational items received.' Library 'issues', 'visits' and 'consultations' are, of course, very much better than nothing in the measurement of library use; we are not concerned to deny their value, but to qualify it by reference to their several limitations.

In the first place, it is not only in recreational libraries that users enter the library without *specifically defined* 'needs' in their heads, and it is arguable that this *can* be the most creative kind of library use, rather than some kind of deficiency on the part of the users. Even if we visualise a library only in terms of 'book force' (11), that 'force' is greater than the sum of those parts with which the reductionist mentality is exclusively concerned. It is important to distinguish between 'specific item/specific information library use' on the one hand, and 'using a library' on the other. The latter is a matter of degree, but it implies much more than 'browsing'. Such 'holistic' use requires fuller investigation (12). It may also be argued that many libraries are not adequately organised for this kind of use. Neither can its value (reader 'satisfaction') be accurately measured in terms of $x$ documents borrowed or $y$ pieces of information received.

*Equating different kinds of transaction*
Secondly, there remains the problem of equating these different kinds of library transaction. Is 'eyeball contact' with five textbooks worth one research monograph? Is one public library book issue in a severely deprived locality worth five issues (in social 'value') to the professional intelligensia? Are all bibliographical enquiries of equal importance—or urgency? Is the issue of material on one subject of greater value than the issue of material on another? How much less 'satisfaction' is there if a borrower has to reserve a book and wait for it? Alternatively, how much less satisfaction is there if the borrower has to return the book at the end of a very short loan period, with no option of renewing the loan because others are waiting to borrow the book? Asking readers themselves to cost bibliographical deprivation and satisfaction may have relevance in certain special library areas where a costing structure is more readily available. However, it has little general applicability, both because of an intrinsic meaninglessness (how would you cost deprivation of all librarianship literature for two years?), and because library use is (with some qualifications) an indivisible social good which is transferred beyond the 'primary' user.

A more fundamental criticism of the mechanistic model of library use, which processes inputs of specific needs with specific documents and specific pieces of information, is that it emphasises the *service* conception of librarianship, as opposed to the *synergic*. It emphasises a stimulus-response system in which users provide the stimulus and the library responds. Yet user demands and expectations are conditioned by what the library already is—or, rather, what the user *thinks* it is. (Hence the not uncommon surprise of a public library user who discovers that the library also functions as a local information bureau, or that it is able to provide him with scholarly and esoteric books.) The service concept of librarianship tacitly accepts and confirms these expectations and assumptions, and

54

scientism's service methodology improves library performance within these assumptions. By contrast, the synergic model emphasises library stimulus and reader response, as well as reader demand and library response, and is constantly striving to expand the expectations and assumptions of actual and potential users.

The central task of a creative librarianship is the synergic transcendence of the service conception examined above. By its materials selection, presentation and display, and its retrieval devices, and facilities and stimulus for exploring the stock and services, by its wide ranging involvement with users and the user community (through dissemination and promotional activities, through education in library use and the subject literatures, through participation in the parent community's deliberative and decision making bodies, through the public library as a major recreational and cultural agency), by all these means does the library become an autonomous and an active agent of change in its community. Synergic librarianship is about the enormous *potential* capacity of a library to stimulate and carry forward the community and to transcend its own original self through this cumulative impact on the community. Individual libraries are more, or less, synergic; it is partly a matter of resources and of community responsiveness, but it is also very much a matter of the creative imagination and responsiveness of librarians. It is our argument that the mentality of scientism threatens that kind of creativity. At the same time, the techniques of quantitative systems analysis and mathematical modelling have an essential part to play in *supporting* that creativity. (In the collection and preliminary analysis of large quantities of user and use data, for example.)

*Service and synergic conceptions*
The contrast between the service and the synergic conceptions is most dramatically exemplified by comparison of the traditional college library with the emergent 'library-college'. In the former the library is envisaged as a service department of the college; in the latter 'the library contains the educational community and acts as the major teaching instrument' (13).

The management of the library's second major resource—staff—is no more amenable to reductionist treatment than are library stocks or users. It is noteworthy that evidence assembled to 'demonstrate' the effectiveness of one style of library personnel management as against another has proved inconclusive (14). There are too many 'soft variables' for any firm conclusions to be generally accepted.

Quantitative management techniques, and the mechanisation which often follows their application, are intended to increase library effectiveness and (usually) to reduce staffing costs. They have achieved important successes in such areas of mechanistic activity as acquisitions, issues, and manipulation of catalogue entries. However, the very strengths of mathematised systems analysis in the processing of things are its weakness in releasing the creative energies of people. In this area, as in others, it tends to have a restrictive and conservative effect. For example, in the smaller public branch libraries there are problems regarding the full employment of professional staff on professional work. In more than one system O & M teams have been brought in to investigate this problem. They have calculated that only $x\%$ of work at branch libraries of a certain size is professional work, and as a result of their recommendations new staffing ratios have been introduced for professional staffs. The point is that this kind of analysis is valid *only within existing conventions of library practice.* Where local library service has been creatively conceived as a complex community 'outreach' activity, professional staffs are involved in almost twice as much professional work as that conventionally practised within the walls of a branch library (15).

### MbO straitjacket
The scientistic mentality also tends to have a restrictive effect upon the creativity of the staff themselves. It sees the library system as a mechanism in which large quantities of data are gathered and processed to enable senior management to identify problems, set objectives, and determine outputs. It is convinced of its ability accurately to dimension problems out there in the field. It has the habit of prediction. It can accommodate a certain amount of staff consultation, but this is conditioned by a hierarchy of Procrustean job descriptions and choice from a limited range of highly specific and quantified targets and objectives. Management by Objectives (MbO) is not in itself a style of management, and does not of itself release staff initiative and creativity. It *can* become something of a straitjacket and a means of forcing up work pressure on a reluctant staff.

The librarian is faced with many complex psycho-social problems, in the fields of education, information, research, culture and recreation. Senior management must be aware of the limits it must set to the usefulness of the increasing amount of valuable data made available to it by computer processing, and must appreciate that, in some respects, the local 'picture' available only to subordinates working in specific areas will have greater validity for decision making.

For example, several field teams of public librarians may be developing a service, each to a different kind of community. They will each have a lot to learn, and should be continually rethinking their objectives and the means of achieving them. Beyond certain common requirements, the work will develop differently, because of the different kinds of community and the different collective personalities of the teams. At any point in time, each team will possess an extremely complex and subtle picture of the problems facing it; it will have the 'feel' of the different communities in a sense not available to senior management, and some of its less straight-forward decisions will have an intuitive rather than a 'rational' basis.

Such as project is at the opposite extreme to the analysis necessary for developing, for example, a new stock accession system. The two kinds of mentality—methodology is not the right word here—are not exclusive to each of these examples, but it is clear where each *should* predominate. And yet it is the 'rational', reductionist kind of systems analysis which at present dominates the thinking of the new librarianship, and this means that the new librarianship is so much less than it could be.

Consider, for example, an academic library. 'A', which invests its re-sources heavily towards achievement of a close and dynamic relationship with faculty and students through development of a team of well-qualified subject librarians, liaising with the different departments in respect of materials selection, bibliographical servicing, and library instruction. It is interesting to reflect whether it would not be making a stronger contri-bution to the institution's educational and research effort than library 'B', where all the effort was going into development of a 'total systems' mechani-sation programme. Admittedly, the two developments complement and support one another, and, admittedly, circumstances alter cases and exten-sive mechanisation may be necessary to maintain a particular library's basic services in the face of rising demands on the system. Our point is, how-ever, that the present climate of opinion is scientistic and places undue emphasis upon the latter kind of development, with a possible loss of potential library effectiveness.

*Priorities wrongly ordered*
It is a commonplace that staff are the most expensive resource in the library budget. Yet it is the resource with the greatest and perhaps most under-used potential, and its achievements and failures tend to be more variable and unpredictable than in the management of other resources. Yet comparison of the resources and attention devoted to reductionist analysis and machine-based systems with the low level of training and development of librarians suggests that perhaps our priorities are wrongly ordered.

Maybe the Bains Report on the management of the new local govern-ment (the biggest employer of United Kingdom librarians) is a harbinger of the change of emphasis suggested above. The Report urges 'a much greater awareness of the importance of personnel management', and it notes 'recent criticisms of the growth of central management services on the grounds that they have become a very costly item and that expected benefits have not been realised. It is said that their cost benefits have not been established' (16).

## An existential librarianship

To conclude this first part of the paper we shall introduce a more comprehensive mode of knowing for the library manager than that offered by scientism. Next month we shall examine some areas of library activity in which the existential perspective seems particularly important.

For 'library science' as for other contemporary technologies there appears to be only one mode of knowing which enjoys full academic respectability. This has been variously termed 'conceptual', 'logical', 'explicit', 'reductionist', and 'rational-experimental', and derives from the methodology of the physical sciences and, more particularly, the technologies. It contrasts with a 'perceptual', 'dialectical', 'implicit', 'existential', and 'experiential' mode of knowing. Donald Schon has argued the decreasing effectiveness of the 'rational-experimental model of knowing' as society moves beyond 'the stable state'. He concludes that 'there are other modes of knowing that are not strange and mysterious, but do require taking seriously: forms of perception which do not fall within the experimental model' (17).

## Immature librarianship, swaddled in tradition

It must be emphasised, however, that scientific method and general systems theory do embrace not one but both of these modes of perception, though commonly believed to relate only to the first. Thus Michael Polanyi, the distinguished physicist, has argued that 'objectivism' is a restriction upon true scientific perception, a 'Laplacean folly', a 'delusion which remains unbroken to this day'. In its place he substitutes 'personal knowledge', which is grounded upon the current scientific consensus of 'objective' realities.

It is the rapidly expanding technologies which have over-emphasised the importance of reductionist perception and methodology. The technologist (or his employer) is not so much concerned with achieving cash results for his client, and with selling kinds of expertise which his client does not possess. In areas where technological knowing is wholly relevant this activity is desirable and necessary (though it is questionable whether there is *any* technology in which the implicit, existential perception is without relevance). To an immature librarianship, swaddled in tradition, reductionist technology has offered a quantitative and predictive methodology which has both improved its effectiveness and given it prestige. Beyond the present reach of this methodology there is seen a dark frontier land, where 'library science' is seen solely in terms of advancing this frontier. Presumably the 'soft' knowledge, dependent upon less structured modes of perception, can be dispersed into certain marginal areas of 'library science'.

Our contrary argument is that both modes of knowing are essential to librarianship. Ronald Benge has argued, further, that 'the key point for understanding is that tacit, or existential, knowledge is the *dominant principle of all knowing,* and that if it is rejected as unscientific or illogical, this automatically involves the rejection of the possibility of any knowledge whatsoever' (18) (presumably leaving only a complex of pieces of information?). Over-exposure to reductionist modes of thinking may lead to inability to comprehend reality in any other way. The far from successful preoccupations of much of the academic establishment in the social sciences with achieving a 'scientific rigour' comparable with that of the high-prestige physical sciences is the most striking example of this 'blindness'.

*References and notes*

1 The 'tools' are examined one by one in Hampden-Turner, C: Radical man: the process of psycho-social development. Duckworth, 1971, Ch I.

2 Reductionism—The reduction of wholes—of 'holistic' phenomena—into constituent parts. The whole may be 'more' than the sum of the parts, may be qualitatively different from them and may transcend them. Reductive analysis assumes that the parts collectively explain the whole, as if a clock, for example, were explicable in terms of the levers, pinions and other mechanisms which constitute it. Similarly, reductionism tends to conceive a 'built' library stock of mutually supportive documents as if it were an aggregate of functionally unrelated items, each meeting a specific potential need.

3 Library Association. London & Home Counties branch. Public library aims and objectives. Library Association record, 73 (12), December 1971, 233-234.

4 There is an interesting discussion in Haak, J R: Goal displacement. Library journal, 96 (9), 1 May 1971, 1573-1578.

5 Rzasa, P V and Baker, N R: Meaures of effectiveness for a university library. Asis: Journal of the American Society for Information Science, 23 (4), July-August 1972, 248-253.

6 Behavioural science, vol 7, July 1962, 395.

7 Meakin, A O: The production of a printed union catalogue by computer. Library Association record 67 (9), September 1965, 315.

8   It is with such a fusion that Robert S Taylor is concerned in his stimulating book The making of a library: the academic library in transition. Becker & Hayes, 1972.

9   Synergy—means here an interaction of different elements to produce a synthesis which is a qualitative development from the óriginal elements and which transcends them. Synergy is not a state or a condition, but a synamic and potentially escalating process. Thus, the 'synthesis' may be no more than the change in a reader's mind after borrowing and reading a library book. When he returns to the library to use it again, to that extent he is a different person. The whole concept of synergic librarianship merits closer examination. This use of the term is explored more fully in Hampton-Turner, C: Radical man. Duckworth, 1971.

10   Colley, D I: Information and management. Library Association record, 74 (9), Sept 1972, 159-161.

. 11   For a discussion of this important concept, see Savage, E A: Library Association record, 58 (9) Sept 1956, 327-331.

12   See, for example, Apted, S M: General purpose browsing. Library Association record, 73 (12) Dec 1971, 228-230.

13   Beswick, N W: The library college: the true university? Library Association record, 69 (6) June 1967, 198-202.

14   Lynch, B: Participative management in relation to library effectiveness, and Marchant, M P: And a response. College and research libraries, 33 (5) Sept 1972, 382-397. Lynch's paper is a critique of Marchant, M P: Participative management as related to personnel development. Library trends, 20 (1) 20 July 1971, 48-59.

15   On this and other aspects of staff management and deployment treated in this paper, see Jones K: Staff deployment. New library world, 73 (864) June 1972, 320-323.

16   Great Britain. Department of the Environment: The new local authorities: management and structure. Report of a study group . . . (Bains Report). HMSO, 1972.

17   (Reith Lectures 1970), Listener, 84 (2177) 24 Dec 1970, 877. (Also available in book form: Schon, D A: Beyond the stable state: public and private learning in a changing society. Temple-Smith, ;971).

18   Benge, R C: Communication and identity. Bingley, 1972; Hamden, Conn, Linnet; 43.


**Part two—the existential perspective**
Beyond its mechanistic support systems, a library is, fundamentally, a *holistic system* in which two plus two never equals four and where the existential mode of perception must be paramount. Most librarians sense this; it is inherent in their daily work. We use the term 'existential' because it emphasises the autonomous and creative human element which is of the essence of librarianship (*Ex-istere*, to stand out), and because it relates the

60

argument of this paper to a comparable polemic in psychology, education, sociology, management theory and elsewhere (19).

The existential perspective seems particularly important in the following areas of library activity;

### (a) Organising progress and gauging achievement

Agreed aims and policies are essential for a library system if it is to develop satisfactorily, and to counteract means-centred tendencies. At the level at which the library operates as a processing and servicing mechanism precise objectives are desirable. However, in the sense that the library organises the creative interaction of materials, users and librarians, the staff will need freedom to experiment and feel their way in the development and work-through of programmes. There are more roads than one leading in the agreed direction of the library's advance, and which proves to be the best may depend on the particular talents and interests of staff involved. (In passing we should note the importance of the *team* in such creative situations, contrasting with a structure of 'fixed function' posts (15).)

In Part One of this paper we criticised the scientistic mentality for its restrictive effect upon staff creativity, and emphasised the importance of 'on the spot', experiential learning and knowing, in contrast to the wholly explicit information available to senior management. We quoted as an example the experience of field teams of public librarians developing a community service, and the same example would serve equally well as a warning against tying staff up with tight, closely worded programmes and pedestrian objectives (even if they have largely devised them themselves! ). Always assuming there is the necessary training, experience and ability, staff are more likely to show originality, imagination and executive enthusiasm where there is an openness about short term objectives and freedom to take risks and make mistakes and learn from them.

Similarly, consider the interaction of library staff, teachers and students in a college, in which, through months of discussion, experiment and partial failure, different interests, attitudes, needs come to be understood, and confidence is established, leading to a programme of education in library and literature use which really does 'bite'. At the outset the library might have some general aims and principles, and some possible lines of advance, beyond which it would 'play it by ear'. The programmes and methods eventually adopted would be of a kind not conceived at the outset of the project. Compare a predominantly non-learning, non-experimental approach, in which information is gathered about the different courses and subjects, formal consultations effected, programmes framed, and target dates set for their implementation. The whole project is completed satis-factorily (but only on its own terms).

Ultimately it is only through feedback from members of the community which is being served and stimulated that a library's *impact* (as opposed to its *provision* and *output*) can be gauged and its effectiveness established. And because users' expectations of libraries tend to be low, we must not exclude the consensus judgement of an exacting and self-critical staff.

Corporate planning and management situations may also provide evidence of achievement, though the estimate of co-workers in other disciplines or professions (who may or may not be users of the particular library service). For example, consider, in local government, a field team of officers from different departments, working on an extended community project—housing officers, teachers, environmental planners, social workers, youth leaders, community relations workers, and public librarians. The members of the team will soon become aware of which colleagues' work and which Depart-ment is making some impact, even though there may be no statistics to indicate 'target achievement'. The teachers will know through their pupils about the impression made by the new stock and activities at the branch library; the youth worker will know that it is the only public building in the neighbourhood that does not receive the attention of vandals . . .

The Delphi technique is an interesting example of the use of consensus as an aid to decision making in 'soft' areas of library management. This uses a consensus of expert opinion for 'forecasting in loosely structured problem areas' (20).

## (b) Creative risk-taking

If chief librarians want a really creative style of work from their staff, then any preoccupation they—and therefore their staff— may have with security, precision and prediction, with familiar routines and with always getting the small things right, will need to be periodically shaken out in order to keep the organisation flexible and adaptable (21). In any case, most effec-tive libraries (if only by virtue of their very effectiveness) are subject con-tinuously to pressures which make such periods of rethinking, of reorgan-isation, of 'suspended judgement', of 'creative risk-taking' desirable for maintaining and increasing that effectiveness. Indeed, there are some loosely structured library systems which appear to be in an almost con-tinual state of flux, distinguishable from chaos by the unusually high morale of the staff and their close relationship with an appreciative body of users amongst whom only the newcomers are surprised. The kinds of situation we have in mind require of the staff a stong sense of professional identity and a keen perception of the possible (which is what professional education and training are really about). Those of us who have worked in libraries of this kind are unlikely to forget the experience. Those who 'work' (or, rather, are 'used') in libraries which are very much of another kind do have opportunities for creative subversion, and sometimes this is the only way in which they can retain a sense of professional purpose and self-respect (22).

*(c) From library service to library synergy*
We have already introduced the idea of the synergic library, which grows out of, and transcends, the service concept. We refer to the synergy of users, documents and staff whose dynamism derives from the sustained and imaginative effort of the librarians to make of their library a positive stimulus to creative use. The library goes beyond being a convenient service, a supplier of required items (or maybe just 'something to read'), and seeks to increase the number of purposive (and non-purposive) browsers, bibliothecal adventurers, users of more than their own corner of the library, users for whom a session in the library *as a whole* ('holistic' use) is as much a creative experience as any single one of the items read in it or any one of the services used. And by the same token the synergic library invites the participation of the non-user. And, of course, it is concerned to stimulate the more conventional *specific* kind of use as well as the more *holistic* kind of use suggested in the following section.

The development of synergy and the shift from an exclusively service role *(and the mentality which goes with it)* implies a new look, a review, covering all aspects of librarianship, ranging from the design and layout of libraries to programmes for the promotion of their use. Its essential starting point, however, is a wholehearted user-centred approach to the work. This means a great deal more knowledge of users, both implicit and explicit, and this needs to go beyond knowledge of library use.

To contrast 'service' with 'synergy' is no more than an introductory convenience, since there are different kinds of ideas. Good service does not only 'satisfy' the reader; it stimulates and involves him further, as does also a good, well-built stock of materials. It is simply that library 'service' is associated with a user-demand, library-supply transaction which is non-synergic in that it is not the stimulus for, and start of, a process of dynamic interaction of user, materials, and staff. This is what we mean when we refer to the 'service concept' of librarianship. Clearly there are certain other library activities which are more explicitly directed to the stimulating of such a synergy. Public library 'outreach' activities, or the shift in learning and teaching from classroom to school library, are examples. Again, a well manned and supported enquiry desk will, variously, provide specific pieces of information on request or it may open up a whole range of possibilities of which the enquirer was unaware. Which it does will depend mainly upon the nature and potential of the enquiry, but also upon *how the librarian at the desk sees his job*. Some enquiries are amenable both to a 'service' type of response or they may mark the beginning of a synergic process. And stimulus is the starting point of the synergic library experience, which will subsequently be sustained by the effectiveness of stock and services or else will languish in unfulfilled promise. An extended and sophisticated enquiry will assume the form of an oral or written dialogue, over a period of time, which is of the essence of library synergy.

In some areas of activity, however, the attempt to stimulate and involve actual and potential users may have to compete for resources with the more conventional provision to meet the highly specific demands of the highly purposive reader (who, we must remember, may reappear at another time in need of a different kind of use). The synergic library has to cater for a wide range of kinds of use. For example, a public library stock informally arranged to attract, interest, stimulate and involve use which is initially non-purposive, and which resembles a popular bookshop in a lounge, will present for specific and purposive use an arrangement less helpful than a shelf stock conventionally ordered systematically by subject. It would be self-defeating to stimulate an interest which cannot readily be followed up because the enquirer cannot easily discover further material; provision, therefore, needs to be made for both kinds of use.

Some types of library have an intrinsically greater potential as stimulators and self-developers. The public library is a particularly interesting example. Its purposes are not readily defined by the community it serves, and its potentialities remain pinned down by the weight of its own past (23).


*(d) Facilitating 'holistic' as well as 'specific' library use*
Contrast the problems of a librarian responsible for the exploitation of a collection of novels with another who has a similar duty in respect of a collection of technical reports in a highly structured subject. Each is concerned to facilitate the use of his stock by making its content more accessible by some logical arrangement of the physical items, and by cataloguing and indexing them according to some helpful characteristic, such as author or contents. Ultimately, both librarians are concerned with maximum acceptable thought transfer from the stock to the users' minds. They have the same purpose, but they have problems of a very different order.

Information science revolutionised librarianship by analysing the subject content of documents into units of 'information' with a degree of sophistication which surpassed 'subject cataloguing', and, through its indexing and disseminating activities, manipulated the information to serve a variety of user needs and approaches. This is essentially a reductionist activity, and a very necessary one. It is concerned with relatively *specific* use of relatively *specific* content. This contrasts with the tendency to 'holistic' use, whether the 'whole' is a book or a subject area or an entire library. These 'wholes' for this purpose are *conceived* as being integral, indivisible, irreducible, and greater than the elements comprising them. An example would be a subject collection or a literature guide *used* rather to illuminate the structure and character of a literature as a whole than to identify specific items.

An existential librarianship is concerned to explore beyond reductionism, and, mindful of the controversy in psychology and other social sciences about 'holistic' as opposed to 'reductionist' conceptions, must consider in what sense it is possible to define 'holistic' content and use in librarianship. This concept has already been introduced in this paper. Evidently there are subject areas (notably in the humanities) in which the reductionist concept of 'information' has limited relevance. Literature provides an extreme example, but it is also obvious that one does not use a library to study the causes of the French Revolution in the same way as to discover the melting point of copper, or even how an internal combustion engine works. The French Revolution tends to be a holistic subject in that it cannot be structured and analysed into constituent units except in a relatively arbitrary and subjective way which is of limited value. The parts are subsumed in the whole. (It is also noteworthy that to the extent it has 'meaning' it has different meaning for different people, so far as history exists in the mind.) In traditional librarianship readers were presumed to know something about the content of the literatures in which they were interested, and the librarian commonly limited himself to providing an author or name catalogue. (Public library fiction collections are still more of a 'lucky dip' for most readers than they should be.)

In the future more thought will need to be given to construction of holistic lines of communication between both individual 'documents' and groups of related materials, on the one hand, and the users on the other. Arrangements of material for suggestive browsing, guides to subject literatures (suited to different kinds of use and user), 'state of the art' reviews, annotated reading lists, abstracts, and education in subject bibliography, are all examples of holistic bridge-building, as is also an enquiry desk staffed by librarians with adequate subject and subject-bibliographical knowledge.

The school learning resources centre is a striking example of the library revolutionised so as to encourage learners with the most ready possible access to the knowledge locked in book materials. Teachers and librarians are mobilised for the purpose, and audio-visual materials are added to introduce as well as to complement less readily accessible or attractive print-bound knowledge. Various materials are combined in study kits and displays to provide the best access to particular subjects. Access in terms of selective analysis (as in the conventional library), is not enough here, and a variety of holistic 'bridges' have to be built.

In some cases users build their own bridges. In a college, the links between students' minds and the contents of the library materials they are enjoined to study are not only formed through conventional teaching but also, in the more progressive places, through duplicated 'study guides' and other 'handouts' which constitute introductions to the subject, and selected readings, carefully adapted to the students' needs. These guides are produced by the different tutors, and are more sophisticated than the conventional reading lists.

We believe that the concept of holistic use could profitably be explored further, though here, as elsewhere in this paper, we are doing no more than suggesting new ways of looking at, and developing, a landscape of library activity which already exemplifies our arguments.

*(e) Education for creative librarianship*
In his book *Lateral thinking: a textbook of creativity*, Edward de Bono observes that 'the emphasis on education has always been on logical sequential thinking, which is, by tradition, the only proper use of information. . . . This selective type of thinking needs to be supplemented with the generative qualities of creative thinking . . . This book is about lateral thinking, which is the process of using information to bring about creativity and insight restructuring.' De Bono sees creativity not as 'some mysterious talent to be vaguely encouraged,' but as something that can be achieved by systematic learning (24).

Just as the various quantitative management techniques are introduced into the education of librarians, so also do we need creativity sessions, for the other kind of knowledge, the other kind of problem solving. Weekend 'workshops' of this kind would give librarians opportunity collectively to break through to existential thinking in the context of their own libraries. Typical methods would be case studies, simulated exercises, brainstorming sessions, T groups, and other kinds of unstructured group work. One problem with which such workshops would be concerned would be the

66

kind of management and training needed to develop staff creativity. Such workshops would be one-sided in the sense that the two modes of knowing and problem solving complement one another; however, some effort of the kind suggested would be necessary in order to correct the imbalance with which this paper is concerned. The implications for full time education in librarianship of all that has been said here would more properly form the subject of a separate paper . . .

The fears which prompted the writing of this paper are those expressed by Ronald Benge:

'Traditional librarianship was historically rooted in the humanities, and subsequently (quite rightly) has been modified by scientific and technical growth, and particularly by the science of information retrieval. But there is now a danger that the technical emphasis will take over the whole field, and that traditional librarianship will become an awkward 'sub-culture' within the main field of library science. . . . Nobody will admit to a deliberate such intention, but 'they', who include some 'library educators' (lecturers) behave *as if* they are possessed of this intention, by ignoring in practice non-technical elements of librarianship activity (25).'

However, over the last two decades there has emerged in several different areas of life and culture a new, existential humanism, which is of cardinal importance in the social sciences. This paper is a first attempt, hesitant and imperfect, to examine its relevance to librarianship, and to argue from a critique of 'library science' forward towards a new librarianship, which will synthesise both the existential and the reductionist modes of knowing and doing (26).

*References and notes*

19 Naming existential humanists is neither easy nor helpful. However, thinkers as varied as the following may provide a field of reference: Noam Chomsky, Michael Foucault, Erich Fromm, Arthur Koestler, R D Laing, Herbert Marcuse, Abraham Maslow, Rollo May, J-P Sartre, and Norbert Wiener. In the field of management theory the work of C Argyris, D McGregor and R Likert shows a similar orientation.

20 Wennerberg, U: Using the Delphi technique for planning the future of libraries. Unesco bulletin for libraries, 26 (5) Sept-Oct 1972, 242-245.

21 Several examples of 'creative risk taking' are to be found in management literature. One of the most dramatic is of Michael Cooley and 'Plant Y' in Guest, R H: Organisational change: the effect of successful leadership. Irwin & Dorsey, Homewood (USA), 1962, 42ff.

22 An entertaining and high spirited guide to positive organisational subversion is Townsend, R: Up the organisation. Michael Joseph, 1970.

23   For a further discussion see Jones, K H: Towards a re-interpretation of public library purpose. New library world, 73 (855), Sept 1971, 76-79, 82.

24   De Bono, E: Lateral thinking: a textbook of creativity. Ward Lock Educational, 1970, 7 and 297. Note also De Bono, E: Lateral thinking for management: a handbook. McGraw-Hill, 1971.

25   Benge, R C: Communication and identity, Bingley, 1972; Hamden, Conn, Linnet; 27.

26   This paper also owes much to other convergent lines of thought—to general system theory, to certain trends in the philosophy of science, and to Marxian dialectic. Noteworthy in this respect are review articles in the Journal of librarianship in which D J Foskett examines the relevance to librarianship of the following three books, and explores in greater detail some of the fundamental ideas introduced in this present paper. They are: Ziman, J M: Public knowledge and the social dimension of science. CUP, 1968 (review: Foskett, D J: Public knowledge and the social dimension of librarianship, Journal of librarianship, 1 (1) Jan 1969, 68-72). Pantin, C F A: The relations between the sciences. CUP, 1968 (review: Foskett, D J: Libraries and the structure of knowledge, Journal of librarianship, 1 (3) July 1969, 191-194). Bertalanffy, L von: General system theory . . . Allen Lane the Penguin Press, 1971 (review: Foskett, D J: Information and general system theory, Journal of librarianship, 4 (3) July 1972, 205-209).

# 2
# Purpose and planning

Traditionally, the librarian 'runs' his library. Purpose and value of the service are seemingly implicit, and only become implicit in the resounding generalisations of such documents as the Unesco Public Library Manifesto (1972).

In the latter half of the 20th century the pace of social change has quickened, organisations have become larger and more complex, and the parent organisations of libraries have invited them to define more explicitly their aims and purposes, and to justify the share of expenditure traditionally assigned to them. The methodology of science has been applied to the management of organisational complexity, and Management by Objectives (MbO) has emerged as an established system for deploying resources for the achievement of specific objectives or targets. The claims of MbO are so compelling, in principle at least, as to be difficult to reject, but in the classic form expounded by Humble (1973) it is open to criticism on several grounds. A brief description of the method will be found in the paper by Dutton in this reader (p 29), but, like so many management methods, it takes its colour from the *kind* of organisation in which it is practised. It has been variously described as a 'straitjacket' and a 'do-it-yourself-hangman's-kit', but since much of the library management literature is prescriptive and anodyne in character it is difficult for the inexperienced reader to form his own opinion of the value of the practice which lies behind the theory.

The paper by John R Haak which follows refers to undergraduate libraries, but his treatment of the problems of formulating objectives for libraries (and particularly the phenomenon of 'goal displacement') makes for thoughtful reading by librarians in other fields. Orr (1973) also offers a valuable introduction to the crucial question of what *is* 'library effectiveness' and how it is to be measured. Several interesting examples of MbO practice drawn from UK public libraries will be found in the pamphlet *Aspects of public library management* (Great Britain. Department of Education and Science, 1973), and Bone (1975) has reported the experience of a number of US public libraries. The problems of framing objectives for special libraries have been discussed by Gilchrist (1973).

The pressures for organised change, and the resources available to achieve change, are such that in many parts of the world completely new national library systems have been created, whilst even in a developed country like the UK the last decade has seen both the refashioning of the National Library and the public library service, and the assumption of some measure of state responsibility for library planning and control. Sewell's article refers to industrialised as well as to developing countries, and emphasises the need to develop well integrated national library services which are, in their turn, related to the educational, social and economic needs—and development plans—of the countries concerned.

Taken together Haak's and Sewell's papers exemplify common management dilemmas faced by the librarian. Haak's emphasis is upon 'tangible goals', yet 'goal displacement' as formulated by Merton (1957) is most likely to take place in bureaucratic institutions where sufficient concern is not given to the overall aims or 'intangible goals'. Sewell pleads for library objectives to be considered in the light of national and international objectives, and on paper a neat hierarchy of objectives, from international through national and institutional down to those of individual library systems and sub-systems, may suit the planner, but the individual librarian's basic concern will be with serving his own community. The higher the hierarchy is ascended, the wider becomes the perception of libraries, so that Sewell can favour integration of library services, whilst librarians aiming basically to serve their own communities can perceive integration as a threat to their own services and personal status. In the United Kingdom both the possibilities and the problems have been discussed by Wilson and Marsterson (1974).

The two papers in this section of the reader point to another development in managing and planning which will affect libraries increasingly in the future. We refer to 'corporate management', by which the work of subdivisions of any organisation are coordinated for the pursuit of common goals. This has been a fundamental idea to emerge from local government reorganisation in the UK (Bains Report, 1972), and is beginning to affect the management of several UK public libraries. There has been complaint that the expensive planning exercises near the apex of the hierarchy have not so far been accompanied by sufficient inter-departmental achievement at the 'grassroots' as would justify them. Here again, the state-of-the-art is more difficult to discover than is the state-of-the-literature. Corporate management, like MbO, has, in principle, many attractions for the library manager, but executive management still appears to have a long way to go in using it to produce a more effective (and more tolerable) organisation. It is therefore necessary still to make a distinction between corporate planning and corporate management. The former is often present but the latter is often absent.

The problem is not only one for local government. In educational institutions, if the library is to be developed as a learning resource centre then some kind of corporate management of curriculum development of the whole business of learning and teaching, which would involve teachers,

71

librarians, administrators, and educational technologists, is surely necessary. A start has been made (for example Fothergill, 1971, 1973), but a good deal more needs to be done.

# THE DEVELOPMENT OF LIBRARY SERVICES:
# THE BASIS OF THEIR PLANNING AND DEVELOPMENT

*P H Sewell*

Perhaps more unconsciously than consciously we are moving in Britain away from a situation where many institutions and categories of institutions are allowed to grow up in an uncoordinated way towards one in which considerable resources are only committed on the basis of proved need and in reference to agreed lines of national development. I have over the past two years been reading in the field not only of library planning, but of educational planning and its links with economic and social planning, particularly in the developing countries. Although I could not claim expertise in any of these fields as a result of this reading, it has seemed to me that by widening our sphere of interest a little beyond library matters we may, as librarians, gain fresh insight into library problems. Such insight may be the result partly of our increased ability to view library services, not just as a basic community service in its own right, but as an integral part of other national and community services. May I attempt to illustrate this proposition?

## Assessing the development of library service

In all probability a librarian's first reaction to the task of assessing the development of library services is to deal with the topic in terms of quantitative development—new libraries established, new buildings erected and increases in the annual input of books, periodicals and other material. He would also be likely to consider improvements of efficiency in carrying out the technical/professional tasks involved in the acquisition, recording and exploitation of library materials. If he were writing in Britain within the last five years or so he would, no doubt, also consider measures taken both to match library service to the expressed needs of library users as shown up by reader surveys and to ensure that library users had received at least some basic instruction in the use of libraries and library materials.

73

It is less likely that he would feel it necessary first to examine the educational, social, cultural, scientific and economic aims and objectives of the country under consideration, then to investigate in conjunction with appropriate experts and practitioners the potential contribution which library services have to make to the achievement of these objectives and finally attempt to assess the extent to which this contribution has been made. Yet, I suggest, such an assessment would be far more meaningful.

Any assessment of the development of library services in these latter terms will, of course, be easier when there are fully enunciated official policies related to the development of various facets of the life of the community. However, even in a country such as the United Kingdom, where in a number of areas of national life communal aims and objectives are to be arrived at by taking a consensus of informed opinion, rather than through a study of statutes and official reports, broad statements of national aims and objectives can, no doubt, be produced which would command a wide measure of support.

The analysis of the potential contribution of library services (and here we must include literature-based information services) to the attainment of various national objectives is unquestionably a complex matter, but one which is certainly susceptible to investigation. Indeed, one can imagine few more stimulating experiences for librarians than participation in a series of working groups with educators concerned with various levels of formal and informal education, sociologists, scientists, industrialists and economists which were seeking to identify the optimum role for library services in contributing to current objectives. One difficulty which is bound to emerge is that in most areas of national and communal life there are a series of overlapping objectives, and at different times one or the other takes priority. This difficulty does not invalidate this approach. Rather it emphasizes both the value of basing library development policies on as thorough as possible a study of all relevant factors to enable policy changes to be seen in context and the need for regular reassessment of library service objectives in the light of changes in objectives in different sectors of community life.

*Library service and educational objectives*
Let us take an example to indicate the way in which the development of library services can become an integral part of educational development. The Main Working Document for the Unesco Expert Meeting on the National Planning of Library Services in Asia, Colombo, 1967 (COM/CS/ 190/3) has a chapter on the 'Role of library services in educational, social and economic development in Asia' which includes the following passage:

'The educational situation, as seen in the social context, demands that large numbers of children should have a thorough educational exposure and that schools should offer programmes calculated to orient the children towards active participation in the tasks of development and modernization. It is noted that in Asia there is a widespread preference for an academic type of education, unsuited to the requirements of modernization and development. The philosophy and practice of teaching in Asian countries often works to discourage inquiry and initiative among students; there is excessive emphasis on conformity and not enough on independent discovery; literary subjects, looking towards prestigious, white-collar appointments take undue precedence over practical and scientific instruction.'

The Report of the Education Commission of the Government of India, had already in 1966 made a plea for turning from a curriculum and text-book-centred teaching to student and library-centred teaching. The Report says, 'Given enthusiastic teachers who teach with books and librarians who can cooperate with them in converting the library into an intellectual workshop, even a comparatively small collection of books can work wonders in the lives of students. . . . Indeed, as Tagore put it, what makes a library big and purposeful is its use and not the bigness of the building or the collection (1).'

It should be noted that the desired educational effect demands equal, or at least, equally purposeful and understanding, contribution from librarians and teachers. Librarians may wince somewhat at the reference to the usefulness of small collections, but teachers sometimes wince at the unsuitability for educational purposes of some large collections and the limited educational impact which they sometimes have. The use of libraries in educational institutions is clearly something which calls for the combined approach of librarians and educators at all levels—those concerned with overall strategy, local tactics and day to day operation.

One of the more obvious roles of library service is in support of literacy, whether it is gained through fundamental education campaigns or through attendance at primary schools. Yet until very recently educational development and library development plans were often not considered together. This was one reason among others for the poor quality and impermanence of the educational experience resulting from some development plans. In economic terms library service may be considered an investment in consolidating literacy, in technical advance and often in social integration. Moreover, by doing something to fill in the gap between the educationally privileged and those less privileged, public library service can act as a social cement. The generation gap can.be even wider when only the young generation has functional literacy.

It would, of course, be wrong to suggest that there is no significant interaction between librarians and library-providing bodies and those groups which are professionally concerned with educational, social, cultural and economic objectives. Clearly interaction and dialogue takes place continually and it comes to the surface especially when budgets are being agreed and resources allocated. Such dialogue and interaction is, however, largely at the tactical and institutional level rather than at levels where overall strategy is the main concern. Further it is likely that in many cases such interaction as exists is frequently less fruitful than it might be because librarians on the one hand and the various groups of experts and administrators on the other are not sufficiently informed of the others' current problems, resources and objectives.

*Some current problems in educational planning.*
It may be instructive to draw attention to some of the matters commented on at Unesco's International Conference on Educational Planning, 1968 (2). It was pointed out that educational planning must be a continuous, integrated, flexible process, concerned with obtaining education of the highest quality and efficiency and must be comprehensive, embracing all levels and types of education. The essential purpose of planning was seen as to rationalize and systematize decision-making for the future,—'it does not necessarily imply centralized decision-making and administration. The organization of the planning process may be very different in a highly centralized developing country, or one with a long tradition of decision-making at the local level, but in each case the country's education system can be planned in relation to local and national needs'. The conference noted that 'in many countries the question of the yield of the educational system, its output and efficiency, and the question of the content of education are today much more urgent than simply educational expansion. The alarmingly high rate of drop-out and repetition in many countries, and possible solutions to these problems are nowadays subjects of great anxiety to planners'. It was further emphasized that, although planning calls for expert work, it ought not to be regarded as exclusively a matter for the specialists. It was pointed out that 'education must be concerned with the individual child as well as the total framework of students and pupils as a whole, and that the family is, and will continue to be, the original and basic nucleus of education.' The conference noted the existing imbalance between the relatively slow rate of economic growth and the rapid expansion of education in certain developing countries and another imbalance between the educational opportunities available to women and to the

inhabitants in rural areas. 'They consequently insisted on the need for a thorough study of the relationship between education and social progress, between education and society, and education and the economy.' On a more mundane level, the conference found that the problem of diagnosing the current situation as regards education involved 'the need for each country to collect, elaborate and make a critical study of statistical and other information' and to attempt 'to develop the standardization and exchange of these various categories of information in the field of education'.

These quotations and comments are given in some detail, partly because experienced librarians will not need me to suggest what kind of contribution an efficient library service could make to the solution of some of these problems and partly because to some extent one can substitute 'library service' for 'education' in some of these passages.

My own experience, as evinced by a comparison of the first and second drafts of my revision of a library planning work, followed by a set of lectures on the same subject, is that one learns from a study of the problems and progress of educational planning to approach the subject of library planning in a much more tentative fashion. One learns how inappropriate it is to be querulous or dogmatic about library development needs before making a fairly close study of the general context and conditions in which the library services in question are to operate.

*Unesco's definition of 'planning library services'*
The most concise statement of the point of view which I have been adumbrating can be found in the definition of 'Planning library services' used in the Main Working Paper for the Colombo Conference, already referred to (which is itself an adaptation of the definition used in C V Penna's *Planning library services*, 1967):

'The planning of library services is regarded as a specific aspect of educational planning within the social and economic planning of a country or region, for only within this context can library planning acquire the support which it needs if it is to be effective. Regarded in that way, the planning of library services necessitates a continuous, systematized studying from the standpoint of their library needs, of educational problems at all levels, including adult education and the problems of scientific research. It also involves determining the aims of library services, setting targets for attaining those aims, and making realistic decisions to ensure that those objectives will be reached through the rational and reasonable use of available resources.

*Library services in industrialized and developing countries*
In large, comparatively wealthy countries the loss of efficiency, resulting from the lack of overall integration between the development of library services and the various sectors of national development, has up to recent years been fairly easily accommodated. Gaps, overlaps and inadequate objectives for library service gradually make themselves apparent, policies are reassessed and eventually new lines of library development emerge. The need for the development of library services to be planned as an integral part of other development plans has not seemed pressing nor of primary importance. However, in those areas of national life which impinge most closely on the policies of those concerned with the disposition of national resources, ie scientific, technical, commercial and, in fact, general industrial and economic development, the need for an assessment of national objectives and of the potential contribution of library service in reaching those objectives has been increasingly realized in recent years. Moreover, the international character of science and the rapid increase in the volume of current publications has, of course, led to an appreciation of the need for the coordination on an international basis of library and information policies as a contribution to identifiable information needs.

When we turn to developing countries, the case for relating library development to national development plans generally is both simpler and more complex. It is simpler because there is the obvious need to avoid overlapping and unnecessary services and to ensure that such resources as can be spared for library services contribute more directly to development objectives. It is more complex because the available resources in skilled manpower, money and materials are commonly out of all proportion to national needs. Nevertheless, such is the competition for resources in developing countries and such is the general lack of awareness of the potential contribution of library service to national development that even modest library development plans seem likely to receive priority only where the library planner and administrator is equipped to inform himself of development objectives, to assess the potential contribution of library service in attaining them and to prepare appropriate plans for the development of library services which are convincing to other development planners and administrators and realistic in terms of resources available. Moreover, such is the likely state of other development plans and the multiplicity of factors affecting policy decisions that the library planner must be prepared with alternative phasings of his plan, alternative priorities of development, or at least be prepared to accommodate, with as little harm as possible, modifications to his original proposals.

78

*The inter-dependence of library services*

One of the implications for the development of library service of this approach to library planning is that the planner can no longer restrict his interest to one type of library. Probably only within the last decade has the interdependence of various forms and levels of education been explicitly acknowledged and it seems to me that the same is true of library service. Certainly references to this theme have become increasingly common in recent years. The contributions and the roles of various types of library must, therefore, be seen in relation to each other and in relation to national objectives. As a result there may be need for some redefinition of library roles and certain libraries may have to assume dual roles.

An interesting example of this new tendency to plan for the total library development, instead of for certain types of library only, may be seen by comparing certain successful post-war schemes of library development with some of the latest developments and plans. The Jamaica Library Service and the Ghana Library Service, for example, are basically concerned with public library service, with agency services to school libraries coming as something of a secondary benefit. More recent schemes, such as the Tanganyika Library Service, are being extended to embrace certain national library functions, and the library needs of government departments. The ordinance to establish a Ghana Libraries Board does, in fact, set out its functions in fairly broad terms. 'It shall be the duty of the Board to establish, equip, manage and maintain libraries in Ghana, and to take all such steps as may be necessary to carry out such duty.' The act setting up the Tanganyika Libraries Board expands this as follows:

1 'The functions of the Board shall be to promote, establish, equip, manage, maintain and develop libraries in Tanganyika.

2 The Board shall have power for the purpose of carrying out its functions to do all such acts as appear to it to be requisite, advantageous or convenient for or in connection with the carrying out of its functions, or to be incidental or conducive to their proper discharge, and may carry on any activities in that behalf either alone or in association with any other person or body (including the Government or a local authority).' (3)

The National Library Services Board proposed for Ceylon at the Colombo Meeting of Experts on the National Planning of Library Services in Asia would have much wider coordinating responsibilities. Having noted the variety of bodies with responsibilities for library provision and the general lack of coordination of library services, the Meeting

'proposed that the most effective way of overcoming the difficulties with respect to library services would be to establish a Ceylon National

Library Services Board which would be an independent, statutory body. Its main responsibility would relate to the:

(a)    organization, development and planning of the library services in general;

(b)    organization and development of the Ceylon National Library;

(c)    promotion and development of public libraries;

(d)    promotion and development of school library services;

(e)    coordination and collaboration in the development of universities, special and government departmental libraries;

(f)    advising the government on establishing minimum academic and professional qualifications for library personnel, and ensuring that they enjoy the status and emoluments commensurate with their qualifications and responsibilities;

(g)    promotion and development of library education.

The Board will be a small high-powered body concerned with general policy, but having such executive authority necessary and at such level to discharge the assignments listed above. Committees as may be appropriate will be set up to advise the Board (4).'

It is also of interest to note that in a Report to the Government of Jamaica in 1968, Dr J Periam Danton recommended 'the creation of a National Advisory Commission on Libraries, comprising educators, librarians economic planners, etc whose first task would be the preparation of a national plan for library development in Jamaica' (5). Similarly, recommendations by a Technical Advisory Committee, which were submitted by the Ghana Library Board to the government in 1965, included a recommendation for 'the establishment of a Council for the coordination of Library Services to assume responsibility for the development of a National Library Service and also for the coordination of library resources generally' (6).

Turning to a country where library services are highly developed, we find a new recognition, expressed in recent legislation in the USA, that not only public libraries, but academic and special libraries must be developed together so that they may all make their distinctive contribution to meeting public needs. In particular, the new act covering 'Interlibrary Cooperation' is leading to the development of state-wide systems of library provision which aim at securing the best overall use from the total investment of library resources in a given state. What seems to me a useful statement of the philosophy underlying development of this kind, backed by substantial public funds, comes in the Conlis Report 'A National Library Agency: a proposal' (7).

80

'The basic hypothesis proposed by the Committee is that the national interest requires assured and ready access by all citizens to all unrestricted information. (Taken here to be understood in its more general sense as the meaningful content of any communication, as opposed to the random, meaningless, etc.) In simplest terms, information as a commodity is essential to our development as individuals, to optimization of our activities, to the strength of our nation, and to the progess and survival of mankind.'

*The need for systematic study of library needs*
The recognition of the need for coordinated development of library services of all kinds is clearly gaining ground. In some cases this coordination will be secured primarily through a central body representing not only various library interests by the interests of various user groups. The Unesco definition of library planning would certainly call for such a body to carry out a coordinating role, but it also calls for systematic study and systematic reappraisal of the library needs for cultural, social and economic development. Two major benefits appear to stem from this approach. First, the potential contribution of library services can be set out in terms which are meaningful to those responsible for allocating resources for general national development purposes and are thus more likely to attract adequate support. Second, the preparatory work involved in producing library development plans, which are well based on the library needs of the various sectors of national and community life, is likely to ensure that the plans are worthy of such support, in that they will contribute to agreed national objectives.

In practical terms, if the points made in this paper are accepted, some librarians will have to become familiar with the concepts and techniques employed in economic planning and some will need to become much more familiar than heretofore with the educational, sociological and scientific and technological needs of the community. To some extent experts from these fields must be part of any library planning team, but also there is an increasing need for librarians who can add librarianship or information science qualifications to one of these basic disciplines. The introduction of first degree courses which include a study of these disciplines along with library studies may also be seen to be making its own contribution to library development. Meanwhile, for the experienced librarian there may be need not only for short courses related directly to his profession, but for more wide-ranging courses enabling him to communicate in a more meaningful way with the section of the community which he serves. Further, the role of library research may be seen as relating not only to strictly professional matters but to the investigation of the library needs which are implicit in various national or sectional development objectives.

It must in fairness to the argument be pointed out that, within the space of this article, the topic has had to be given cursory treatment (8). We have not attempted to look at the role of library service—particularly public library service—in making up for the deficiencies of an educational pyramid in which the provision for secondary and higher education tapers off rapidly from the broadly based provision for primary education. Nor have we examined the potentialities of public library service in improving the community and economic development of people in developing countries. The need for parallel development of national publishing and library services has not been touched on. Finally, we have given scant consideration to the fundamental need for a sound, systematically organized library service to be created in each country if it is fully to benefit from the international, scientific and technical information systems which are being established (9).

## References

1  Quoted by S R Ranganathan in 'Blueprint for national education' in The education quarterly (India), 18 (72) January 1967, 3-6, 11.

2  Unesco: Extract from the Final report of the International Conference on Educational Planning. Paris, 6-14 August 1968, 11, 12, 13, 16.

3  Evans, Evelyn J A: Library legislation in the developing countries of Africa. (Paper given to the Public Libraries Section of the IFLA Conference, 1967), 12.

4  Unesco: Meeting of Experts on the National Planning of Library Services in Asia, Colombo, Ceylon, 1967. Final report (COM/CS/190/6), 14-15.

5  Communication from Miss Cynthia Washington, May 1969.

6  Communication from Mr. David Cornelius, April 1969.

7  ALA bulletin, 62 (3) March 1968, 255.

8  For a fuller treatment of this topic see: Penna, C V: The national planning of library and documentation services, Second edition revised by P H Sewell and Herman Liebaers. Paris, Unesco (1970), and Sewell, P H: The planning of library and documentation services. Paris, International Institute for Educational Planning, 1969, 87 p (IIEP/S20/1). Document prepared for participants in the Seminar on the 'Planning of library and documentation services', held by the IIEP from 21-23 July 1969. Mimeo.

9  Perez-Votoria, A: Towards a world science information system: a ISCU-Unesco joint venture. Unesco bulletin for libraries 23 (1) January-February 1969, 2-7.

# GOAL DETERMINATION

*John R Haak*

For many undergraduate libraries (1) the honeymoon period is now ending. This period may be characterized by the excitement and the frenzy of activity which is inherent in any pioneering effort. During this time the plant is developed, the staff hired, and the collection begun. Idealism, coupled with predictions of a new utopia in library service, is accompanied by the more practical impetus of a patient and cooperative library management which is willing to supply the funds, freedom, and time necessary for the library to grow up. But the day finally dawns when the issue of the undergraduate library's effectiveness is raised, and the honeymoon is over.

The uneasiness, doubt and questioning which accompany the end of the honeymoon spring from a number of sources. First, during the honeymoon we are dealing with activities which are more familiar to us, as librarians, and for which we find precedents in older undergraduate libraries. The processes involved in creating buildings and acquiring book collections are familiar and concrete, and their results may be viewed by visiting established undergraduate libraries or by reading about these libraries in the literature. The providing of buildings and collections is akin to creating a stage setting for the play itself. When the scene is set and it comes to creating and acting out the play itself, the undergraduate librarian is on his own. As he turns from a period of preparation to a period of providing services for undergraduates, the teacher of undergraduates, and the undergraduate curriculum, he finds fewer cues to prompt him, either in other libraries or in the literature. Often he is forced to learn his lines or improvise while on stage.

Second, the operation of undergraduate libraries is no longer a hypothetical activity. The hard facts of experience have shattered any fantasies which we may have conjured up in which faculty embrace our undergraduate libraries like a newly discovered cause. Experience shows that pious statements of purpose are not of sufficient attraction and must be

83

followed by a solid service program. The play, to carry the analogy further, must have substance.

Finally, once the issue of effectiveness is raised, it means that a period of evaluation will soon follow. This period is bound to be somewhat painful, for organizations, just as individuals, find it more comfortable to ignore their most troublesome traits rather than to correct them.

Perhaps at this moment we undergraduate librarians are better equipped to create the set than write the play, but we are entering into a period during which the play must be written and performed, if our libraries are to significantly improve undergraduate education. It is our responsibility to develop our specialty so that these libraries may offer substantive service programs.

## The problem of goals

While there may be no such thing as a purely undergraduate level book, or even book collection, there are services which are more appropriate for undergraduates than for other members of the academic community. It is these services that make the library uniquely an undergraduate library. Before such service programs can be planned and before evaluation can take place, institutional goals must be defined.

While perusing programs for a number of undergraduate library buildings, I was struck by the amount of detail they contained. They all specified the exact number of reader stations as well as the number of volumes the new building would contain. Descriptions of furniture were supplied in minute detail, as were heights of doorways, locations of desks, the number of lavatory fixtures, and on and on; everything seemed magnificently accounted for.

I then began a search for comparable documents which would specify service programs, documents which would inform me of what intended results would emerge from this mixture of librarians, students, faculty, books and buildings, and how these intended results would be produced. I searched in vain. There were a number of phrases which expressed, abstractly, purposes or goals of undergraduate libraries. Some of the typical statements of goals are as follows: to stimulate undergraduates to read good books, to encourage the life-long habit of self-education through reading (2), to be a center of learning for undergraduate students (3), to continually respond to the changing educational needs of the students (4). These may be defined as intangible goals—goals which express intended states but do not indicate the processes or activities which lead to their accomplishment. Intangible goals are important, as they provide the ultimate purpose for organizational activity.

84

However, since intangible goals by their nature do not provide for order, direction or coherence, they cannot by themselves guide group action and therefore must be supported by sets of tangible, or operating, goals which do. For example, much religious activity has been centered around the intangible goal of 'gaining the kingdom of heaven'. This goal is usually supported by a set of more tangible goals to accomplish this end—the Ten Commandments, the beatitudes, etc. In some cases, an evaluative system is even built in through private or public confession and repentance. So, too, our libraries need tangible goals (5) to bridge the gap between means (acquisitions, cataloguing, circulation, book collections, listening rooms, etc) and the intended results as expressed in intangible goals (6). All too often library planners and undergraduate librarians have neglected to develop such sets of tangible operating goals.

Most undergraduate libraries claim the intangible goal of acting as an agent for enriching the educational experience of undergraduates. We must implement it through a series of related tangible goals that are subordinate yet instrumental to this larger achievement. One such goal then becomes close faculty-librarian understanding and cooperation. An entire series of more specific goals may be built under this heading. Another tangible goal becomes productive student-librarian relations with a ladder of varied activities leading toward this important aim. Book selection is another subordinate tangible goal that can be made instrumental to the primary intangible goal. Some of the characteristics which tangible goals should possess to be both effective and practical are as follows:

1 Tangible goals should be a guide to action and sufficiently explicit to suggest a certain type of activity. They should be helpful to decision-making and not pious statements.

2 Tangible goals should suggest tools to measure and control effectiveness.

3 The goals should be challenging. It is the goals which create organizational vitality. It is necessary to distinguish between the possible and the impossible, but to be willing to get close to the latter.

4 The whole set of goals should make sense. With rare exception, there is no single overriding goal. Goals should be balanced in relation to one another.

5 Goals must take into consideration external opportunities and constraints. Experience shows that it is not possible to sit down and write a reasonable, practical, and specific set of goals. It is first necessary to consider the internal challenges and opportunities as well as the external ones relating to the organization's environment.

Principles to follow in goal setting:

85

1  Limit initial statements of goals to questions which are of practical concern. Select a limited starting point, cover it well, and then branch out into other items on the list as the need becomes recognized.

2  Goal setting, to be effective, calls for group participation. It is a well-recognized principle that people work harder to achieve objectives that they have helped to establish.

3  Set a half dozen specific goals for each position. These goals are usually reviewed and revised annually. Users of this approach have found that it usually results in superior individual achievement. The employee not only knows the purpose of his effort but is then also able to relate his work to the overall goals of the organization.

For a more complete discussion of the process of setting goals, see Franklin G Moore's *Management organization and practice* (Harper, 1964, p 78-96).

The following program for the Earlham College Library illustrated the principles enumerated above:

1  Advise entering freshmen that they will be tested on their knowledge of the following basic reference sources: *Encyclopaedia Britannica; Readers guide,* card catalogue, and about six other sources. Freshmen who do not demonstrate competence on these reference sources are given 50 minutes of additional library instruction during freshman orientation week. This time is divided among the librarians who man the reference desk.

2  Give library instruction on the following basic reference sources to all freshmen doing research papers in required courses: *Social sciences & humanities index, Public affairs information service, Essay and general literature index, Biography index, New York Times index,* and *Subject headings used in the dictionary catalog of the Library of Congress.*

3  Ask for invitations to give library instruction to all classes which are making intensive use of the reference services. At first, note the classes in which students ask for similar information at the reference desk and talk with their instructors. After you have a reputation for giving effective library instruction, ask individual instructors before a new term whether they will want library instruction.

4  Give one to ten hours of library instruction related to a course required of all majors, as they begin concentrating on their discipline.

5  Make the library instruction concrete and relevant: a) Ask the instructor to describe the assignment for which library instruction is needed. b) Meet with the class when students are beginning their literature search. c) Hand out annotated bibliographies especially prepared for each class. Arrange the bibliographies according to categories of reference sources in

a logical order for doing a literature search. d) Use the bibliography to work through the literature search for a sample term paper topic. Use an overhead projector to show transparencies of sample pages from about ten of the most important and/or complicated reference sources. Do not demonstrate sources already known to most students in the class. e) Ask the teacher to attend this presentation and make comments. f) Caution students that an hour of library instruction is only the beginning. g) Encourage faculty to require a working bibliography at least four weeks before a major paper is due.

Creating tangible service goals requires the same attention and concentration on detail that is exhibited in building programs. It is by developing tangible goals that we make intangible goals attainable. Since this attention has not generally been displayed by the planners of undergraduate libraries and since some of the older undergraduate libraries are beginning to waver in their commitments to provide professional service to undergraduates, I wish to draw a connection between these two problems—lack of tangible goals and wavering commitment—by probing into a process described as goal displacement.

*Goal displacement*

Social and service organizations, such as undergraduate libraries, which orient their programs to abstract ideas are most susceptible to goal displacement (7). Goal displacement is a process through which means, unwittingly, become substituted for claimed goals. For example, custodial functions tend to displace treatment or rehabilitation functions in prisons, juvenile halls, and mental hospitals. So, too, in libraries clerical processing tasks, rules, and even the collection itself become the operating institutional goals, supplanting the more intangible service goals. Therefore, unless a structure of tangible goals or programs is developed to bridge the gap between means and ends, the means gradually surface, and, through default, function as the tangible goals (8).

Goal displacement is not really a conscious process; it occurs gradually as intangible goals are replaced through the day-to-day decisions which create more secure operational habits and minimize uncertainty, insecurity, frustration and risk.

Reports which emphasize activities which may be counted serve to legitimize these activities as ends, contributing to goal displacement. Annual reports of libraries often exemplify this fault. These reports generally highlight attendance and transaction counts, the number of volumes added to the collection, the number of reference questions answered, the amounts of fines collected, the problems with the building, etc. It is not that these statistics or conditions are unimportant, for this data is what our masters need to justify plant and staff. But often the data we accumulate about libraries is just a pulse-taking operation. It indicates something about the level of activity without measuring its quality or ascertaining whether the library is meeting its goals.

The basic result of intangible goals which are unsupported by tangible ones is goal displacement; goal displacement cuts an institution away from its philosophical moorings and sets it adrift. Displacement takes its toll by directing an institution away from its original purpose and towards the means which were established to accomplish the purpose.

Perhaps it is this failure to develop tangible goals which has contributed to the skepticism which a number of undergraduate librarians feel toward the intangible goals so often used to justify undergraduate libraries. It is very difficult for an organization or its staff to have success experiences which can be related to unsupported intangible goals. Also, unsupported intangible goals may be taken literally by some staff members, students, and faculty, who will then develop expectations that the library will accomplish them, thus leading to misunderstanding and frustration. Undergraduate libraries need meaningful service goals that are possible to attain if they are to earn long-term support and respect.

A further product of unsupported intangible goals is that they make it possible to assume that an organization is effective. According to Warner and Havens:

'Accumulated experiences, precedents, rules, and traditions assert that certain tangible facilities, processes, and practices increase effectiveness, and these assertions are accepted as proven. . . . Obviously, assuming effectiveness as a given prevents adequate evaluation. Yet an organization is severely handicapped if its effectiveness is not tested, for lack of evaluation and feedback may force the organization and its program into more nonrational forms and programs (9).'

Therefore, goals are necessary not only to guide undergraduate library programs and to coordinate them with the programs of other campus libraries but also to evaluate results. Effectiveness then becomes a function of the degree to which an undergraduate library accomplishes its goals, and tangible goals serve as the standard for measurement.

By not rigorously examining goals, and by succumbing to the process of goal displacement, an organization risks destruction in the same manner as a home attacked by termites. It is not until the house suddenly collapses that its owner becomes aware that anything is wrong, and then it is too late. So, too, undergraduate librarians who fail to assess library goals

might soon find their libraries abandoned (10) by their superiors or unwittingly transformed into different kinds of libraries as commitment
weakens or as goals become confused or displaced.

*What do we mean by service?*
Before tangible goals can be developed to guide the service programs of
an undergraduate library, a clear conception of what is meant by service
must be achieved. There is a great tendency in discussions of undergraduate
libraries to confuse resources with service. Are open stacks, selected book
catalogs, audio rooms (all the elements we have described as providing the
set for the play) services? We often speak of them as if they were.

Irene Braden, in her survey of undergraduate libraries, identified six
ways in which they have differed from traditional university libraries (11):
1) by providing open access to the collection to avoid the difficulties of
the closed stack system; 2) by centralizing and simplifying services to the
undergraduate; 3) by providing a collection of carefully selected books,
containing the titles all undergraduates should be exposed to for their
liberal education, as well as incorporating the reserved book collection;
4) by attempting to make the library an instructional tool by planning it
as a center for instruction in library use, to prepare undergraduates for
using larger collections, and by staffing it with librarians interested in
teaching the undergraduate the resources of a library and the means of
tapping those resources; 5) by providing services additional to those given
by the research collection; and 6) by constructing a building with the
undergraduate's habits of use in mind.

As Patricia Knapp rightfully points out, these differences are not very
useful for clarifying a unique function for undergraduate libraries (12).
Most are really antidotes to the ills of older university library systems.
The objective of providing additional services to those offered by the
research library has often meant that undergraduate libraries have become
a refuge for a mish-mash of special music, poetry, and art collections,
most of which have only very tenuous roots in the undergraduate curriculum. And no undergraduate library has yet been allocated the staff and
other resources necessary 'to make the library an instruction tool by
planning it as a center for instruction in library use.'

Braden's six categories may be divided into two basic capabilities which
the undergraduate library should have if it is to complement and support
the teaching trends on campus: a self-service capability and an active-
service capability (13). The first capability provides the library with a
self-service potential where the student or teacher uses, or is encouraged
to use, the physical means which the library places at his disposal. The

more common elements of this self-service capacity are as follows: a) the library environment, including its location, building, atmosphere, and interior arrangement of books; b) the book and periodical collection, including the reference collection; c) the reserve book, honors, and browsing collections; d) the self-instructional devices and programs, including programmed texts, tapes, recordings, educational television, radio, and films; e) the finding devices, including the catalog, periodical lists, and information pamphlets; f) exhibits; g) special facilities for the physically disadvantaged.

Each of the elements of the self-service capacity may be approached directly by the library user without reference to the library staff. In providing these self-services, the library staff acts in a technical capacity as administrator, provider, and processor. The self-service elements contribute to the teaching function of the university by providing a place for, and access to, materials which complement the classroom efforts of both students and teachers.

There is no doubt that undergraduate libraries have been extremely successful in these self-service areas. Good selective collections, a centralized location for heavily used stacks, and attractive buildings have encouraged library use by students. Undergraduate libraries have broken down barriers which so often have stood between the undergraduate and library materials in large research libraries.

The second capability the undergraduate library must have to complement and support university teaching is what I shall call an active-service capability, one which revolves around the concept of the undergraduate librarian as teacher rather than technician. Active library service is totally dependent on the library staff and on its ability to work with faculty and students, and requires the participation of the librarian inside and outside of the library building. It is with these active services that the librarian binds the library to the curriculum and guides the student in the use of the library's resources. With the proper training of staff the following services can potentially be offered through the undergraduate library:

a) Teaching undergraduate students and their teaching assistants, through formal or informal classes, ways to use the library effectively, including the different ways to search for information, the uses of bibliographical and informational tools and their purposes and limitations, and the features and peculiarities of the total university library system.

b) Stimulation of reading by students through counseling, library sponsored seminars, and cultural events.

c) Providing reference and reader advisory services, including work with students on library related assignments.

90

d) Serving the faculty in an advisory capacity, exploring with them the ways of using the library's staff collection, and services to enrich the undergraduate teaching program.

e) Working with the faculty in evaluating and improving teaching programs which require students to use the library.

Active services generally have not been clearly defined. The unhappy result has been that such services have received meager support. By dividing goals into self-service and active-service categories, we can begin to develop appropriate tangible goals for each one as well as evaluation criteria and procedures. We can also establish appropriate qualifications for staff and can begin to assess our libraries, not only on the basis of what *they have,* but what *we do.*

## *Institutionalization*

One of the conditions and limits of undergraduate libraries is that they have no monopoly on campus library resources. The books and periodicals in the undergraduate library collection may also be found in other campus libraries. The undergraduate library, therefore, is in a position of having to compete for clients (students and faculty). The long and short of an undergraduate library's success will rest with the ability of its staff to achieve *institutionalization* (14) or, in other words, to solicit support for the library's service goals from faculty and students.

Goals give direction to an institution and also mark a standard for its evaluation. But even if the library staff meticulously develops a program of tangible service goals, their efforts are wasted if these goals and the justifications for them are not familiar to the faculty and students and supported by them. The problem of defining goals in a service organization is not ended once a logical set of goals and priorities is set to paper. It still remains to broadcast goals and to determine whether or not these goals and the programs devised to accomplish them are meaningful and useful to the library's patrons.

People are generally more willing to accept and support goals that they have helped to set. They are also more willing to accept an institution and its purposes if they know, like, and respect its staff. On most university campuses the fact that one is a librarian does not automatically place one in the center of a communication network which includes faculty and students. The librarian must work to build these relationships.

Traditionally, service organizations have recognized the value of encouraging the people they serve to participate in decision-making. This practice not only keeps the organization keyed to the ever changing needs of its clients but also fosters vital personal contacts between staff and customer. Banks have men on their governing boards who represent local industrial and financial interests; federal regulatory agencies solicit advice from the industries they regulate, and their customers, as well as from related state and local government bodies; research libraries also have their faculty library committees. Service organizations, including libraries, which make no attempt to involve those they serve in the life of the institution, foster the attitude that the organization is created and operated for the convenience of the staff.

Most undergraduate libraries do not have an active advisory committee made up of students or faculty. Whether or not such a committee is the answer to a particular library's need to institutionalize is dependent on a number of factors, such as the inclination and the personality of the librarian, the degree of formality or informality of the campus, and the interests of faculty and students. However, if the committee method is rejected, then other ways should be found to formulate goals and programs which are pertinent to the needs of faculty and students and are acceptable to them. So, too, other ways should be sought to increase personal contact between librarians and the people they serve.

Once contacts are made, support for any particular library goal is dependent on three basic factors. First, a goal is more likely to be supported if the value it implies is compatible with the values of clients. For example, if a faculty member encourages his students to read independently and explore the library collection, the librarian's role was reader advisor is much more likely to be accepted than if a faculty member binds his students to a reserve reading list. Second, goals are more likely to be supported if clients concur with the library staff in the importance or degree of emphasis placed upon them. A number of librarians have applied this principle by postponing library orientation until that point in the semester when students are assigned to write papers and so have an immediate need for help. Lastly, goals are more likely to be accepted by students or faculty when they see that librarians themselves are accomplishing them. If undergraduate libraries claim a reference service but a student's first attempts to have questions answered by a librarian are unpleasant or unsatisfactory, or if the reference desk is only occasionally staffed, the student's confidence in the ability of the library to provide reference service is nil.

Several undergraduate libraries have attempted to involve faculty and students in the life of the library in a way other than through an administrative committee. This 'way' is by encouraging the university community to look upon the undergraduate library as a cultural center. The undergraduate library at the University of Michigan provides a large multi-purpose room for a variety of educational programs. For five years the College Library at the University of California, Los Angeles, has had a successful series of informal seminars featuring popular faculty members as well as numerous and varied programs of chamber music. And, during this coming academic year, the Cluster Library (the undergraduate library) at the University of California, San Diego, will begin sponsoring a series of concerts, poetry readings, informal seminars, and art exhibits.

Some university librarians as well as undergraduate librarians object to undergraduate libraries engaging in such activities. They major negative argument seems to be that these activities are really peripheral to the central purposes of an undergraduate library (15). My view is that such events make the library visible and soften its formal institutional and bureaucratic image. These activities and the process of planning for them provide opportunities for increasing the dialogue between librarians, faculty, and students.

Institutionalization may also be increased if undergraduate librarians join social, recreational, cultural or official campus organizations whose memberships are primarily comprised of students or faculty or both. It would not hurt at all if a few more librarians were good surfers, basketball players, musicians or energetic and effective committee members. Participation in campus activities transforms the librarian from a title into a person. Recent surveys have shown that all too often undergraduate librarians remain cloistered in their libraries and as a result know few faculty members or students.

Successful institutionalization is dependent on personal relationships and 'image'. Whether institutionalization is fostered through formal or informal committees, cultural events or participation in campus activities, each one of these methods requires personal contacts between the undergraduate librarian and faculty members and students. Such personal relationships take time to develop. For this reason turnover of effective undergraduate library staff members can be particularly crippling to institutionalization. Whether we like it or not, people categorize libraries and other service institutions according to the way they perceive the staff. If the library staff members are friendly and helpful, the library is a friendly place. If the staff is arrogant, impersonal, and bureaucratic, the library is a hostile place. Let us hope that we might eventually attract for our undergraduate libraries the support recently expressed on a petition by a group of University of California, San Diego, students for a cafeteria threatened with closure:

'We request that the Matthews snack bar remain open. This is the only cafeteria on campus which gives its customers friendly, personalized service. In a world where most people don't give a damn, it's great to go to a place where the employees have a smile for you and even know your name.'

*Staffing the undergraduate library*
One of the barriers inhibiting the development and reward for staff in undergraduate libraries is that there has often been little recognition of the possibilities that special training or skill is necessary to serve in them. A typical attitude of library administrators seems to be that any young person with an attractive personality has the necessary qualifications (16) and that 'turnover is of no importance because what is important is that they are willing to help people and to go to some lengths to help them' (17). One assistant university librarian told me that a nice young person was running their undergraduate library but that the real creative work was performed by the administration before the library opened.

These views of certain representatives of library administrations, are rooted in the short history of undergraduate libraries. These libraries have often been a fashionable and practical solution to the problem of providing needed additional space for books and readers. In order to reduce development time, they have borrowed from each other in cannibalistic sequence, with each new library copying much from its predecessor.

The induced birth of many undergraduate libraries has meant that often they have been planned and built by the campus director of libraries or his immediate subordinates. They consult with another library director who has an undergraduate library; they select the site and develop the building program; they choose a relatively handy and up-to-date list of 'basic books' to guide book purchases; and the finally put the undergraduate library into business by hiring a nice but relatively inexperienced group of young people to operate the library. As a result, the post of undergraduate librarian has been seen as one where minimal creative or independent work is required.

A second attitude seems to be that, yes, a very well-qualified individual is needed to serve as the chief administrator for the undergraduate library but that the few other professional positions assigned to the library require librarians with only a minimum of experience. Undergraduate libraries expressing this philosophy place their emphasis on the novel self-service capabilities of the library rather than on the personal service that may be supplied by staff.

However, as more undergraduate libraries are turned over to us undergraduate librarians to create and operate, we, rather than the general

94

library administrator, become the true spokesmen for these libraries. It is up to us to develop our specialty as undergraduate librarians; to ask what is really the rationale of the movement; to build a service program of substance and worth; to improve our capabilities in order to carry out these programs; and to fight for more adequate support. We can begin by specifying tangible goals to guide us and to foster institutionalization. We can also begin working with one another.

*References*
1 In this paper an undergraduate library is defined as follows: 1) a special library for undergraduate students; 2) located in a university or other institution supporting graduate work to a significant degree; 3) housed in either a separate building or in a self-contained section of a general building; 4) consisting of a collection designed to support and supplement the undergraduate curriculum, and a staff and services which promote the integration of the library into the undergraduate teaching program of the university.

2 Frederick H Wagman as quoted in Braden, Irene: The undergraduate library. ALA, 1970, p 49.

3 Sub-Committee of the Undergraduate Library, Report, University of Texas, Austin, 1968, p 1.

4 Statement of program for the undergraduate library, University of Pittsburgh, p 1.

5 Tangible goals can be stated in such as way as to be subject to evaluation, whereas intangible goals cannot. This is an important point, since it is organizational events which are tangible and measurable that are most often used in evaluation and sanctioning.

6 If the library is to have an educational impact on students, goals must be clearly specified. If specification is lacking, students may not know whether their own purposes and those of the library coincide. For a stimulating study on the effect of goals on student values, see Vreeland, Rebecca and Charles Bidwell:'Organizational effects on student attitudes: a study of the Harvard houses', Sociology of education, spring 1965, p 233-50.

7 For this discussion of the process of goal displacement I am indebted to W Keith Warner and A Eugene Havens and their article 'Goal displacement and the intangibility of organizational goals', Administrative science quarterly, March 1968, p 539-55.

8 Kenneth Keniston seems to argue that institutions in a technological society are culturally susceptible to goal displacement, since technological values concentrate on means rather than ends—telling us how to proceed rather than where to go. In the absence of other positive values the instrumental values of our society are often unconsciously elevated to ends. The 'deification of instrumentality' has two basic aspects—pursuit of sheer quantity and the quest for expertise. See Keniston, Kenneth: The uncommitted: alienated youth in American society. Harcourt, 1965, p 335-36.

9 Warner and Havens, op cit, p 545.

10 Abandonment is not as far-fetched as it sounds. The Undergraduate Library of the University of South Carolina, Columbia, will be abolished in 1973 and a science library will occupy the building instead.

11 Braden, op cit, p 2.

12 Knapp, Patricia: The library, the undergraduate and the teaching faculty. 1970, 49p. Mimeographed paper presented during the Institute Training for Service in Undergraduate Libraries, sponsored by the University Library, University of California, San Diego, August 17-21, 1970.

13 Naturally, fundamental to both of these capabilities is the whole supportive apparatus of ordering, cataloging, binding stack maintenance, etc.

14 Institutionalization may be defined as the degree to which a system of action obtains support for its decisions or goals from the environment.

15 For an example of the point of view see Orne, Jerrold: 'The undergraduate library', Library journal, June 15, 1970, p 2230-33.

16 Braden, op cit, p 89.

17 Ibid.

# 3
# Organisation

The large library organization was, and to some extent still is, a bureaucratic hierarchy. It comprises an establishment of several professional grades, wherein each officer performs prescribed and relatively specific duties appropriate to his office, and for which he is responsible to his immediate superior. Within this bureaucracy 'professionalism' manifests itself in various—sometimes convoluted—forms, and even flourishes in the more favoured spots. This is the 'classical' management structure, which provides us with a base line from which various modifications are being made.

The above model has been subjected to three kinds of change in recent years.

The first of these changes *can* be accommodated within the bureaucracy, but is potentially revolutionary. We refer to the historic shift in the principle of organisational division, of departmentalisation, that has been evident in the last two decades in large UK public and academic libraries. Traditionally the library has been organised around the technical processing of materials and information. The public library had—and has—its Accessions Department, its Cataloguing Department, its Reference Library, and its Lending Library. This pattern has been paralleled in large academic libraries. The orientation now is increasingly towards the library user (or potential user). Hence many large academic and public libraries are now organised along subject specialist lines. A useful analysis of the position in UK academic libraries will be found in Scrivener (1974), although the important contribution of the polytechnic libraries needs stressing. Overington's *Subject departmentalised public library* (1969) still provides a valuable review and assessment. Similarly, the emphasis is shifting from 'running a branch library' to 'developing a community library service', whilst in college and school libraries there is the move towards developing the library—in close cooperation with the teachers—into a learning resource centre. As for special libraries, this kind of user/subject orientation has always been fundamental to their organisation and activity.

The creation of a strong user/subject dimension in a library organisation immediately poses the question of its relationship to the technical/functional system. What, for example, is the relationship of subject librarian to cataloguer? This is the staff-and-line problem which figures so largely in 'classical' management textbooks. Is dual responsibility to be invested in a single individual, with the danger of one responsibility being subordinated to the other? Should the activity be carried out by completely separate divisions of the organisation? There are a number of alternative possible arrangements. For example, Burgis, in the paper which follows, strongly argues for a matrix type of organisation, to which further reference will be found in the paper by Dutton. Matrix problems of responsibility are found in a number of UK public libraries, where a (geographical) divisional librarian may also have all-county responsibility for, say, prison library services, or a divisional bibliographical officer (stock editor) may have all-county responsibility for a particular subject field.

The problem of the *geographical* principle of division (that is, the problem of the multi-site library system) has increased with the growth in size of library systems. These include the new 'super-county' library authorities, for example, or the many multi-site polytechnic libraries to which college of education libraries are now being added. Moreover, an increasingly sophisticated service is required from this complex of service points or departmental or faculty libraries, with a corresponding need for greater back-up from the library system as a whole. The second part of Ashworth's paper offers a starting point for the study of problems of multi-site systems, and emphasises their relatively high costs.

The problem of diversification or centralisation of libraries is a difficult one, be the question directed at a single library system, or at the level of regionally or nationally coordinated services. As we adopt performance measures (see section 5) it is becoming easier to determine the optimum distribution of services and there are a number of studies on this subject such as the work by researchers Elton, Orr and Schless using document delivery as a performance measure. The problem is a standard one for management and the solutions are often arrived at by a mathematical analysis of the situation (Woodburn, 1969), (Brookes, 1970).

Very little material exists on the organisation structures of different types of library. Not only has there been little research into optimum patterns of organisation; here as elsewhere there is a need for state-of-the-art reports at the Linnaean level of collection and classification of information. The work of Scrivener (1974) has already been mentioned, but Peter Woodhead's paper on *Subject specialisation in three British university libraries* (Woodhead, 1974) is a good example of the kind of work that is needed.

Earlier we referred to three kinds of change which could be discerned at work in library organisations today. The first we have just covered. The other two are bodies of theory which have undoubtedly influenced many library organisations already, but which may work in a subtle and elusive way.

First, over the past two decades there has been a 'human resources' tendency or school of thought in personnel management which, as we shall see

99

in the next section, has had considerable influence on libraries on both sides of the Atlantic.

Second is the idea of an organisation as an 'organism' rather than a 'machine', which was first developed by Burns and Stalker (1968) and is introduced in the first part of Ashworth's paper below. This is embraced in the wider concepts of General Systems Theory (Bertalanffy, 1971), and has been imported into management on the one hand in the form of general management methodologies such as Management by Objectives (MbO) and Corporate Management, and, on the other, in the form of systems analysis and the problem solving approach of Operational Research, introduced in order to improve the cost-effectiveness of various library operations and procedures and stimulated, often, by the considerations of mechanisation. The general effect of systems theory upon the traditional relatively static library bureaucracy, endlessly processing its stock and users ('my library runs itself') is to modify it in the direction of a dynamic, 'mission-orientated' system. This comprises a number of interlocking sub-systems, the workings and 'outputs' of the system being subject to continuous evaluation in the pursuit of programmes of objectives.

The system ought not to be managed as an end in itself and the objectives ought not to be achieved accidentally as it were (or in the case of some libraries in spite of the system; see a telling article by Blasingame and Lynch (1974). It is intolerable that departmental librarians should operate in ways that conflict with the goals of the central library managers, but the remedy does not necessarily lie with more centralisation, or more decentralisation, and certainly not with a proliferation of committees.

To think in this new way is not at all easy, heavily limited as we are by our bureaucratic culture. It involves an appreciation of cybernetics and the laws of variety and of constraint. All this is not to say that the bureaucratic structure is outmoded. It has its place in task oriented, relatively stable, situations (in the jargon—closed systems) as research has shown. Under conditions demanding change and where organisational goals are unclear or diffuse the organic, systems approach offers a chance of survival and development towards greater effectiveness. There is little doubt about which of these two situations apply to libraries today. This conception of the library as a system should take us up from the level of debate which is concerned with 'centralisation or decentralisation' to a level where we perceive that the nature of the decision determines the nature of the decision-making process. On p 115-6 Ashworth refers to decisions being best made by the person most informed and capable. Quite clearly this could be anyone in the library from the porter to the chief. It is the job of the managers of the system to see that everyone taking decisions has the necessary information about alternative courses of action and that they are able to select the alternatives that are beneficial to the system as a whole. In other words, to see that the system is so arranged that self interest, and organisational interests coincide enough to make the systems effective overall.

Further reading into systems theory would be helpful here. Unfortunately the most carefully worked out readings are not easy to understand. One might start with Simpson (1968) and Bellomy (1968) as easy introductions to the application of systems thinking to library problems as well, of course, as Mackenzie's article in section 5 of this reader, but the writings such as Morse (1968), or Raffel and Shishko (1969), reporting the applications of systems analysis and operational research to libraries require a lot of study.

In a more general context the work of Beer (1975) for his essay 'Operational research as revelation' pp 56-69 and, more difficult, Beer (1966, Part III) 'The relevance of cybernetics' are much easier to understand but require a fair amount of mental effort and experience to relate this kind of thinking to the library situation. The Open University's manual on systems (Beishon and Peters, 1972) is also a good guide and includes one or two case studies.

Perhaps the most important feature of the systems approach to library management is its emphasis on the evaluation of library effectiveness, and the measurement of the library's achievements against specific objectives or standards. Stecher (1975) offers an excellent introduction to the whole range of quantitative studies in library evaluation. However, our commentary has now carried us round to the concluding section of this book, on library evaluation.

# A SYSTEMS CONCEPT OF ORGANISATION
## AND CONTROL OF LARGE UNIVERSITY LIBRARIES

*G C Burgis*

The traditional organization structure in large university libraries is in an obvious state of collapse. The situation is not peculiar to any one university but is endemic to most large university libraries in North America. The changing role of the library in the university community and the external forces being brought to bear upon it are demanding a more modern organizational approach if the library is to fulfil its functions in the immediate future.

Several months ago Mr M W Eagles, a visiting executive faculty member of the College of Commerce, at the University of Saskatchewan, spoke at a technical services seminar in the University Library on 'Emerging concepts in management'. At that seminar Mr Eagles discussed the highly successful reorganization of the Advanced Devices Centre, Ottawa (1). The systems concept of organization and control was so well received there, and was so highly praised in the business community, that the prestigious Harvard Business School conducted a special study of its establishment (2).

The organization structure of the Advanced Devices Centre is based upon the *matrix concept.* Essentially it is a network of *product teams* and *functional teams* with a Systems Operation Council acting as the administrative body. Working as a multi-disciplined management group, under the leadership of the Chairman, the Council has provided a deeper reservoir of knowledge and skills with which to encourage the Centre's business. It has provided better use of technical and business know-how by incorporating this knowledge into the operation of each team. It has facilitated decision making and has resulted in prompter action being taken upon those decisions. This team approach has also helped to bypass the usual barriers caused by different levels of rank in management.

The main purpose of such a manufacturing organization is to produce products which are marketable*. The Advanced Devices Centre, operating in a competitive electronics field, discovered that its old organization, run with traditional staff and line management, could not react quickly enough to the rapidly changing market demands. It discovered that by the time a new product was ready for sale it might already be out of date, and that the end product very often was not of the design originally conceived by marketing management.

Although in the library profession we do not sell a product, we do provide a service to the university community, namely its information needs and services. I suggest therefore, that the approach adopted by the Advanced Devices Centre to correct the problems of unresponsive management and outdated end products, is applicable to present day library organization.

*Library administrative and operational committee*
The work of most large university libraries can be divided roughly into Public Services and Technical Services. These two aspects of library service permeate all library departments to a greater or lesser extent. For example, Circulation and Reference are clearly Public Service aspects of library services and, as such, represent the *services* or *end products* of the library. The Acquisition and Cataloguing Departments belong traditionally to the *technical*, or *functional services* of the library. The functional organization chart shows how these two aspects of library service could be divided and produce an organization similar to the organization matrix supporting the Advanced Devices Centre. The chart illustrates how these two types of library services interrelate: a) public service teams (teams on the horizontal axis), b) technical service or functional teams (teams on the vertical axis). Any library problem can be solved by the meeting of any two teams on the matrix, ie where there is an intersection of interests. A team could consist of the professional staff only or, if desired, the entire staff of a department. Two teams may meet to resolve a problem at the request of a Department Head, the Assistant Directors, or the Library Administrative and Operational Committee.

If such a distinction is made on a functional basis, obviously some division will be arbitrary, and for the benefit of the discussion, Systems Research, Production and Office Management and Collection Department have been designated as Technical Services and grouped with the *Functional Teams*. Similarly, Serials **, Government Documents, Automated Reader Information Services, Coordinator—Branch Libraries, Audio-Visual Services and Special Collections have been designated as *Public Service Teams*.

The *matrix concept* demonstrates the adaptability and flexibility needed to incorporate new library departments into the library organization. Similarly, new departments that may be needed by libraries as technology advances in the future could also be easily included in the matrix organization. It is important to remember, however, that each library department head has direct access to both the Assistant Director—Public Services and the Assistant Director—Technical Services, for those departmental problems related specifically to either director.

The functional chart further reflects the Advanced Devices Centre organization by the composition of the Library Administrative and Operational Committee. This Committee consists of the top library administration, including the positions of the Director, Associate and Assistant Directors. It would be the responsibility of the Library Administrative and Operational Committee to define the role of the library as a university institution, in conjunction with university and faculty advisory bodies, and to define its service goals in the university community. It would be the Committee's responsibility to interpret these in the practical and specific terms of policies, priorities, and procedures in the library system, its departments and branches.

The Committee members, in addition to their own particular and specific responsibilities, would have—as a Committee—the overall responsibility for all libraries in the university library system; overall responsibility for budget preparation and allocation of resources; overall responsibility for long-range planning and institution of changes in the system, and overall responsibility for salaries, job classification and departmental definition.

However final executive authority must remain with the Director of Libraries. He must retain the authority to demand cooperation between teams, schedule overall work loads and be able to delay a decision of his advisors in the Library Administrative and Operational Committee if he feels it is necessary and in the best interests of the university community. Within the individual service and functional teams, the traditional line and staff relationships can be maintained. Each Department Head would maintain executive authority over his professional and clerical staff and be responsible for their direction.

*How it operates*

As an example, the Library Administrative and Operational Committee could ask the Head of Circulation Services and the Head of Cataloguing to meet, with their teams, to solve a problem in circulation. The meeting

# FUNCTIONAL ORGANIZATIONAL CHART

LIBRARY ADMINISTRATIVE AND OPERATIONAL COMMITTEE

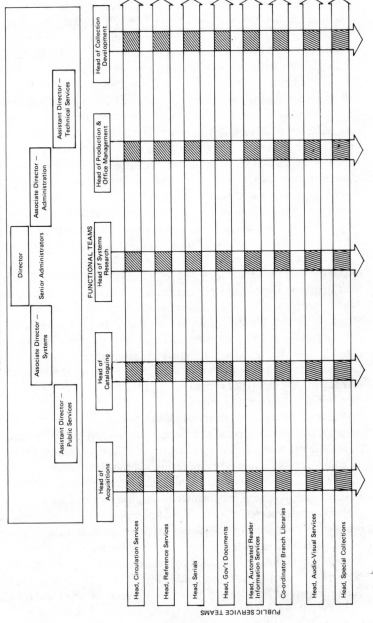

Director

Senior Administrators

Associate Director — Systems

Associate Director — Administration

Assistant Director — Public Services

Assistant Director — Technical Services

FUNCTIONAL TEAMS

Head of Acquisitions

Head of Cataloguing

Head of Systems Research

Head of Production & Office Management

Head of Collection Development

PUBLIC SERVICE TEAMS

Head, Circulation Services

Head, Reference Services

Head, Serials

Head, Gov't Documents

Head, Automated Reader Information Services

Co-ordinator Branch Libraries

Head, Audio-Visual Services

Head, Special Collections

of these two teams, as illustrated in the cross-section of the matrix, would bring together those members of the staff *directly* involved with the problem and, therefore, most capable of finding a solution. An example interdepartmental problem is the keypunching of punched book cards (PBC) for an automated circulation system. If the PBC design includes a fixed author/title field, then rules have to be devised which meet the standards and which are mutually acceptable to both the Circulation Department and the Cataloguing Department. What type of truncated entry would facilitate easy matching of the author/title entry on the PBC with its counterpart in the public catalogue? On the other hand, what problems or extra work would be incurred by the Cataloguing Department in devising such a shortened entry for the keypunch staff? Would some sort of vocabulary control to govern truncation be necessary?

In other words, the best ideas and brain power could be drawn upon from the two teams, and the staff should be able to get together and resolve the problem. The teams having participated in finding a solution would consequently be more willing to put it into effect. The end product or service would have been designed to the knowledge and satisfaction of the Circulation Department, the Cataloguing Department and the Library Administrative and Operational Committee. This type of teamwork, in effect, means that the staff of the various teams involved in the decision making process will be continually aware of the evolution of the final product. Likewise, the teams will be constantly aware of any changes necessitated in their work in order to effect the change desired. There would be no need for any group not complying with the decision to change or modify the end service as agreed upon.

The team approach to library administration guarantees that any new or developing service is equally represented in the participative management arena. *Library journal* (3) in its February 1969 issue, mentions the possible inclusion of people from other professions in the library organization. An example of such a person would be a Head of Production and Office Management. A competent graduate in business administration (6) could probably manage a clerical typing pool for catalogue card production, and oversee the buying and maintenance of typewriters, better than the average professional librarian, who by nature has little interest in such things. This concept is not unlike an industrial concern which employs the specialties of people from many educational backgrounds to fulfil its corporate needs. The University of New Mexico has recently confirmed this trend by advertising for a Business Administration Librarian. This does not mean that that professional librarians need to fear the takeover of their libraries by outsiders. If the president of a manufacturing firm expressed such a fear, he would probably be considered extremely unrational. It is clearly understood that bibliographic control and content must always remain under the direction of professional librarians.

*Criticisms and advantages*

A major criticism of any attempt to include a majority of the executive branch of an organization in the decision making process is that of wasted time. However, experience suggests that the time currently wasted because of inadequate consultation and arbitrary decision making, probably far exceeds the supposed time loss incurred by operating within the framework of the proposed Library Administrative and Operational Committee. A case in point would be, should the library establish or not establish a new branch library? What are the wishes on the part of the faculty proposing the branch in question, and are they well expressed to the Library Administrative and Operational Committee? If such views were adequately expressed to the Library Administrative and Operational Committee, the pros and cons in opening a new branch could be discussed simultaneously with the entire management team present. The advantages and disadvantages of any course of action would be adequately expressed to the representatives of the *Public Service Teams* and the *Functional or Technical Service Teams.* In effect, this would mean that the best in professional ability would be brought to bear upon the problem in arriving at a suitable decision. It would also mean that the Assistant Directors would know exactly what was expected of their departments in order to arrive at the 'end service' decided upon. The Assistant Directors could then hold a series of meetings with the various teams to plan and execute the actual work brought about by a Committee decision.

Today, most large university libraries have systems research facilities of some sort or another. Many already have systems analysts and programmers on their library staff. The problem is, how do these people relate and interface with the rest of the library's professional staff? The functional chart readily provides for their participation in the management arena by including them with the rest of the *Functional Teams* of the library. This makes the systems research team readily accessible to the total library organization. Although in practice this department would tend towards an advisory staff function, yet in the organization chart it does have the advantage of definite responsibilities through the directive channels and offices of the Assistant and Associate Directors and the Library Administrative and Operational Committee. Any department or branch library may request direct aid of Systems Research in solving internal and immediate problems. The Assistant Director—Library Services and the Associate Director—Systems may also direct the Head of Systems Research to conduct studies in spheres of broader concern and future planning.

University libraries are also rapidly developing automated information services for their faculties. Whether these services develop within the library itself, or originate on a regional or national basis, technical staff and trained personnel to run such services need to be included in the library organization. The sooner such services are integrated into the on-going library processes, the more effective they will be. The University of Saskatchewan has participated in the CAN/SDI Project (4) since its inauguration in April 1969. This Project is one of the first national automated information storage and retrieval systems, providing a current awareness service for Canada's scientific community. The Library Search Editor at the University of Saskatchewan has prepared and manages over forty profiles which serve over one hundred faculty members for the University's Science Faculties. Although in the beginning these services could exist as a section of Reference Services, with growth and development in the seventies, a department of Automated Reader Information Services is likely to become a necessity.

*Conclusion*

The systems concept of organization and control of the Library Administrative and Operational Committee should bring the best human resources of the library into the decision making arena, and should overcome the present communication gap which exists in most university libraries. There is still, however, a problem of how and where library management interfaces with other university organizations. The Advanced Devices Centre of Northern Electric Co Ltd recognized the need for coordinating its activities with other parts of the company and with outside organizations. They have conceived a system of directorates to act as 'links' or channels of communication to and from the Advanced Devices Centre. Each directorate is comprised of 'linking-pin' individuals*** from within the Centre and from the outside organization. Similar establishment of channels of communication to and from the Library Administrative and Operational Committee is imperative. An adequate and meaningful interface between the Committee, faculty, students, and other academic services must be developed. Such interaction however, is the concern of many university administrators, and emerging patterns of communication are developing with local emphasis.

*Notes*
  * In achieving this purpose the Advanced Devices Centre did not over-
look the tremendous contribution that social goals could add to their total
productivity. These were:
  — To match an individual's capabilities to certain jobs so as to provide
security, challenge, and opportunity for growth;
  — to provide continuous assessment of recognition for achievement;
  — to provide a program of additional training and education each year
for all members;
  — to improve and advance communication, internally and externally;
  — to consider and contribute to the external environment in a responsible manner (5).
  This attempt to integrate personal and organizational goals implies a
need to consider all aspects of the situation so that no one element is en-
hanced at the expense of others. In other words a *'systems' view* is required
in which all elements of a system are specified and their relation to and
dependence upon all other elements of the system are clarified and made
explicit (6).
  ** Serials has traditionally been a Technical Services department of most
libraries. However, with increasing computer applications in the department,
it is possible that the serials staff may in the future, be 50 per cent highly
technical personnel, and 50 per cent public service trained. For example, as
computer search techniques are applied to searching the ever-increasing
technical and professional literature, then more personnel with public service
know-how will be needed in the Serials department. Such searches of technical report literature are even now included as a regular service at the University of Guelph (7), and at Laval University in Quebec City.
  *** The expression 'linking-pins' was originated by Rensis Likert of the
Institute of Social Research at the University of Michigan. 'Linking-pin'
members belong to more than one group and provide integration and information exchange between the two groups.

*References*
  1  'Employee adaptability'. Financial post, 8 October 1966.
  2  Three papers on the subject bearing the copyright of the President and
Fellows of Harvard College:
Northern Electric Company, Ltd: A) Cambridge, Harvard Business
School, 1968 (HP 659)
Northern Electric Company, Ltd: B) Cambridge, Harvard Business
School, 1968 (HP 660)
Northern Electric Company, Ltd: C) Cambridge, Harvard Business
School, 1968 (HP 661)
  3  Wilder, David: 'Management attitudes; team relationships', Library
journal, 94 (3) 1 Feb 1969, p 499.
Smith, Eldred: 'Do libraries need managers?' Library journal, 94 (3) 1 Feb
1969, p 502.
  4  Brown, Jack E: 'The CAN/SDI Project', Special libraries 60 (8) Oct
1969, p 501-509.

5  Northern Electric Company, Ltd: The Advanced Devices Centre in review 1965. Ottawa, 1965.

6  Northern Electric Company, Ltd: A) Cambridge, Harvard Business School, 1968 (HP 659), p 3.

7  Markuson, Barbara Evans: 'Automation in libraries and information systems', in Annual review of information science and technology. New York, John Wiley & Sons, 1967, Vol 2, p 273.

# THE ADMINISTRATION OF DIFFUSE COLLECTIONS

*Wilfrid Ashworth*

There is a story of the tourist who, after a special package tour intended to show the British way of life, complained that he had not been shown the Church of England! I meet much the same situation when people ask me to show them the Library of the Polytechnic of Central London for it has seven separate divisions dotted around its fourteen buildings and to show it all involves a walk of several miles. Perhpas this is why the Winter Meetings Committee decided to ask *me* when they thought it time that some attention was focused on the problem of administering diffuse collections. I have been a member of that Committee myself and can imagine the discussion. First the doubt–'but he hasn't been there very long', and then the hopeful–'well, at least he'll have had to *think* about it', and that's another meeting as good as fixed!

Many library systems have to operate a number of branches or service points at geographically-separated places. This has happened for a long time in municipal and county library systems where it is a natural consequence of attempting to provide a service within a reasonable distance of everyone in a widely-distributed population. Such a service parallels that offered by banks, multiple stores or large-scale dry cleaners, where loss of business ensues if there is no branch within easy reach. More recently, however, a new kind of multi-site situation has begun to develop in the library world. Industrial mergers have brought together separate companies which continue operations after re-organization and need to be supplied with information at scattered points. Universities in their growth have sometimes spread too widely to be served adequately at a single centre. Finally the polytechnics, formed by amalgamation of colleges, often widely separated, present the split-site problem in its most exaggerated form. It might be thought that the knowledge gained through years of experience of public and county branch systems could be drawn upon for help. Unfortunately it proves to be not entirely relevant. In the first

111

place such libraries offer a homogeneous service which, considered in a rough and ready way, is not basically different if enough copies of each book needed to serve the population are either concentrated centrally or are spread out, like the population, into groups. In the second place the rate of growth of public libraries has been sufficiently slow to allow the development of an acceptable hierarchical system of administration. Neither of these factors is applicable to special libraries. As will be seen later both their state of flux and their primary concern with the advance of knowledge prove disruptive factors to the administration of a group of special libraries, and it is this type of library with which my talk mainly deals.

There used to be a subject called 'Library Organization' taught in library schools but it consisted largely of a set of rules culled from the experience of wise old librarians who had learnt them by trial and error. Lacking such guidelines, and hoping to avoid the error side of experiment, it seemed to me reasonable that we might, together, start by attempting to see whether any established principles of management offer useful pointers. For obvious reasons the most-studied type of organization has been the industrial manufacturing concern but in most cases emphasis on the interaction between people rather than on the firm itself makes the findings relevant to other systems.

However dogmatically they may end, in their introductory pages all textbooks of management seem to agree that there is no single set of principles or ideal system to which all administrative practice must conform, but rather a series of sets of rules which only succeed when applied to their own particular set of conditions. So the first task of management is to identify the nature of the organization and its set of conditions.

It does not require much consideration to identify the earlier type of multi-site library. Its established service—the loan of books for home reading, reference work, and extension activities to stimulate interest in books and library use—form a stable 'product'. The case is similar to that which Donald Schon, in his book *Beyond the stable state* (1), recognizes as a centre-periphery style of organization. As stable examples he quotes the American Coca Cola company and the Roman Catholic Church. The former empire depends upon the sale of a product of secret composition for which licences are issued to approved retail outlets under strictly controlled conditions. In the second case the product is not for sale but is still under central control. For such organizations a bureaucratic administration is satisfactory, indeed desirable. The individual in the system has his precise function defined, together with his responsibilities and powers.

By implication he is thus also told what is not his concern and what he must leave to the decision of higher authority. Such an organization, now usually called 'mechanistic', operates according to a consistent body of rules and has a strongly hierarchical framework which carries with it an inbuilt career structure. Promotion is according to seniority or achievement and is decided by superiors. There is never any doubt whether a particular appointment is promotion, demotion or a sideways move, since the status of each post is overt. It is interesting to see another similarity between public libraries and industries of this kind. The annals of the library profession are rich with legends about the great chief librarians of the past. These exactly parallel those which in industry gather about the personality of managing directors! Tom Burns and G M Stalker in *The management of innovation* (2) refer to a study of twenty organizations and say that the one constant element was the extraordinary importance ascribed to the heads of the concerns. Everyone interviewed referred to their 'outstanding personality', 'flair', 'wisdom' and even 'genius'. These estimates can persist in retrospect even when there could be no personal benefit associated with their expression, so they have to be taken as having some basis in genuine belief. In fact it is suggested that the existence of such beliefs is necessary to the success of the mechanistic organization and that the head fails if he does not inspire them. As a corollary, because he has a powerful influence over the destiny of his subordinates, he also has to endure social isolation and the loneliness of command. There is no reason why this form of administration should not persist in public libraries so long as there is no marked change in the service offered. Nor need it necessarily be affected by even major regrouping, as has been shown in the London Boroughs reorganization. However, it would seem that the bureaucratic approach has innate weaknesses where the product of an organization is subject to innovative change, which is the case in the newer multi-site libraries. They are all experimenting with systems, developing information services and introducing unfamiliar routines. Further, the information they provide is often on the frontiers of new knowledge in science, technology and the social sciences. All the prophets, McLuhan, Schon and Toffler have been at pains to point out that our society and many of its institutions subjected to the disruptive effect of the new technology are entering on a phase on continuous adaptation to the changes it brings. Schon, for example, traces the pattern of failure in a centre-periphery organization subject to innovative change. Instead of the centre issuing instructions to the outstations while they in turn report back directly in a manner creating a balance (as do the centrifugal and centripetal forces in a flywheel), the branches on the phery start to m 113 periphery start to make connections with each other without informing the centre. Instability develops and full control is lost. It is almost inevitable that this should happen in a changing situation where some of the outstations have a common problem not shared with the others. In an attempt to regularize what cannot easily be prevented a new organization system is drawn up. It remains a centre-periphery model but some, if not all, of the branches become secondary centres with partial autonomy, though there is still central oversight. In this state the functions of the primary centre become specialization in training, deployment, support monitoring and determination of overall policy. In such circumstances the customers of each secondary centre approach it as if it were autonomous and are dissatisfied whenever reference has to be made to headquarters. Thus centre-branch conflict arises with the familiar complaint of regional offices that headquarters is slow in decision, unresponsive to suggestion and out-of-touch with local conditions. The situation is readily recognizable when it occurs in libraries. For example, a local academic librarian can be faced with demands from a Board of Studies which conflict with total Library policy and an embarrassing division of loyalties ensues. If the secondary centres take independent action, the whole model fails. Schon sees the solution in the development of a network system of communications which formalize controlled interconnecting channels of authority, information or decision between the centres. The network differs from direct contact in that there are multiple interconnections or nodes in which several connecting stands meet. Such a network may have a powerful effect. Sometimes when a formal hierarchical organization becomes sluggish through overgrowth even an *informal* network superimposed on the system enables people to get things done.

It is doubtful, however, whether a network system alone is the answer to administrative problems in the diffuse library situation, though some network features may be of assistance. A more promising solution seems to be that offered by Burns and Stalker. They, too, recognize that in a changing situation the constant need to find answers to unfamiliar problems sets up an intolerable degree of strain in a mechanistic system of government. They examine the progress of breakdown in a different manner. Each difficult problem as it arises is sent higher and higher up the organization tree in the hope of finding a level where sufficient responsibility exists to settle it. Eventually executives lower down the scale claim that they can only resolve matters if they by-pass the senior managers and and directly consult the head of the concern. When he becomes overloaded responsibility has to be delegated, so the organization chart is

114

redrawn with stronger barriers against by-passing. As the situation usually recurs relief proves to be only temporary. Instead of this method a ruse which is sometimes tried is to pass unfamiliar problems over to a 'super-person': in other words a committee, though Burns and Stalker dub this device pathological!

The solution they propose, which has been found successful in changing industrial situations, is to move towards a newer form of management which is termed 'organic'. The mechanistic system has all the hierarchical controls and innate career structure we have already noted. It also has a rigid approach with clearly-differentiated functional tasks which some-times leads to those tasks being performed as an end in themselves, rather than to accomplish the aims of the organization. The organic system is stated to be more appropriate to those changing conditions which give rise to unforeseen problems and call for action which cannot be dealt with automatically. The system seeks to develop a 'common culture', a manner of dealing with people and problems, and of making judgments which is the 'way' of the organization. Amongst the character-istics of the organic structure which seem especially relevant to a library situation are the following:

1  Special knowledge and experience are applied to the common aims of the concern.

2  Individual tasks are continually re-defined and adjusted through interaction with the staff.

3  Shedding of responsibility on to others is eliminated.

4  Commitment to the interests of the concern is not limited to the pre-defined narrow confines of one job.

5  The network structure of control, authority and communication.

6  Omniscience is no longer imputed to the head of the concern. Knowledge of the technical nature of any task may be located anywhere in the network, which point then becomes the *ad hoc* centre of control, authority and communication.

In respect of the network structure the organic system parallels Schon's advice, but he makes no provision for the building of a corporate approach to decision-making. However, good communication in an organic system is an important cohesive force. It takes place when necessary, irrespective of relative rank, and in the form of consultation rather than command. The content is therefore more often information and advice than instruc-tion and decision.

While organic systems are not strongly hierarchical in the same sense as are mechanistic systems they can still be stratified, levels being differentiated according to seniority or expertise. It is assumed that the lead in joint decisions will be taken by the person who, on the occasion, shows himself most informed and capable. It is interesting to note that Burns and Stalker see that the simplest way of explaining the necessary commitment of individuals to their work is to describe it as of a 'professional' nature, which ties in with the nature of librarianship.

Having examined current management thought let us now try to see how it can be applied to diffuse library collections. Clearly I can do no more at this stage than identify pointers and lay down some general guidelines, but I hope this will prove useful. The first lesson would seem to be to reject a completely bureaucratic control. It is not, however, so easy to do this. In the inherited situation the 'Powers that Be' will expect that each major branch will be put in charge of a librarian or information officer with defined responsibilities and so the stage is already set for breakdown from all the causes we have seen. If Burns and Stalker are right such breakdown can be avoided if a sufficiently good interactive communication network can be set up and especially if a feeling of total involvement in a common professional purpose can be fostered. As a first stage in achieving this happy state it is advisable to isolate the unavoidable clerical routines, and, by making their performance as mechanical and as little time-consuming as possible, to remove them from the scene as creators of friction. In the interests of economy and interchangeability of staff, uniformity of routine must be aimed at, which requires common agreement. One can begin by setting up interbranch working parties to collect opinions and make recommendations on routine systems. These working parties should be composed of staff from different strata levels. The aim in this case is not to create a super-person in the form of a committee but to take the first step in encouraging working interaction. It also ensures that in several of the libraries there will be individuals who, as authors of selected systems, have a vested interest in preventing erosion by local modification. Thus a network system has been started, which, later on, when experience of this form of interaction has been gained, can be applied to more fundamental matters like the design of new services and eventually to development planning. Of course a curb must be placed on the amount of time spent in round-the-table discussion. Instead in each case the most appropriate 'nodal' individual through whom interaction can continue must be identified as quickly as possible. If this method proves successful not only will a basic network have been created to bring coherence to the centre-periphery framework on which it has been imposed, but a 'style' of approaching situations will begin to permeate the library.

It is interesting to see that the role of the chief librarian is no longer to be omniscient but by his deep and extensive professional experience to be able to recognize the more critical factors in any situation. He will pilot his staff so that they become sensitive to potential snags in the solutions they choose to the problems they meet. It therefore is unimportant, as Toffler points out, when, because technical change is now so rapid, most managers have to administer staff more competent than themselves in some of the newer advances. In such matters a chief librarian may, without loss of standing, be merely part of a team examining a new development. It is his *way* of handling situations which determines the policy style of the library. He need in theory no longer be in social isolation as in a mechanistic organization, although it is extremely difficult in practice to develop an entirely free relationship, because all responses to him tend to be tinged with circumspection.

The total commitment of an individual within an organic system clearly makes more call on his resources, and may cause him to wonder exactly what is expected of him. To this there will be no detailed and specific answer in terms of a particular post, but Don Kennington, speaking to an Aslib Transport Group meeting a little over a year ago, suggested that the answer is apparent if one focuses on the contribution individuals can make to the results of the organization. 'In my experience', he said, 'good staff can be stretched and developed well beyond the limits which individuals would set for themselves (3).' This, of course, is intensely rewarding both for them and for the organization to which they are responsible. The new organic approach suggests that in fact individuals can, in the right circumstance, be encouraged to stretch *themselves* and set their *own* 'reach for the stars' standards.

We must now leave the management side and concentrate for a time on the other aspects of administration mentioned in my synopsis. The one fact which unfortunately cannot be escaped is that it costs a great deal more to operate libraries on multiple sites. I refer, of course, particularly to the case where there are separate special libraries serving limited groups of users. In such a case any forced duplication of stock (for example, reference works which must be locally available, or duplicate copies required because there is an overlap of interests between two or more libraries) generally means wasted money. In consequence overlapping interests have to be considered most carefully. It must be decided whether to designate one of the libraries the centre for each particular interest or discipline, or to spread one's resources for that interest rather thinly between two or more libraries. There is no easy answer to the dilemma and it may not be feasible to make a uniform decision for all cases. Because the expense of unavoidable duplication will already be high most librarians will tend to favour the designation of the one most appropriate library as the centre for each particular discipline, notwithstanding the known unwillingness of users to travel far for the information they seek. However, special cases will undoubtedly have to be acknowledged where two different topics have to be studied at different places, each in conjunction with a common third topic. Legal, management or social aspects of problems form good examples of this kind. Unfortunately we in the polytechnic libraries are victims of the modern tendency towards the development of interdisciplinary courses in the departments which are the centres of the particular disciplines. Thus students will already be working in different buildings at different times and therefore it is no hardship to them to use the appropriate libraries.

Another major factor in the increased expense of a multi-site library is the staffing problem. In the first place there is a minimum staff level needed to cover the hours of opening at even the smallest service point. In the second place each branch is in the condition of a small special library which lacks flexibility in staff usage and which cannot readily divide the duties to be performed into professional and non-professional categories. In order to assemble sufficient professional expertise at each separate location one is forced to appoint assistants at a generally higher professional level than would otherwise be justifiable. There are then too few juniors adequately to support their seniors and sometimes no staff at all of intermediate professional status. Interchangeability of members of staff between branches is also made difficult because they will have been chosen for particular libraries on the basis of specialist subject knowledge and if moved cannot be so effectively used. With each library falling into the 'small' category even a large system may still show all the disadvantages of smaller libraries, and be continuously vulnerable to overloading the remaining staff during periods of illness, holidays and re-appointment following resignations. As the total staff number rises these effects diminish, but experience shows that until the staff level at each library reaches more than ten inefficient usage will remain significant.

Unfortunately no quantitative study has yet been made of the extra cost of multi-site libraries, though such a study is very much needed to support requests for funding them. It would be especially valuable if it could be carried out by an independent body for an organization such as the Department of Education and Science: the results would then carry some weight. Several librarians have made inspired guesses at their own supercosts but a great deal depends on their definition of what is a true extra. I am indebted to E J Ellis of the Polytechnic of North London for a suggestion that the figure for increased running costs is certainly not less than 5 per cent per site, that is to say, for two sites one would add 10 per cent, for three 15 per cent, and so on. This is a rough and ready figure but seems to tally with the estimates I, and some other polytechnic librarians, have been able to make. I have reason to believe that in an industrial situation the position would not be appreciably different.

These estimates cover material and staff but not communications which depend too much on local conditions for any estimate to be generally applicable. Communication costs can be quite high as they include telephone charges, postages (internal and external), transport of books and periodicals and, often forgotten, a large item for unproductive staff time and fares of staff members in inter-library movements. Part of this is chargeable at the highest level as the chief librarian and his deputy keep in touch with the branches and need to consult with major users of each library in order to monitor the local acceptability of the service. Another item not included in the above estimate of increased running costs is equipment, such as photocopiers, optical-coincidence punches and light boxes, and even typewriters and duplicating machines. They have to be made available at each centre though perhaps they may be under-utilized in consequence. The installation of a visible index system for recording periodicals, to take an example, can require the purchase of as many cabinets as there are libraries, with an increase in cost of several hundred percent, a cost which becomes daunting even when written off over the notional life of the equipment. When, however, even more expensive equipment comes under consideration the cost may become not daunting but prohibitive. It is one thing to install electronic theft detection devices when one exit controls the whole collection, quite another matter if $x$ black boxes have to be acquired and maintained. Yet the alternative may be an uncontrollably high rate of loss of material—a hidden aspect of the unfavourable economics of split-site operation. To go one stage further, suppose the matter under consideration is a computer issue system. Though it could well remove a load of finicky routine from the staff and offer a much improved service to users, the idea, at the present stage of technology, is out of the question, because of the cost of terminal equipment.

The unfavourable economics of carrying out routine processes at several separated locations naturally drives one towards consideration of centralization of matters like acquisition, mechanical processing of books, cataloguing and classification. But would this really be economical? The truth of the matter is that nobody knows. No investigation in depth has yet been made which would balance the cost of transport and communications against possible reductions resulting from better use of staff and equipment and potential savings through more experienced and bulk buying. Centralization of routines also leads to frequent enquiries from branch to centre and reduced effectiveness as seen by users who may have to be kept waiting for replies. It is hoped that if the Cambridge University Library Management Unit turns its attention, as expected, to Polytechnic Libraries the economics of central unit working will be one of the earliest problems to be investigated.

It might be thought from what has so far been said that diffuse collections are all debit and no credit, but that is not so. Again, there has ·been no study of the relation of size to effectiveness in libraries but there is little doubt that the larger libraries too easily become impersonal and make less appeal to users, even though their greater stock and wider range of resources are obvious advantages. Where information services are offered there is distinct advantage in having a workable number of users whose needs can become more effectively known through personal contact. Everyone familiar with the branch library situation knows how strong users' affinity to their own branch can be. This, of course, conflicts with the desire of the Chief Librarian to foster the image of the library as a unified service and provides yet one more problem to be resolved by compromise as both attitudes are in themselves meritorious. A decidedly positive advantage arising out of the community spirit in smaller, departmentally-based libraries is that library misuse, particularly losses by theft, can be significantly reduced by the social pressures which develop from a feeling of involvement and 'ownership'.

Another feature which often results from branch-loyalty is that the users of each branch may demand a local committee and wish to have some control over *their* library and especially over the way in which *their* share of the total library budget is spent. Public and county libraries are in a different position as their committee structure is imposed upon them by the nature of local government, so there is little point in commenting on them. However, in industrial, academic and other special libraries there can be little doubt that local committees are a mixed blessing. A single advisory committee can be useful in giving support to the librarian and in helping to determine general policy. It cannot be overstressed, however, that its function must only be advisory. It should have no powers over the administration of the library nor any control over professional work like, for example, book selection or budgeting. It is perhaps

120

more acceptable that departments of the firm or organization should be asked to appoint liaison officers through whom (though not uniquely) departments' views and needs can be made known and to whom the local librarians can go for advice when necessary on matters of subject-interest. In this way users can be brought into a community relationship with the library to mutual advantage.

I hope this review will be regarded as an interim report on a subject of developing importance. Much more study is needed and far more evidence must be collected and collated before definitive administrative policies will emerge. In the meantime we who have the administration of diffuse collections can, paradoxically, regard ourselves as fortunate. A challenging job brings its own enjoyment and rewards.

*References*
1 Schon, Donald: Beyond the stable state. London, Temple-Smith, 1971.
2 Burns, Tom and Stalker, G M: The management of innovation. London, Tavistock, 1961.
3 Kennington, Don: Managing effectively: some tips for special librarians. Aslib proceedings 23, 6, June 1971, p 287-91.

# 4
# Personnel

Intertwined with the idea of a library as a managed system (from which has grown a quantitative, technologically orientated library service), over the last two decades a human relations philosophy of personnel management has become no less influential. This derives from certain behavioural science research, most notably into the needs and motivation of people at work. The paper by Dutton which follows introduces the reader to the seminal theory of Maslow and Herzberg on which the new personnel management is founded. That of Plate and Stone concludes, from a replication of Herzberg's research, that librarians are motivated at work much the same as other people. Evidence from UK academic libraries will be found in Roberts (1973) and Smith (1973). For further readings in the relevant behavioural science we would recommend two other 'readers'— Vroom and Deci (1970) and Pugh (1971). A useful overview is provided by Schein (1970).

It should be noted that researchers in this field are not agreed that organisations which adopt this 'human relations' or 'human resources' philosophy (McGregor's 'Theory Y', below) become more effective organisations as a result. There are so many variables at work that validation by formal research would be difficult indeed. In library management the dialogue between Lynch (1972) and Marchant (1971) would seem to confirm this.

Most of the literature of librarianship has been concerned to expound these ideas and to advocate their adoption, rather than critically to assess their relevance to the management of libraries. Moreover, looking beyond libraries, there is a tendency to neglect the wider world in which alienated twentieth century man spends his free time, and to see him only as the Orwellian Organisation Man so well pictured by Whyte (1957) and more than hinted at in some of the writing on Organisation Development (OD) (Lumsdon, 1975). This question of organisation commitment is already more than an academic matter for the many librarians who find themselves in the hands of dynamic library managers who are trying to motivate them. . . .

Again, such an impressive edifice of management theory has been erected upon such a slender foundation of simplified Maslowian existential psychology as to exclude other modifying influences that might have been drawn from the behavioural sciences. For example, would not a little Adlerian concern for that balance between a sense of security and insecurity, which is so important for individual mental well-being, perhaps lead managers to temper their policies of wholesale push towards self-actualisation?

After he has studied section 4, the reader has reached a point at which we may attempt to synthesise the various approaches to library management introduced previously. The idea of Burns and Stalker (1968) of 'mechanistic' and 'organic' patterns of organisation seems to us to offer a basis for this synthesis. This idea has been introduced in the early part of Ashworth's paper (above). It relates back, like all the 'new' personnel management, to McGregor's Theory X and Theory Y (McGregor, 1960).

Theory X assumes that the average human being has an inherent dislike of work and will avoid it if he can. Therefore people have to be directed, controlled and even threatened, in order to get them to put forth an adequate effort. They prefer to be told what to do, and reluctant to assume much responsibility for organising their work, are relatively unambitious and mainly interested in a secure, predictable work situation.

Against this Theory X McGregor argued Theory Y—that the expenditure of physical and mental effort is as natural as play or rest, that people will exercise self-direction and self-control in the service of objectives to which they are committed, and, under proper conditions, will learn not only to accept responsibility but also to seek it. The capacity to exercise a relatively high degree of imagination, ingenuity and creativity in the solution of organisational problems is widely, not narrowly, distributed in the population. Under the conditions of modern life, the potentialities of most average human beings are only partially utilised.

Should we be inclined to bask in this optimistic view of mankind as a relief from contemplations of awkward staff members or trouble in the typing pool a glance at Silverman (1970) might prove a valuable corrective:

'The emphasis, however, on the multi-dimensionality of needs, and the selection of self-actualisation as the highest-level need of all is not necessarily convincing. One cannot escape the impression that the humanistic psychologists, like the human relationists, too easily move from 'ought' to 'is', too easily see what they want to see'.

Burns and Stalker's mechanistic and organismic tendencies in organisations may be paradigmed as on page 126.

The mechanistic/organismic paradigm is not, of course, a description of two separate types of organisation. Rather does it define two opposing tendencies to be found in any organisation, or the two ends of a continuum at some point along which any specific organisation may, arguably, be located. Moreover, in real life, beyond the organisation chart, one of these tendencies may predominate in some parts of the organisation and the other in other parts. This is not uncommon in a professional/bureaucratic organisation like a library. Most readers will have little difficulty, we suspect, of recalling examples from their own experience. This mix may be intended by senior management. Arguably, the acquisitions

## Mechanistic/organismic paradigm

| | Mechanistic | Organismic |
|---|---|---|
| AUTHORITY | Authority concentrated at 'the top'; little delegation. | Dispersed; much delegation. |
| PROFESSIONAL EXPERTISE | Low and localised; bureaucracy tends to take its place. | High and dispersed. |
| STRUCTURE | Hierarchical. Favours centralisation. | Network. Favours decentralisation. |
| STAFF DEPLOYMENT | Closely defined job descriptions; sharp division of duties; fixed function of posts; emphasis on PROCESS (routine). | 'Open-ended' job descriptions; duties defined rather by purpose and staff interrelationship; team organisation; emphasis on PROJECT. |
| COMMUNICATION | Little. | Much. |
| – lines of; | One way, 'top' to 'bottom'. | Multi-directional. |
| – content; | Mainly instructions, 'cut-and-dried' decisions. | Mainly information, advice, opinion-seeking. |
| – format; | Emphasis on written communication. | Oral, 'face-to-face' is important. |
| JOB SATISFACTION | 'Hygiene' factors important; reward and—punishments. | Herzberg's 'motivators' important. Opportunity for self-development and socially useful work. |
| COMMITMENT | Obedience and loyalty to an individual leader or/and a part of the organisation. | To the organisation as a whole, or, or, more likely, to professional goals, or, more likely, to a sense of social 'mission'. |
| STAFF DEVELOPMENT | Claims a relatively small share of the organisation's resources; confined to formal training in new skills and introduction of new knowledge. | Claims a relatively large share of the organisations's resources; employs a wide range of means to assist self-development; is concerned with attitude-change, as well as acquisition of knowledge and new skills. |
| DEVELOPMENTAL CAPACITY OF THE ORGANISATION | Works best in relatively static environments, meeting predictable demands; inflexible, and unreliable under stress. | Adapts readily to rapidly changing and unpredictable situations; flexible, and reliable under stress. |

department might be organised more successfully on mechanistic lines than might a group of subject librarians. The continuum does not run from EVIL to GOOD, as might be suggested by some writing on the subject.

On the other hand, the above mix may have developed 'unofficially' as a result of professional and other pressures within the interstices of the bureaucracy. Thompson (1968) has observed that 'the growth of specialised expertise in organisations results in the separation of AUTHORITY and KNOWLEDGE. As fewer and fewer supervisors know more than their subordinates, less and less can hierarchical command carry the load, and a new form of influence appears.' This theme of professionalism and bureaucracy cannot be pursued further here, and the reader is referred to Etzioni (1959), Hall (1968) and Rayward (1970).

The mechanistic/organic continuum offers a valuable frame of reference in the study of many different areas of library management. For example, staff appraisal practices (as described and discussed by Williams (1972), Peele (1972) and Messenger (1975)) assume quite a different significance when refracted through opposite ends of the continuum!

The organic pattern accords well not only with the human relations/ human resources approach in management, but also with the systems approach to the subject. Thus, in a standard textbook on systems theory we find that: 'One of the basic tenets of the systems concept is that the people associated with an operating system should do their own planning. This is a basic change from traditional management, where the planners are separated from the doers' (Johnson et al, 1970).

On the other hand, Mason (later in this reader) favours a systems approach, but with a more mechanistic management style: 'each person knows the range of his activities and authority, and that there is no overlap or underlap'.

The most striking manifestation of the organic idea in many libraries has been the redeployment of staff in teams, rather than in the traditional isolated fixed-function 'post'. The theoretical origins of this development will be found in the work of Likert (1961), and its development in UK public libraries has been described by Jones (1972).

It will by now be evident to the reader that the theory of management is no more divisible than is its practice. The separation of 'executive management' from 'personnel management', or 'personnel management' from 'training', or of 'library managers' from 'librarians with management responsibilities' (and few have none) is, beyond necessary division of labour, hardly practicable in a complex, developing library organisation. Similarly, the reader of this book is advised to view its subdivisions as no

127

more than a convenient scaffolding within which to build his own understanding of a very tightly integrated subject. The practical guide to organisation development offered by Mangham, Shaw and Wilson (1971) affords a very good example of this.

# STAFF MANAGEMENT AND STAFF PARTICIPATION

*B G Dutton*

There is a traditional tendency to think of managers and the managed as two quite separate classes of individual and I should like to make it clear therefore that when I refer to ways in which a manager can improve his effectiveness I am talking about anyone of you who, at a particular moment in time, is achieving his objectives through the agency of at least one other person. I would suggest that by this definition we are all managers, for even those few who in their jobs do not work through a subordinate must, in order to approach their objectives most effectively, manage either their peers or their seniors.

Staff can seem at times to behave illogically, perversely, and unpredictably. Contrary to the belief of some, the good management of staff is not just a matter of common sense. It is common sense in the context of an environment which has been moulded by social influences, technology and other large-scale forces, and group behaviour, whether in the office or at a football match, is not the sum of a set of individual behaviours. To manage staff well requires a formal effort to grasp the import of these influences so that our individual attitudes can be controlled and developed to meet the day to day staff situation in a way in which empirical common sense will have difficulty.

It is particularly important that the manager of a service organization like a library or information unit makes this effort for two reasons:

—firstly, his product, being service, is closely linked with the attitudes of serving staff themselves and it is not possible by inspection to reveal a faulty service in the easy way that faulty materials can be detected, and

—secondly, the cost of labour is likely to continue rising at a greater rate than that of the manager's other main tools, machinery and materials, and he must therefore use the staff he really does need to best advantage.

To set the perspective for my remarks on participation I would like to spend a few moments outlining the four major styles of Western staff management which have been practised since the Industrial Revolution.

The earliest of these rested in the notion that one's life on earth and entrance to Heaven were predetermined and so no action was necessary to better the condition of one's staff. This, so far as I am aware, is no longer overtly believed—the poor may sometimes justly deserve to be poor but they no longer expect it. The other three styles are all in evidence.

The earliest was 'scientific management' and had, as a main postulate, that man was an inefficient machine motivated solely by money; hence the most efficient form of organization ought to be one where each job was broken down into simple components, with the worker skilled in only one aspect of the job. On a piece-rate basis this led to his earning more; hence it was concluded that the most efficient organization would also be the most satisfying. Although piece-rate practice is not characteristic of libraries the job breakdown approach is still in evidence; a good example is the splitting of tasks associated with the key-punching of information.

In the late 1920s, humanist theories of behaviour developed which recognized the influence of the working group on the individual member and argued that the job should be fitted to the worker. In particular, very extensive series of experiments on worker behaviour were carried out in the US at the Hawthorne Laboratories of the Western Electric Company and from the results of these it became clear that output was affected more by management interest in the job than by variation in physical work factors. This influence has always to be borne in mind when personnel experiments are carried out. Thus the tenet of scientific management was turned round—the most satisfying organization was expected also to be the most efficient.

More recently, a major consequence of the changing social environment has been a decline in the concepts of work and of conforming as virtues in favour of a more permissive and persuasive approach, both at home and at school. This has conditioned younger people in particular to expect to be consulted and to have some part in deciding courses of action that they must follow.

Behavioural scientists sought to rationalize these changing attitudes by suggesting that an individual is motivated by two classes of need—basic needs and those that are socially determined and that both of these must be satisfied to allow emotional maturity. These various needs have been helpfully portrayed by an American psychologist, Maslow, as a five-level hierarchy (1) and he suggested that as one type becomes satisfied, and only at that point, the next higher type begins to exercise a subconscious motivation on the individual. Maslow's hierarchy of needs is shown in Figure 1.

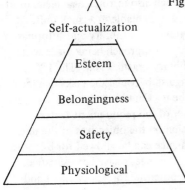

Fig 1—Maslow's 'hierarchy of human needs'

Self-actualization

Esteem

Belongingness

Safety

Physiological

*Self-actualization* — the climax of the individual's needs whereby his own potentialities are realized fully

*Esteem* — the social needs of success, esteem, prestige, etc come into play

*Belongingness* — the individual develops the need for belongingness and love

*Safety* — attention is turned to safety, security, order and routine

*Physiological* — a seeking to satisfy basic primary needs

Looking at this we can see that the needs expressed by the two lowest layers of the pyramid are, for the most part, automatically satisfied by Western society — basic physiological needs such as food, clothing and shelter on the one hand, safety on the other, are all built into the normal working environment. Thus these needs are no longer motivators. It can be said that man lives by bread alone only when he has none.

Management techniques become valuable in developing high work involvement from the satisfaction of needs from the third level upwards — social, ego and self-fulfillment needs. Thus, if we consider social needs, a recruit to an organization is seeking membership of a work group and acceptance by the group depends on his conforming within a reasonable time to their ways. These ways will include quality and quantity of work performance. External courses of the type run by Aslib can play a valuable supplementary role in the training process — indeed this is important justification for my own Division being in Aslib — but the existence of external courses should not become an excuse for the neglect of in-house training or the integration of the individual into the unit will suffer. More benefit accrues if the individual comes to the external course generally knowledgeable on the way his own unit does things. A facet of training which could usefully be further developed is the provision of courses or course materials to create trainers themselves.

Once a new member feels that he belongs securely, Maslow suggests that he becomes receptive to signals of esteem for what he does; he wants to do worthwhile things well, to be recognized as a good performer, to be accorded prestige for what he is doing. An important technique in this area of needs is the well planned job evaluation scheme. This can provide a means of recognizing benefit from training and development, as well as a standard of grading for initial entry. It can also introduce an element of promotional incentive not otherwise readily available in a small unit. Boodson, at an Aslib conference on In-training of Library and Information Staff two years ago (6), discussed a practical approach being made within ICI to staff job assessment in a special library organization. The ICI method lays stress on the need to distinguish between the tasks in a job and the personal qualities of the incumbent. Careful distinction between the two results in a much smaller number of job requirement factors being necessary and concentrates attention on the objectives of the unit. This is important since personal performance can be allowed for by means of salary increments. Finally, when all other needs have been satisfied, man seeks self-fulfillment—he has a basic potential for achievement and self-development and needs to fulfil it (10).

An extention to the theory of needs which has important practical implications is due to Herzberg (2) who made an extensive examination of claimed job satisfactions and dissatisfactions among various classes of professional and non-professional staff in developed industrial countries and found that the causes of satisfaction were not the same as the causes of dissatisfaction. If factors providing satisfaction in a job-situation were absent and Herzberg called these 'motivating factors', the result was not dissatisfaction but simply indifference. Likewise, if causes of dissatisfaction were absent and Herzberg called these 'hygiene factors' the result was not satisfaction but, again, indifference. The factors identified are shown in Figure 2.

In this figure, lines to the left of 0 relate to active dissatisfaction and lines to the right relate to active satisfactions. The length of a line relates to the relative number of occasions on which the factor was raised and the width relates to the persistence of feelings generated.

Thus, when company policy was poor, many staff felt active dissatisfaction, but only for short periods, whereas a good policy raised very little interest—it was taken for granted.

Again, absence of opportunity to take responsibility caused little active resentment whereas in those environments where there was an encouragement to take on responsibility, not only was there marked satisfaction but it was of long duration.

If we look at the factors involved, it is clear that the factors which gave active satisfaction when present are in the highest strata of Maslow's hierarchy, whilst those which caused most dissatisfaction when poor relate to the lower three Maslow layers.

These studies suggest that in developing staff we need to recognize two fundamentally different types of effect on motivation relating, respectively,

132

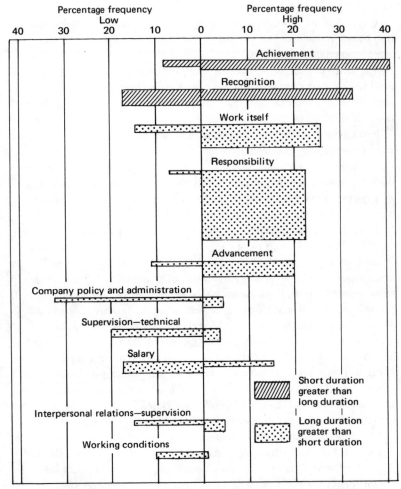

Fig 2–Comparison of hygiene- and motivation-factors (Reproduced by permission from Herzberg, F, et al: *The motivation to work*, 2nd ed, Wiley, 1959)

to hygiene factors and to motivation factors. Further, whilst the hygiene factors must be considered first, it is only necessary to ensure that these do not get out of line. The only practicable method for doing this is through comparison with other similar units. It is not profitable to become continually pre-occupied with improving these aspects of the work. Rather, we must concentrate on trying to improve the motivation factors through the better organization of work, and experience points to staff participation as being a highly effective means for doing this.

What is meant by staff participation? It is essentially an active cooperation between manager and subordinates in the setting up and pursuit of
agreed job-related objectives.

The unit's overall long-term objectives within any larger organization will
need to be determined initially, but once this has been done the medium
term objectives and the short term improvement targets must come from
the staff themselves.

Participation is not synonymous with downward consultation. Downward consultation is motivational only to the manager who is trying to
make the right decision and get it accepted by the group. The subordinate
does not have to live with responsibility for the consequences and indeed
may become frustrated since, although consultation is involvement, it
denies him the exercise of personal responsibility.

Participation demands real commitment by everyone involved. Commitment by the management must come first because there lies the authority.

Any suggestion of a blow-hot, blow-cold attitude to styles of staff
management can be very damaging to the unit's objectives. The manager
must be in full control of his own job—if he is excessively preoccupied with
his own worries his sensitivity to the perceptive limitations of others will
be low. He must be fully prepared for all his unit's activities to come
under question. Commitment of the subordinate, to be effective, must
be self-generated, and hence will come about only as a programme develops.
There will then arise upward consultation in which both parties are motivated—the subordinate is motivated by the need to make the best decision
and the manager by the need to develop his staff.

At this point I make no excuse for digressing to discuss the most fundamental of all the management techniques—communication.

Drucker has made three pertinent observations on this subject (3):

1  It is the recipient who communicates; the so-called communicator
only utters.

2  People can only understand within the limits of their experience (a
point long recognized by teachers of rhetoric, but forgotten again and
again by practitioners of communication).

3  People as a rule perceive only what they expect to perceive—here I
am not thinking of the few who might resent the truth but the many who
do not absord the unexpected at all or, worse, who mis-see or mis-hear as
the expected.

The problem of communication cannot be solved simply by listening
more carefully, since if a manager cannot communicate downwards, it is
even more difficult for a subordinate to communicate upwards.

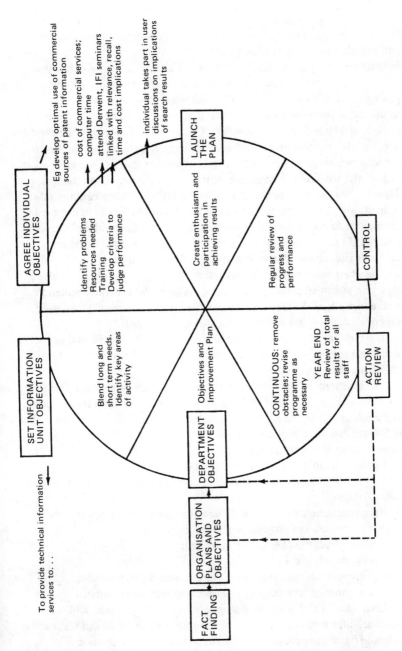

Fig 3: Management by Objectives—a dynamic system (after Humble)

135

An appreciation of the true nature of communication is essential to give meaning to the most important step in fostering participation—this is for manager and subordinate to develop a dialogue focused on objectives that are real to both parties. A first step in such a dialogue is for the manager to ask his staff to think through what they, as individuals, see as the major contributions to the unit that they should be expected to provide and be held accountable for. The answer will rarely be the expected one, but the first aim of the exchange is precisely to bring out this divergence in perception—once both parties realize that they see the same reality differently, we have the beginning of true communication. As the dialogue develops, the intended recipient of communication—in this case the subordinate—is given access to experience which enables him to understand. He is given access to the reality of decision-taking, the problems of priorities, the choice between what one likes to do and what the situation demands and, above all, the responsibility for a decision. He rarely will see the situation in the way his boss does—perhaps he should not—but he may gain an understanding of the complexity of the superior's situation and, above all, of the fact that the complexity is not normally of the superior's making, but is inherent in the situation itself.

The concept of the individual being encouraged to suggest and adopt individual job targets has been formalized as a specific management technique—Management by Objectives (4).

The first steps in any formal MbO programme are to establish Departmental and Unit objectives with higher management and to identify those key areas of activity which must be undertaken for their achievement. The individual can then be encouraged to relate his own working to these objectives by an iterative approach as indicated in Figure 3.

Firstly, personal objectives need thinking out;
—then, resources needed, training required, and likely problems all need identifying;
—the programme can then be agreed with the manager and criteria developed to measure progress and judge performance;
—at this stage, the plan can be launched;
—subsequently, performance is reviewed periodically;
—improvements are consolidated into standard performance;
—new improvement targets are agreed and objectives updated.

Even when it is thought inappropriate to operate a formal MbO programme, information application of the principles involved can form a valuable framework for developing motivation and participation.

Whether a staff participation programme in turn should be formal or informal will depend on the circumstances of the unit involved. A formal programme may be decided on if a clear increase in productivity seems called for (and this was the case in ICI), or if morale is low, but I must stress that adoption of a particular style of personnel management will rarely solve problems *per se* but should be used to provide a framework for constructively synthesizing a working environment. Changes in attitude do not occur overnight. In the ICI programme, for example, it was anticipated that at least two years would elapse before the work attitudes developed during the formal Staff Development Programme became a normal mode of behaviour. Particular care must be taken that a change in style does not sew the seeds for its own destruction—thus, to cite an extreme situation, an increase in productivity must not be followed by the creation of immediate enforced redundancies.

A formal programme, in turn, can be introduced on small or large scale—the advantage of the latter is that everyone is in step, otherwise changes which involve inter-action with a non-participating unit may fail for lack of motivation on the other side; again, a more systems-based approach is practicable, lessening the chance that an increase in productivity of one part of the unit will lessen that in another part; also more productive use can be made of commercially available supporting material, such as films, etc.

Some criteria which were developed to measure progress by my own information unit are set out in below:

1  Adoption of individual targets—deep knowledge of areas of technology, information services, languages, etc.

2  Definition of training needs—having established individual objectives, staff were encouraged to select meetings, courses, etc to promote relevant expertise and subsequently to pass on information gained at in-house seminars. This proved a good test of their own understanding and replaced, in our case, an earlier attitude of a ration of courses for everyone regardless of value.

3  Extent to which all aspects of work are subject to self-examination. One of our counter staff spontaneously did a quantitative comparison of borrowing success rate for books between other ICI divisions and the NLL which resulted in us reversing our standard practice.

4  Openness in discussing and solving problems. Involvement of counter staff from the beginning in studies on a mechanized loans control programme resulted in valuable suggestions on practical points.

5  Elimination of unnecessary work, eg by identification and justification of the least important tasks done. Excessive checking is often detected here.

6   Acceptance of more exacting work—shortening lines of communication through effective delegation with decision-taking nearer the sources of information and action. More exacting work should not be confused with more work and whilst any major increase in responsibilities can be rewarded financially at an appropriate time, direct linking of increased participation with financial reward should be avoided—this is partly because, as I have said, money is a hygiene factor and as such has only a transient effect on work attitudes and partly because to do so is effectively to prostitute the increased motivation.

7   More optimal use of mechanized methods.

If an organization elects to send any of its staff on an external course it is imperative that it either operates or is actively sympathetic to the type of management covered; otherwise the learning could be disastrous by putting the attendee severely at risk.

A useful technique which enables the manager to relate his own particular style of management to the many possible is representation of style as the interaction of two variables—concern for output and concern for people. These variables are conventionally assigned a range of intensities from 1 to 9 and by representing them as the x and y axes on a grid, it is possible to chart a wide array of managerial styles (see Figure 4, the 'Managerial Grid') (5). In particular, the four corners of the grid and the centre represent five major styles of management and if one can recognize that one's attitude to a particular job situation stems from one of these styles, a deeper understanding of one's overall approach to staff management can be gained. Colley, for example, has linked attitudes to training library staff with managerial style (7).

The (1,1) manager has minimum commitment both to output and to people—in the training context, to quote Colley, he will quickly pass his staff onto his subordinates or to the training officer.

The 9,1 manager concerns himself only with production—he sees people as tools—if he can get a better tool he does; otherwise he puts his staff in for training and expects immediate improvement. Although such a manager can often achieve good results his subordinates may be driven to adopt defensive 1,1 attitudes; he also tends to precipitate win/lose situations.

The 1,9 manager is the converse and believes that if you look after people, production will look after itself—thus he sends people on courses to keep them happy. This style is particularly common in a service organization because quantitative performance criteria are more elusive—the danger lies in its obvious cost-ineffectiveness in times of crisis.

The 5,5 manager is also common in a service organization—he tries to balance people against output, believing that too much emphasis on either

138

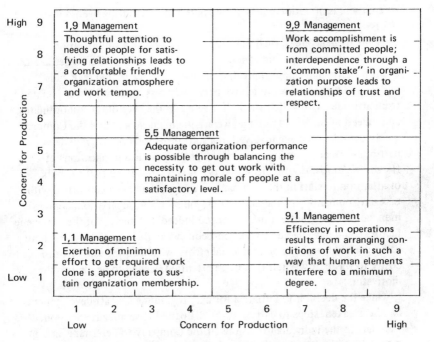

High 9

1,9 Management
Thoughtful attention to
needs of people for satisfying relationships leads to
a comfortable friendly
organization atmosphere
and work tempo.

9,9 Management
Work accomplishment is
from committed people;
interdependence through a
"common stake" in organi-
zation purpose leads to
relationships of trust and
respect.

5,5 Management
Adequate organization performance
is possible through balancing the
necessity to get out work with
maintaining morale of people at a
satisfactory level.

9,1 Management
Efficiency in operations
results from arranging conditions of work in such a
way that human elements
interfere to a minimum
degree.

1,1 Management
Exertion of minimum
effort to get required work
done is appropriate to sus-
tain organization membership.

Concern for Production

Low 1

1       2       3       4       5       6       7       8       9
Low                     Concern for Production                High

Fig 4—*The managerial grid* (reproduced from Blake, R R and Mouton, J S:
*The managerial grid,* with permission from Scientific Methods Inc, and
Gulf Publishing Co).

can only be detrimental to the other. The weakness of this style lies in the
large amount of effort needed to maintain such a balance—this results in
traditions and precedents being invoked to promote stability. The manager
becomes preoccupied with administering rules and regulations or establishing
new precedents and has little time either to encourage initiative by his staff
or to solve new problems of output. It is a second-best style which shows
up poorly when innovation is called for.

The 9,9 manager on the other hand sees that a desire for high output and
an intense interest in people, far from being incompatible, are complementary
qualities and his unit is likely to benefit most from staff participation—in the
context still of Colley's example, he sees that training is continuous and
needs to satisfy the needs of both trainee and unit, and in turn he seeks
commitment from both.

In both formal and individual approaches to participation hygiene
matters are likely to be raised first; some trivial, some more deep-seated and
they must not be dismissed with impatience. Cases will usually be found

where there is no rational reason for something not having been put to rights.

Some hygiene areas, such as Company Policy and Administration, we may consider too large and general for any meaningful action to be taken, but it is particularly important that, as managers, we should seek full understanding. However much we personally may wish to be disassociated from attitudes with which we do not agree, in the eyes of our subordinates, and indeed of the world at large, we are the management and the Company.

My own unit became involved in a staff development programme as part of a formal Company exploration of the practical implications of Herzberg's motivation/hygiene theory. It was considered that the bulk of attention to staff in the Company in the past had been concerned with task environment—pay and conditions, job security, supervision, communications and joint consultation, and indeed any neglect of these hygiene factors could have had disastrous consequences. But at a time when there was a premium existing on individual effort, with labour becoming too costly to waste, it was felt that more attention needed to be paid to the motivators.

Once the decision to initiate a formal programme of staff development had been taken, steps to carry out the dialogue I have already mentioned were left to the individual Divisions of the Company to determine and, in turn, within the Divisions each operating unit was left free to develop its own approach. The only contribution provided centrally was initial management training in behavioural science theories for a small number of key individuals to ensure a competent and informed start for individual programmes.

Library and Information Centres equally with other units, both service and line, partly selected and partly elected members to receive training in turn so that an effective dialogue became possible through groups at all levels. To encourage the widest sharing of experience, in addition to homogeneous work groups, representative groups comprising staff of different grade levels and in different disciplines also explored common problems.

As anticipated, hygiene factors predominated initially but a constructive approach to these resulted in attention moving towards motivational factors. Thus individual staff from the most junior began to analyse and discuss their individual jobs, in the light of library operations; to single out and express the important elements and existing shortcomings, and to suggest methods for improvement. A number of such operations, previously spread over several individuals, were reconstituted and total responsibility alloted to one person.

140

With regard to interpersonal relationships within a unit, use of individual objectives to measure performance can make much more pleasant one of the more disliked staff management techniques—that of performance assessment. Traditional procedures seem to range from complex form filling to informal observation. The prize in the former area would seem to go to a New York library system which is reported to expect supervisors to assess staff on 373 qualities before writing an overall summary (8).

In a participative atmosphere using some form, even qualitative, of MbO, the assessment can become more constructive. Both sides have a good lead-in; criteria of performance have been jointly developed and performance reviewed periodically during the year. I personally have always felt a suitably written form to be helpful in directing thought to the most important issues, but this has now become essential in the light of the Industrial Relations Act in that in the event of a dismissal on the grounds of lack of capability, a tribunal can call for written assessment records as evidence.

For a meaningful discussion the assessors must of course be familiar with the subordinate's work and this means not being too far removed from the assessee's own level. The assessee must at the same time feel confident that his assessors are people with authority to recommend meaningful action on his behalf; hence the system depends on effective liaison and delegation in this respect from the personnel department.

Thus I would suggest that in developing and assessing staff, emphasis should be on job objectives. Consideration of personality traits as such should play little part. The human personality is a complex and highly abstract concept and attempts to judge the individual in terms of his personality are likely to induce long-term hostility and block fruitful communication.

However, to refrain from judging personality is not the same as ignoring either its strengths or weaknesses—a work situation which strives for congeniality, homogeneity and conformity may exclude the innovator and change agent.

In much team work the personalities of those concerned can play a major role in determining the degree of success. Considerable attention has been given by behavioural scientists to the formal study of interpersonal relationships with the aim of encouraging a deeper insight into the background to motivation and behaviour specifically in a work context. It is in the specificity of context that such studies which have variously been called Group Dynamics, Sensitivity Training, T-Group Training, etc differ sharply from psychotherapy.

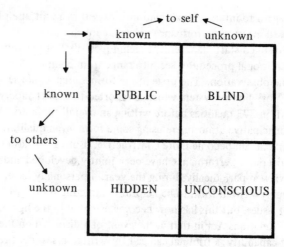

Fig 5—Classification of interpersonal behaviour (known as the Johari window)

Four major behavioural areas can be distinguished and are illustrated in Figure 5. These are Public, Hidden, Blind and Unconscious and the object of Sensitivity Training is to increase public area, decrease the blind and hidden areas but to ignore the unconscious area. Any group of individuals acting together can be observed at two levels:

a) what is said and decided;

b) what is felt: the stresses and strains within a group—the existence of these vitally affects the outcome of group actions and the difficulty of interpreting them, even at first hand, is a major reason why very senior people are prepared to suffer considerable inconvenience to attend meetings in person rather than, say, by TV link-up.

Not only does sensitivity training try to reduce the unknown aspects of personality but identification of these aspects can often lead to their being put to constructive use; apparent weaknesses can become strengths.

In its purest form, the training builds up from unstructured sessions in which participants are left to choose their own topics for discussion in the presence of observer trainers. In this form, there is always risk of generating undesirable destructive hostility between participants and a more useful approach for groups in which the members know each other, or even work together, is to use structured problem-solving sessions or courses under trained leaders to cover both task objectives and also the influence of personal attitudes.

The third area of staff management I wish to consider concerns relations with staff outside the unit. There are two classical approaches to organizing staff in relation to their work: the functional approach, which groups together like means; and the project approach, based on identity of purpose. Each has its merits and disadvantages. The functional approach is reported to be most successful in a stable work environment. Here the disadvantages of having discipline-based groupings with little motivation actively to serve users' needs is relatively unimportant—the traditional library worked in this way, and only five months ago a contributor to *New library world* felt able to write that: 'Many public libraries are grotesquely remote from the mentality of the majority of the public they are presumed to be serving' (9). On the other hand, the advantages of the project approach, with its concept of a multi-disciplinary mobile work-force which can quickly be switched from problem to problem, must be off-set against difficulties of effective conservation and deployment of specialist resources and a lesser sense of security among staff involved. A third approach which has recently received attention is the technique of Matrix Management.

In a Matrix organization each member of the staff is responsible to two managers—a project head with mission responsibility and a subject head responsible for overcoming the insecurity which can arise in a project-oriented management system as projects come to an end, since it should be the professional subject head who is responsible for handling personal problems and career development of his staff.

Under such a system, the subject head surrenders that part of his traditional responsibility dealing with control of the performance of his staff whilst actually on a given job, but his subject responsibilities are increased in that he must ensure that his staff are fully aware of and interact with the present and future needs of the project groups. The project head in turn must facilitate the arrangement by ensuring that each member of his team is given a job that requires solid capability and is achievable.

A number of British public library systems appear to be actively exploring an informal approach to matrix management. Thus the structure of the Leicestershire County Library system is reported (9) to include a number of field terms whose individual members each have responsibilities in four distinct areas: functional (such as local history); user related (with a particular community); project-related (eg developing relations with industry); and service-related (responsibility for a specific group of libraries).

In the case of the industrial library's staff member whose primary qualification is usually in a subject discipline, a matrix system can be valuable in imparting a sense of belonging to the users' team; he ceases to be regarded as an outsider.

A group of staff who require very careful managing by the information service unit are the by now well-known 'gate-keepers'.

A 'gate-keeper' functions best as a mini information analysis centre with his gate keeping being almost unconsciously ancillary to his creative work. It is wise to take special pains to meet his requests and ensure that your junior staff can distinguish him from the squirrels and butterflies but leave him his freedom! A simple technique worth bearing in mind when trying to get things done voluntarily through others is to maximize overlap of objectives. The person you approach may be in full sympathy with your own objectives, but unless you can demonstrate some overlap with his, he may well be too busy to act for you.

Finally, one may ask whether the management techniques which I have described will ward off redundancies and dismissals. The answer is a qualified yes—if the line side of an organization has to be cut back, the service side cannot expect to avoid a proportional cut and the wise manager as part of his long-term strategy tries to strike a balance in his staff which will allow a limited flexibility under such circumstances, but the keyword is 'proportional'. If one has developed an atmosphere of staff participation within the unit so that the essential is being continuously distinguished from the trivial, then it can be expected that the key customers of the service unit will be continuously exposed to the full benefits of a good service which really fulfills their needs; and during any temporary phase of organizational stress one can expect enough key people to stand up and demand that undue discrimination is not practised against the unit in any reduction plan.

*References*
1 Maslow, A H: 'A theory of human motivation', Psychological review, 50, July 1943, p 370-96.
2 Herzberg, F: Work and the nature of man. World Publishing Co, 1966.
3 Drucker, P: 'What communication means', Management today, March 1970, p 91-3, 150-1.
4 BIM Library Bibliography Management by objectives is a useful guide to basic reading.
5 Blake, R R, and J S Mouton: The managerial grid. Gulf Publishing Co, 1964.
6 Boodson, K: 'The significance of staff structure and promotion policy', Aslib proceedings, 22, 6, June 1970, p 267-75.
7 Colley, D I: 'Cooperative schemes for in-service training', Aslib proceedings, 22, 6, June 1970, p 276-81.
8 Peele, D: 'Some aspects of staff evaluation in the UK and the USA', Library Association record, 74, April 1972, p 69-71.
9 Jones, K: 'Staff deployment', New library world, June 1972, p 320-23.

10 Two recent items of general interest in the libraries/information field are:

a) Stone, E W, ed: 'New directions in staff development', American Library Association.

b) Stone, E W, issue ed: 'Personnel development and continuing education in libraries', Library trends, 20, July 1971.

# FACTORS AFFECTING LIBRARIANS' JOB SATISFACTION

*Kenneth H Plate and Elizabeth W Stone*

In any organizational setting the problem of job satisfaction is a pressing one. Whether it is labeled motivation, loyalty, contentment or organizational health, the theme recurs again and again in management literature. The literature of personnel management, in particular, abounds with articles dealing with job attitudes—and their correlate, motivation—and much of the writing centers around the diagnosis, treatment, and, occasionally, prevention of negative employee attitudes, manifested in such problems as absenteeism, turnover, underproduction, and even sabotage. While much of what is written is facile off-the-cuff accounts of what one organization or manager has done to ameliorate difficulties related to job attitudes, there is an increasing amount of research evidence which provides some principles for those engaged in personnel management.

When a manager asks, 'How can I motivate my employees?' or the equally compelling question, 'How can I instill positive work attitudes in my employees?' or even the more specific, 'How can repetitive tasks be made more interesting?' it is obvious even to him that the answer—if indeed there is an answer—will be a complex one and will not be contained in any single article or research report. Organizations are far too complex to allow for formula solutions.

Like other complex organizations, libraries, despite their apparent homogeneity, differ considerably with regard to their organizational history, leadership climate, and even goals and objectives. Library procedures vary from library to library and so must personnel practices and supervisory styles according to the peculiar development, needs, and personnel in any given library. Library managers must therefore be skilled in the adaptation of existing principles of motivation to local requirements*.

What is known about job satisfaction and motivation? What is generalizable from what is known and how can it be applied to the library? These are questions we asked ourselves at the outset of this study. Without attempting to review all the pertinent literature available, we decided to base the present investigation on a widely accepted and empirically tested theory that we believe has immediate practical application in library organization. This theory was developed by Frederick Herzberg and follows the work of Abraham Maslow

## Maslow's 'Hierarchy of needs'

Basic to an understanding of human needs and how these needs relate to the phenomenon we call motivation—as evidenced in job attitudes—is the work of Abraham Maslow, who developed a hierarchy of needs: (1) basic physiological, (2) safety and security, (3) belonging and social activity, (4) esteem and status, and (5) self-realization and fulfillment (3). What is important about these needs is that they have a definite sequence of domination. That is, need 2 is not perceived and its fulfillment is not sought until need 1 has been at least partly satisfied.

Maslow classifies needs 1 and 2 as lower-order needs, while needs 3-5 are called higher-order needs. Lower-order needs are essential to life. They stem from the inherent wish to survive. These lower-order needs, however, are essentially finite; that is, having achieved a certain level of fulfillment of these needs, man tends to become satiated. From this point onward, increases in the level of fulfillment do not generate corresponding increases in human satisfaction.

It would be safe to say that in the industrialized countries of the world today, most of the lower-order needs have been met for most people, and we are now concerned with needs at the higher level. And it is at this point that man is motivated to fulfill those needs which have to do with the mind and the spirit. These needs are essentially limitless and can be met both on and off the job. In fact, 'belonging and social activity' and 'esteem and status' have long been cornerstones in human relations theories and managerial styles, beginning with Elton Mayo's experiments at the Hawthorne plant of Western Electric (4). The work of Rensis Likert (5), Douglas McGregor (6), and Chris Argyris (7) treats various aspects of these need priorities.

The need priorities thus far are relatively simple to comprehend. The highest need in Maslow's hierarchy, however—self-realization and fulfillment—is somewhat more nebulous, perhaps because it is relatively inconstant. Many and perhaps most individuals even in North America never experience extended self-realization and fulfillment, and the majority of the world's population has still not consistently satisfied the lower-order needs. But, at the present time, in Western countries, particularly North America and especially among the professional, white collar, and managerial classes, there is little doubt that increasing numbers of employees are now looking for and expecting work which is meaningful to them as individuals and which they feel also has meaning in the context of our society and culture. The search for meaningful work is not always based on idealism and altruism, but there is evidence that librarianship at both the professional and support staff levels attracts individuals because they perceive library work as being socially significant and as an occupation in which the objectives of the individual and those of the organization are compatible**.

If this is so—that is, that the library milieu offers potential for self-realization and fulfillment—why do motivation and job satisfaction appear as issues in library personnel management? This is not precisely the question that Herzberg in his motivation-hygiene theory attempts to answer but his research does provide insight into the problem.

### Herzberg's 'Motivation-hygiene theory'
Herzberg, unlike Maslow, is primarily concerned with the individual within the organization and it is essential to note that he also divides human needs into two categories. The first set of needs, roughly synonymous with Maslow's lower-order needs, are called hygiene factors (10, p 74). Research studies by Herzberg and others have shown that while hygiene factors are essential to job satisfaction, they do not play a great part in job motivation. That is, their absence leads to job dissatisfaction, but their presence does not guarantee employee motivation. The following hygiene factors are commonly thought to be essential to 'good personnel practice': company policy and administration, supervision, relationship with supervisor, relationship with peers, relationship with subordinates, salary, job security, personal life, working conditions, and status. In other words, poor personnel practices such as low salaries, autocratic administration, and wretched working conditions will make an employee dissatisfied. But the rectification of these conditions will not, in itself, inspire or motivate the employee. The hygiene factors are important, however, because, like primary needs, they must be met in order to prevent job dissatisfaction even though they have little effect on positive job attitudes. The reason is that the hygiene factors are mostly related to the environment external to the job, that is, to the job *context.* Herzberg explains that 'hygiene factors fail to provide for positive satisfaction because they do not possess the characteristics necessary for giving an individual a sense of growth. To feel that one has grown depends on achievement in tasks that have meaning to the individual and since the

hygiene factors do not relate to the task, they are powerless to give such meaning to the individual' (10, p 78).

Motivational factors, on the other hand, are mostly related to the job itself or to job *content*. The motivational factors include achievement, recognition, advancement, work itself, possibility of growth, and responsibility. These factors produce motivation and high job satisfaction. However, as will be shown, their absence rarely proves strongly dissatisfying.

Herzberg's conclusions are based on the results of numerous studies in which employees were asked to recall a time when they had felt 'exceptionally good' about their jobs. Interviewers then proceeded to look for the reasons the employees had felt as they did. The same procedure was followed to determine those factors which led to job dissatisfaction. The analysis of the incidents reported by the subjects involved in-depth interpretation by both the respondents and the investigators. The principal finding was the one just mentioned, that is, the distinction between the dissatisfier factors and the satisfier or motivational factors. It is especially important to remember that one cluster of factors relates to what a person does (the job), and the other cluster relates to the environment in which he does it. The studies which led to the motivation-hygiene theory are fully reported in two monographs by Herzberg, his *Motivation to work* (11) and *Work and the nature of man* (10). Applicability of the theory has been determined through empirical testing of groups such as lower-level supervisors, agricultural administrators, men about to retire from management positions, hospital maintenance personnel, manufacturing supervisors, nurses, food handlers, military officers, engineers, scientists, housekeepers, teachers, technicians, female assemblers, accountants, Finnish foremen, and Hungarian engineers. The present study is an attempt to apply the theory to a cross section of practising librarians.

## Methodology

Two groups of librarians, one American and the other Canadian, provided the data for this study. Although the groups convened in different geograpical locations, the conditions under which the data were gathered were approximately the same: both groups were attending workshops on motivation, and the format of the presentation and of the data-gathering instrument was the same. Before the motivation-hygiene theory was presented, each person was asked to record incidents illustrative of times when they felt 'particularly good' and 'particularly bad' on the job. The subjects were also instructed to explain why they had felt the way they did. Group leaders then tallied the responses in the motivating and hygiene groups of categories, and these data were combined for discussion at the workshop. The records of individual incidents were retained by the investigators for a more consistent and detailed analysis; the data presented in this report are derived from the raw data and not from the group tallies.

In the original Herzberg study, methods of data gathering and analysis were somewhat more structured than the method used here. In the major study that led to the development of the motivation-hygiene theory, a team of researchers administered short questionnaires and conducted interviews in order to elaborate upon and clarify the critical incidents reported by respondents to the basic questions' 'Think of a time on your job when you felt *particularly good.* Describe the circumstances briefly and explain *why* you felt particularly good,' and 'Think of a time on your job when you felt *particularly bad.* Describe the circumstances briefly and describe *why* you felt particularly bad.' While there have been many exact replications of the original methodology, there have also been a number which eliminate the interview or otherwise modify the method either of data gathering or of analysis. Minor deviations in method notwithstanding, Herzberg invokes these studies as further verification of his theory.

In the present study, the incidents as written were the only data source. The investigators followed Herzberg's succinct descriptions of criteria for each of the factors, independently categorizing each incident in terms of a first-level factor. This was done for each group separately. While the possibility of subjectivity in coding incidents is always present in a study involving attitudes, Herzberg's criteria for factor coding ensure—insofar as is possible—that other investigators using the same data would arrive at the same conclusions. For example, the description of the factor 'responsibility' reads in part as follows:

'[It] includes those sequences of events in which the person speaking reported that he derived satisfaction from being given responsibility for his own work or for the work of others or from being given new responsibility. It also includes stories in which there was a loss of satisfaction or a negative attitude toward the job stemming from a lack of responsibility. However in cases in which the story revolved around a wide gap between a person's authority and the authority he needed to carry out his job responsibilities, the factor identified was 'company policy and administration.' (10, p 196)'.

*The population*
*Group A (American):* Of the 200 librarians attending three one-day workshops sponsored by the Oklahoma State Library Association, the State

150

Library of Oklahoma, and the School of Library Science of the University of Oklahoma in March 1971, 180 completed the forms used in the job attitudes study. Eighteen of these were library science students, and since they were not working in libraries, their forms have not been included in the analyses presented here. The 162 remaining subjects represent a fairly equal distribution among school, public and academic librarians. There were a lesser number of special librarians.

*Group B (Canadian):* Of the ninety-nine librarians attending a workshop sponsored by the University of British Columbia School of Librarianship in June 1971, seventy-five participated in the job attitude study. Nearly all were in managerial positions, with the middle managers predominating. The majority were academic librarians, followed by public, special, and school, in that order.

A population of 237 cannot be considered large and would not be adequate for some studies, but in the present instance we believe it to be generous for the purpose of ascertaining whether librarians respond similarly to other groups to which the motivation-hygiene theory has been applied. Herzberg has reported on many follow-up studies of this sort in which the population or sample size ranges from a low of fifty to a high of 203 (10, p 122-23). It should be noted that although the population consists of self-selected workshop attendees, it is binational and representative of types of libraries. Nevertheless, it must be stressed that this group is self-selected, and consequently the results can only be generally suggestive for librarians as an occupational group.

*Findings of the study*
Summaries of the responses to the questions concerning job satisfaction and dissatisfaction in relation to hygiene and motivational factors are shown for Group A and Group B in tables 1 and 2, respectively. Table 3 combines the findings for the two groups. A composite of the factors involved in causing job satisfaction and job dissatisfaction as found by combining the results of Group A and Group B is presented in figure 1. The results of the two experiments follow the pattern of the Herzberg theoretical framework and indicate that motivators were the primary cause of satisfaction, and that hygiene factors were the primary cause of unhappiness or dissatisfaction on the job. As in the Herzberg studies, the relations are not perfect, but the trends are definite and substantial, especially as related to satisfiers.

Figure 2 summarizes the relationship that exists between sources of dissatisfaction and satisfaction and shows that of all the factors contributing

151

Table 1

Responses to job attitude study questions—Group A (*N*=162)

| | Dissatisfaction | Satisfaction |
|---|---|---|
| Motivators: | | |
| Achievement | 20 | 86 |
| Recognition | 9 | 47 |
| Work itself | 0 | 20 |
| Responsibility | 0 | 5 |
| Advancement | 0 | 1 |
| Professional or personal growth | 0 | 2 |
| Hygiene factors: | | |
| Institution policy and administration | 53 | 0 |
| Supervision | 37 | 0 |
| Interpersonal relationships | 31 | 0 |
| Working conditions | 12 | 0 |
| Status | 0 | 0 |
| Salary | 0 | 1 |
| Security | 0 | 0 |

to job satisfaction, 99 percent were motivators, related to job content. Of all the factors contributing to the librarians' dissatisfaction with their work, 81 percent involved hygiene factors found in the work environment (context factors).

Table 2

Responses to job attitude study questions—Group B (*N*=75)

| | Dissatisfaction | Satisfaction |
|---|---|---|
| Motivators: | | |
| Achievement | 9 | 32 |
| Recognition | 6 | 23 |
| Work itself | 1 | 7 |
| Responsibility | 0 | 6 |
| Advancement | 0 | 5 |
| Professional or personal growth | 0 | 0 |
| Hygiene factors | | |
| Institution policy and administration | 15 | 0 |
| Supervision | 19 | 0 |
| Interpersonal relationships | 13 | 2 |
| Working conditions | 2 | 0 |
| Status | 4 | 0 |
| Salary | 2 | 0 |
| Security | 4 | 0 |

In summary, the data from these two experiments fall into the pattern provided by the Herzberg theoretical framework, indicating that (1) the factors involved in producing job satisfaction (and motivation) are distinct and different from the factors that lead to job dissatisfaction; and that (2) the factors producing job satisfaction (and motivation) are concerned primarily with the actual job content (or work-process factors); the reasons for dissatisfaction (or hygiene factors) deal primarily with factors relating to the context in which the job is done—the job environment.

*Satisfaction*
Achievement and recognition, both highly personal factors, appear to be most important in job satisfaction followed by 'position-related' factors such as work itself***, responsibility, and advancement. Typical incidents related to achievement are the following: success in lobbying for a minority-group member to sit on the library board, anticipating need in collection building, successful completion of difficult or complex projects and programs, playing a major part in achieving the passage of a county by-law affecting library service, and generally a feeling of a job well done. One librarian wrote: 'Having given a series of booktalks in a school, I was visiting the branch library closest to the school, and while there, received three calls from students placing reserves on books on which I had spoken. I felt particularly good about my job that day.'

Table 3

Responses to job attitude study questions A and B combined (*N*=237)

|                                          | Dissatisfaction | Satisfaction |
|------------------------------------------|-----------------|--------------|
| Motivators:                              |                 |              |
| Achievement                              | 29              | 118          |
| Recognition                              | 15              | 70           |
| Work itself                              | 1               | 27           |
| Responsibility                           | 0               | 11           |
| Advancement                              | 0               | 6            |
| Professional or personal growth          | 0               | 2            |
| Hygiene factors:                         |                 |              |
| Institution policy and administration    | 68              | 0            |
| Supervision                              | 56              | 0            |
| Interpersonal relationships              | 44              | 2            |
| Working conditions                       | 14              | 0            |
| Status                                   | 4               | 0            |
| Salary                                   | 2               | 1            |
| Security                                 | 4               | 0            |

**Factors Characterizing 237 Events on the Job that Led to the Librarian Feeling "Particularly Bad" on the Job**

Number of Responses: 120 110 100 90 80 70 60 50 40 30 20 10 0

**Factors Characterizing 237 Events on the Job that Led to the Librarian Feeling "Particularly Good" on the Job**

Number of Responses: 0 10 20 30 40 50 60 70 80 90 100 110 120

| Factor | Particularly Bad | Particularly Good |
|---|---|---|
| Achievement | 29 | 118 |
| Recognition | 15 | 70 |
| Work Itself | 1 | 27 |
| Responsibility | 0 | 11 |
| Advancement | 0 | 6 |
| Professional or Personal Growth | 0 | 2 |
| Institutional Policy and Administration | 68 | 0 |
| Supervision | 56 | 0 |
| Interpersonal Relationships | 44 | 2 |
| Working Conditions | 14 | 0 |
| Status | 4 | 0 |
| Security | 4 | 0 |
| Salary | 2 | 1 |

Fig 1—Factors affecting job attitudes, as reported in two studies of librarians

Recognition may come from the public, from superiors and subordinates, or from the profession. The incidents recorded, however, did not indicate the profession as a source, perhaps because the question asked specifically about the job. Respondents in this category most frequently mentioned recognition from sources external to the library itself; library users were most often mentioned, with library boards and committees, university administrators, principals, and company presidents also listed. Although it is difficult to determine with any degree of certainty the amount and frequency of recognition for librarians, it would appear that concrete appreciation is not overwhelming in the librarians' experience. One gathers while reading the incidents that librarians treasure the acknowledgements that are forthcoming, however, and that recognition from both clients and colleagues contributes to positive job attitudes. Several librarians wrote of times when collections were praised or when clients indicated increased respect for librarianship as a result of personal service. Other librarians wrote of letters of appreciation from institutional users, public recognition by university administrators, gifts received, and flattering results from a survey of users. Internally, the librarians recorded incidents indicating recognition from both superiors and subordinates.

The factor 'responsibility' was indicated less frequently than either achievement or recognition but it is a strong satisfier at all levels of library work. Several librarians wrote that the responsibility they felt as a result of participative management made them feel particularly good about their jobs.

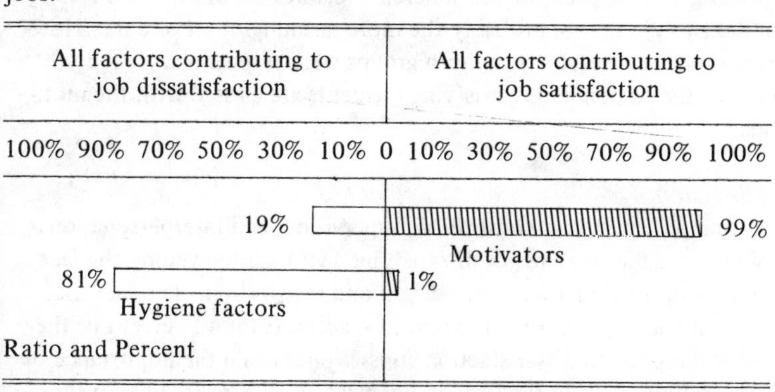

| All factors contributing to job dissatisfaction | All factors contributing to job satisfaction |
|---|---|
| 100% 90% 70% 50% 30% 10% 0 | 10% 30% 50% 70% 90% 100% |

19% |_____| ||||||||||||||||||||||||||||||||||||||| 99%
                                  Motivators
81% |_____| |] 1%
        Hygiene factors
Ratio and Percent

Fig 2—Relationship between sources of dissatisfaction and sources of satisfaction in the job situation.

Even though the 'work itself' worried one librarian, who felt that this was a Calvinistic factor, he and others simply stated that the basic elements of their jobs were intrinsically satisfying.

Advancement, though not a particularly strong factor, was indicated by some respondents who cited instances of promotion and recommendations as highly satisfying experiences in their jobs.

Among the hygiene factors listed as satisfiers, only interpersonal relationships (two respondents) and salary increase (one respondent) were mentioned at all, indicating that in spite of what sociologists say, female-dominated professions do not necessarily place a premium on satisfying interpersonal relationships, at least when it comes to priorities in job satisfaction. It is surprising that only two incidents can be recorded relating to professional or personal growth as stated by the participants. A few more incidents might have been placed in this category but because of their interpretation in context were placed instead in either achievement, work itself, or responsibility. The following incident, for example, indicates professional growth but focuses on satisfaction derived from being given new responsibility: '. . . when the chief librarian asked me for help in suggesting an outline for a survey to be used by a government agency. As a result I acquired some useful skills and learned a lot but more important to me was the fact that my responsibilities were increased—at least for a time—and thus my job was more challenging.'

It should be apparent that factors such as achievement, work itself, and indeed most of the satisfiers can be highly interrelated. Such was found to be the case as the incidents were analyzed. In many instances precise dissatisfier groups may vary somewhat according to the interpretation of the investigator. Because of this inherent weakness, the combined results from the two groups are probably the more meaningful set of data. However, as noted, the results from both groups were very similar; in fact, 99 percent of the respondents' satisfying incidents are classed with the motivators.

### Dissatisfaction

Institution policy and administration, supervision, and interpersonal relationships were the three major dissatisfying factors, followed by the *lack* of the motivational factors, achievement and recognition. The fact that supervision and interpersonal relationships account for 42 percent of the factors leading to job dissatisfaction stresses once again the importance of human relations skills in the library organization. There are obviously great rewards in supervision, but it seems that much unhappiness comes with the supervisory job. It should be pointed out that while fifty-six incidents categorized as supervision reflected failure on the part of superiors, many of the forty-four incidents placed in the interpersonal relationships category referred to a time when the respondent felt that he himself had failed as a supervisor. Furthermore, 21 percent of the incidents categorized as institution policy and administration concerned personnel practices detrimental to organizational health.

The catalog of bad experiences indicates that communication with supervisors, delegation of authority, and support in policy decisions are areas of conflict in supervisor-subordinate relationships. A number of librarians described circumstances in which they had felt 'let down' by their supervisors. Others wrote of arbitrary decisions made without consultation. One librarian wrote:

'A few months after beginning a new job which was an 'upward step' I realized that I was in fact hamstrung in nearly all areas where I wished to take definite (hopefully effective) action, hamstrung by the reluctance of my immediate chief to tackle any problems head on and hamstrung by the ill-defined range of my own authority. This resulted in an overwhelming sense of being the 'superfluous man' and indeed went on for some months where I felt I was drawing a fairly decent salary and achieving nothing whatever.'

Institution policy and administration encompass the broad area of governing bodies, including top administration and personnel policies. Respondents attacked rigid policies, the tenure system, staff cutbacks, inadequate budgets, misguided priorities, and the lack of information necessary to make rational decisions. Some expressed a general feeling of helplessness in the face of institutional policy and administration. One Canadian librarian's experience is typical:

'Two highly valued employees who were being considered for upgrading on my recommendation are being threatened with dismissal on grounds of insufficient bilingual skills. Their loss would mean that the library would have to accept unskilled bilingual personnel and train them in the professional skills already developed in the two employees dismissed. This would be impossible in the case of one, since her special skills in the computer field had been acquired during five years experience in a highly computerized library. In addition this dismissal would mean hardship for these individuals who are well liked not only by colleagues but also by clientele.'

While this example may be peculiar to the Canadian civil service, it contains dilemmas common to many responses in this category. The following is an example from the American study: 'I saw another staff member suffering from very bad treatment by the administration, and I was in no position to do anything about the situation. This led to frustration, bitterness, and a definite deterioration in job interest, and probably performance.' These and other incidents make plain that a person need not himself be the victim of the institutional policy and administration, but that empathy with other victims also causes dissatisfaction.

As mentioned earlier, many of the librarians whose responses indicated dissatisfaction with interpersonal relationships gave examples of times when they felt they had failed as supervisors. The experiences contain accounts of false charges and reports being made to a higher authority, unpleasant dismissals, personnel disputes in which the issues are not clear cut, and staff hostility. The responses clearly indicate a high degree of sensitivity on the part of the supervisors to the fact that altercations with staff members are not all in a day's work but, rather, evidence of supervisory shortcomings. Upon dismissing an employee one librarian concluded: 'I felt particularly bad because I could see the just side of his argument and I have some vague feelings of guilt and failure—in fact some vague notion that the whole affair was my fault.'

Working conditions ranked sixth among the dissatisfiers and were mentioned by fourteen librarians. The cited instances referred largely to exceptional conditions, such as overheated rooms, lack of sufficient shelving, or special problems, such as the following: 'Trying to serve many teachers with films and all the projectors broke down and I was unable to get replacements or repairs.' A small number of librarians mentioned the other hygiene factors of status, security, and salary.

It must be noted that twenty-nine librarians signified a *lack* of achievement and fifteen librarians a *lack* of recognition as dissatisfiers, although these are not hygiene factors. The importance of achievement and recognition as motivators is again emphasized.

## Conclusion

As stated at the beginning of this paper, this study was undertaken with the aim of providing answers to the following questions: What do we know about job satisfaction and motivation? What is generalizable from what is known and how can it be applied to the library? The findings suggest that librarians respond positively to such motivational factors as a sense of achieve ment, recognition, and work that is intrinsically satisfying. Many library jobs are not rich in self-achievement potential and tend to be impersonalized to the extent that incumbents infrequently experience personal recognition from clients and colleagues. Furthermore, many job contain elements of repetitive work. When the job content is deficient in one or more of the motivational factors, lack of motivation will almost certainly result. Such deficiencies can be remedied to a large extent by planned organizational development that involves enriching the work****.

Job enrichment pertains mostly to the position-related motivational factors of work itself, responsibility, advancement, and professional or personal growth. This is not to say that job enrichment has no effect on the other motivational factors of recognition and achievement. Enriching a position should ideally increase the potential of the factors as motivators. Given the very personal nature of these motivators, however, there is no guarantee that this will happen. In the first place, if job enrichment is used by management simply as a tool, if it is presented to employees as a demand rather than an opportunity, or if employees are not considered as individuals, then job enrichment has little chance of really succeeding in increasing job satisfaction. Further, in the theoretical context of motivation presented earlier, it was pointed out that employee wants stem from needs. Herzberg tells us that some employees are in fact motivated only by hygiene factors 'because of their training and because of the things that have happened to them' (10, p 80). He concludes that these 'hygiene seekers have not reached a stage of personality development at which self-actualizing needs are active. From this point of view, they are fixated at a less mature level of personal adjustment' (10, p 80). Thus job enrichment is not likely to increase that level of motivation of such individuals to any considerable extent. Motivation comes only from within the individual, and all managers can do is create the environment and the job in which this self-actualization is facilitated.

The results of this study suggest that these generalizations apply with as much force to librarianship as to the other occupations on which Herzberg based his conclusions.

*Notes*

\* We agree with those who posit a 'situational theory' of management, for example, that there is no one 'best way' to organize. Although this theory has been generally applied to problems of organizational design, it may also be germane to supervisory style. A good summary of this approach to the study of organizations is found in Mockler (1). An application of the situational or contingency theory in library science is found in Vorwerk (2).

\*\* See Denis (8). See also the recent study of Canadian and US librarians in all types of libraries in Presthus (9).

\*\*\* 'Work itself' relates to the specific job, rather than to a more general 'work ethic'. 'This category was used when the respondent mentioned that actual doing of the job or the tasks of the job as a source of good or bad feelings about it' (10, p 197).

\*\*\*\* Those considering job enrichment are directed to the following articles which deal with the mechanics of this technique and an assessment of results in several organizational settings: Herzberg (12), Roche and MacKinnon (13), Paul, Robertson, and Herzberg (14), and Myers (15).

159

*References*

1   Mockler, Robert J: 'Situational theory of management', Harvard business review 49, 1971, p 146-54.

2   Vorwerk, Richard J: The environmental demands and organizational states of two academic libraries. PhD dissertation, Indiana University, 1970.

3   Maslow, A H: 'A theory of human motivation', Psychological review 5( 1943, p 370-96.

4   Mayo, Elton: The human problems of an industrial civilization. New York, Macmillan Co, 1933.

5   Likert, Rensis: New patterns of management. Toronto, McGraw-Hill Book Co, 1961.

6   McGregor, Douglas: The human side of enterprise; Toronto, McGraw-Hill Book Co, 1960.

7   Argyris, Chris: Integrating the individual and the organization. New York, John Wiley & Sons, 1964.

8   Denis, L G: Academic and public librarians in Canada: a study of the factors which influence graduates of Canadian library schools in making their first career choice in favor of academic or public libraries. PhD dissertation, Rutgers University, 1969.

9   Presthus, Robert: Technological change and occupational response: a study of librarians. Toronto: York University, 1970.

10   Herzberg, Frederick: Work and the nature of man. Cleveland, World Publishing Co, 1966.

11   Herzberg, Frederick, Bernard Mausner and Barbara Snyderman: The motivation to work. New York, John Wiley & Sons, 1959.

12   Herzberg, Frederick: 'One more time: how do you motivate employees?', Harvard business review 46, 1968, p 53-62.

13   Roche, William J and Neil L MacKinnon: 'Motivating people with meaningful work', Harvard business review 48, 1970, p 97-110.

14   Paul, William J, Jr, Keith B Robertson and Frederick Herzberg: 'Job enrichment pays off', Harvard business review 47, 1969, p 61-78.

15   Myers, M Scott: Every employee a manager: more meaningful work through job enrichment. New York: McGraw-Hill Book Co, 1970.

# 5
# Evaluation

The key to this section is found in a phrase used by Mason at the beginning of his article 'sufficient information must be made available to demonstrate to top management that the resources are being used effectively'. The argument could be extended that this kind of information (appropriate to the task in hand) is required by everyone at all levels of the system if each operation in the system is to be effective. The amount of information should also be *no more* than is needed to see that the library is being managed effectively. The problem in most libraries is that too much of the wrong kind of information is produced.

Mason's article is concerned with management techniques. Many would argue that it is wrong to include systems analysis and operations research (operational research to the British) amongst a battery of techniques as it misrepresents these aspects which are essentially ways of looking at problems not techniques for solving them (see commentary on Section 3). These approaches employ the techniques appropriate to handle the problems. Operational research could adopt, for example, linear programming or critical path analysis as ways of analysing and solving a problem. The significance of the distinction between a management technique and an approach to a problem is that it is probably not possible for many librarians to master the techniques, but it is important that they comprehend, even if only in a limited way, approaches to problems. Mackenzie's article is an example of both the application of techniques and the problem solving approach.

Mackenzie's paper on 'bibliotheconomics' has been included in this selection because it provides what is perhaps the simplest and most encouraging introduction to a subject which tends to intimidate beginners in the study of library management. For the reader who has struggled with the necessary task of accommodating each successive contribution in this book on his own personal 'map' of the library management field, it may help to explain that Mackenzie is writing within the system model of a library. He describes how the relationships between certain library operations and conditions (such as period of loan, duplication of stock) may be represented quantitatively as a 'mathematical model'. By observing the effects of changing each of the variables, this model can be manipulated experimentally in order to simulate the effects of applying different library policies.

It will be helpful if the reader studies this article in the light of Jones' contribution in Section one of this reader. Mackenzie sees the first step as the definition of objectives in quantitative terms and thus concentrates on areas most amenable rather than, for example, on the perceptions of users and non-users of the library whose definitions of their own satisfaction

162

levels may be at variance with his quantitative measures. To understand a library and its impact involves 'soft' as well as 'hard' areas and Mackenzie's article neatly demonstrates how quantitative measures pose questions of explanation not answerable in quantitative terms.

A rather more sophisticated and updated treatment of the same subject will be found in another paper by Mackenzie (1973). The, by now, historic early work of the Lancaster University Library Management Research Unit has been reported by Buckland, Hindle, Mackenzie and Woodburn (1970). Elton and Vickery (1973) provides a general assessment of operational research in libraries and information services. In addition, a useful paper by Hamburg (1972) offers some introduction to library objectives and performance measures and their use in decision making, before going on to a relatively advanced treatment of this area. These essays in 'library science' lead logically, perhaps, to Salton's futuristic 'Proposals for a dynamic library' (Salton, 1975).

The effect of all this is seen clearly by the trend to add to, or supplant, the use of traditional measures of the input of resources by output measures, or measures of performance, as more reliable indicators of the effectiveness of the library's operation. Look again at Haak's article.

These terms, measures of performance, output measures, etc seem to be interchangeable. Though their use varies there are distinctions to be made. An output measure relates to the end product (any end product) of the operation. For example: number of volumes borrowed. A measure of performance is similar to a measure of effectiveness, that is, a measure of the degree to which the operation is achieving the desired objectives (eg the proportion of documents that are catalogued within $n$ days of arrival, or the probability of finding the document you want on the shelves). Another term often used is 'impact measure'. This assesses the extent of the effect of the service on the community served (eg the proportion of the population registered at the library). A measurement of benefit of a library service is very difficult to find (some would say impossible), as the value of information to an individual is, in most cases, impossible to ascertain. This is unlike other operations whose benefits can be calculated, for example, in cash equivalents. In health services a value can be given to the restoration of a person's ability to work, even if the total value of good health cannot be determined. Articles by Philip Morgan and Arthur Jones in Brown and Surridge (1974) present an understandable analysis of the problems of output measures for most libraries.

Within our profession there have been attempts to measure benefit. A report by Flowerdew and Whitehead (1974) presents a usefully comprehensive discussion of the subject in the context of information science, with a comparison between information and other products, and a framework for relating costs, effectiveness and benefit. Cooper (1973) also discusses the value of information in the same context. When we move to academic and public libraries, these valuations become difficult to apply as absolute measures, though there may be a case for relative values to be assigned. For example, is one use of the Encyclopedia Britannica worth 5 romances read? One feels that this kind of evaluation is actually practised by library managers, even if not systematically and openly pursued.

If one cannot value benefits, one can, in theory, add up the costs of achieving certain objectives. The PEBUL study (University of Durham, 1966), though a very detailed one for the student to follow, gives relative costs for different services. Magson (1973) gives a ranking of cost-benefits in information centres. Smith and Schofield (1971) reports a framework for establishing unit costs in university libraries in a way that will allow comparison between libraries. Special libraries tend to be cost conscious (Vickery, 1972), but few public libraries know, for example, the true cost of adding a book to stock, or of keeping it in stock. Until we have measures of both costs and effectiveness it is obvious that we cannot manage a library system in a way that will minimise costs and maximise effectiveness.

We are on easier ground when we consider measures of effectiveness. If the objectives of a library are clear (and these objectives should relate, however subjectively, to the goals), then measures of the extent of the attainment of these objectives must be found. Mackenzie's article should be read as an extension of Haak's discussion of goals. Lancaster University Library Research Unit, in its operational research study, sought to optimise the provision and management of bookstock resources in the attainment of the measures of the probability of a document being available, together with the percentage collection bias and the total number of hours of document exposure.

Orr (1973) provides a clear account of points of contact between non-users and users and the library service at which some assessment of the effectiveness of the service might be made. The most useful form of measure for the management of libraries are those which are a resultant of the supply and the demand—that is, the extent to which resources are meeting the demands of the clientele. (See Line (1974) for an elaboration of the distinction between *wants, needs* and *demands.*)

There is a rapidly growing literature reporting research work and experiments in which library performance has been measured. A handy package is the issue of *Library trends* January 1974, devoted to the subject of evaluation. Two notable reports referred to in our article by Evans, Borko and

Ferguson are those by Orr, Pings, Olson and Pizer, and the work of Wessel reporting the Atlis project, of which a handy summary appears in *Aslib proceedings* (Wessel, 1968). Wessel considers a matrix of management methods and criteria of performance measures as a means of evaluation of a library.

If measures of benefit are unattainable, there is still a Holy Grail to be sought in the single performance measure which serves as an indicator of the total effectiveness of the library. Hamburg (1974) and Hamburg, Ramist and Bommer (1972) argue that this is contained within the measure of document exposure—that is, the time of eye-to-page contact which the documents of the library achieve in a given period of time. There are, clearly, many difficulties still to be resolved, but the measure has many attractions. If one cannot ascribe a value to reading (eye-to-page contact), one might reasonably argue that, on balance, people do not continue reading that which has no value for them, and that, on average, reading of any one document from a given library's stock is as valuable as any other document from that same library. If this argument is accepted, then a measure of reading time as a gross figure, or a figure per volume or per capita is a valuable indicator of overall performance, if the overall objective of the library is to bring people into contact with documents for the purpose of reading them. The addition of audio visual material does not alter the logic of this argument, though it makes measurement more difficult.

If a single performance measure is not attainable, then a profile of the effectiveness of the service may be had by a systematic schedule of a variety of measures. An example of such a profile for public libraries in America can be seen in DeProspo, Altman and Beasley (1973).

To sum up, libraries, rather late in the day, are coming round to measuring their level of performance, rather than just the level of their inputs. There is a large and growing literature on this, and a reference to published bibliographies (Rodwell, 1975) (Reynolds, 1970) (Noble and Ward, 1976), is a sensible note on which to end this commentary.

# REVIEW OF CRITERIA USED
# TO MEASURE LIBRARY EFFECTIVENESS

*Edward Evans, Harold Borko and Patricia Ferguson*

Libraries are always seeking better ways to evaluate performance and always running into difficulties. Some of these difficulties arise from the lack of available techniques for measuring and evaluating the quality of a service or function. One fundamental problem is that none of the current evaluation methods seems to consider total library performance as critical to making a valid evaluation. Also, most of the present evaluation techniques do not seem to be sufficiently sensitive to both quantitative and qualitative factors of library service and are therefore not completely acceptable to either librarians or nonlibrarians.

This is a report on a literature survey which was part of a study undertaken for the National Library of Medicine*. The study objectives were to develop a list of issues and criteria relating to the measurement of medical library effectiveness. When appropriate, other types of libraries were considered, since there exists a rather broad common bond between all libraries. The procedure employed was to review the literature on the subject of library evaluation. Each criterion encountered was listed and examined in terms of its potential significance and validity for measuring library performance.

Many measures have been employed in attempts to evaluate library performance, as we discovered in our review of over five hundred articles, books and abstracts. Obviously, not all of these measures were unique; they were in fact slight modifications of one another. In order to make sense of the extensive list which we had accumulated, we grouped them in accordance with the aspect of the system that was being evaluated. These we called 'criterion concepts'—for example, accessibility of materials, cost, and user satisfaction are some of the important concepts in evaluating library effectiveness. The specific techniques or data used to measure these concepts we called 'criterion measures'. In the list below, the six criterion concepts are labelled with Roman numerals, while the specific criterion measures are ordered by Arabic numerals. We believe that this distinction between concepts and measures is meaningful and that it eliminates a good deal of confusion in the literature on library evaluation. In addition, the list enabled us to organize and classify the various evaluation procedures we can across in our review of the literature, for most of the reported measures turned out to be slight modifications of one of six basic criteria. The complete list that follows indicates the criterion concepts (Roman numerals) and the various specific criterion measures (Arabic numerals) that fall into the basic categories.

I Accessibility
   1 Number of services and degree of services provided various classes of users.
   2 Ratio of services requested to services available.
   3 Ratio of holdings to total user population (actual and potential).

II Cost
   1 Staff size.
   2 Staff skill and characteristics.
   3 Unit cost.
   4 Ratio of book budget to users.

III User satisfaction
   1 User satisfaction with services rendered.
   2 Number of user activities in libraries.
   3 Percentage of items in collection as listed in some checklist.
   4 Percentage of items in collection by type of materials (books, serials, reports, etc).
   5 Percentage of items in collection by type of material compared to various classes of users.
   6 Quality-value of items in collection based on expert opinion.
   7 Ratio of documents used to materials requested.

IV Response time
   1 Speed of services.
   2 Ratio of number of services offered to average response time for all services.
   3 Ratio of response time (to secure document) to total time document is of value.
   4 Ratio of holdings to response time.

V Cost/benefit ratio
   1 Ratio of services provided to total cost.
   2 Ratio of total service expenditures to users (actual and/or potential).

3 Ratio of item cost to item value or utility.
4 Ratio of a given service (including overhead cost) to response time cost.

VI Use
1 Gross use of services (reference questions answered, bibliographies completed, etc).
2 Ratio of actual users to potential users.
3 Total library use (attendance figures, circulation, etc).
4 Ratio of a given service to total number of users.
5 Ratio of total use for all services to total number of services provided.
6 Percentage of materials used by type and by class of users (student, teacher, researcher, etc).
7 Ratio of documents circulated to various classes of users.
8 Ratio of documents circulated to number of users.
9 Ratio of total use to total holdings.
10 Item-use-day (a measure based on the number of items used in a twenty-four hour period).

## Background comments

Perhaps the most surprising aspect of the literature review was the lack of concern with the how and why of the evaluation process. It would seem to be self-evident that any evaluation of library performance should include a discussion of the purpose, the method of evaluation, and the reasons for evaluation. There are a surprising number of reports and studies on the subject of evaluation that fail to make it clear just what the purpose is. Consequently, confusion arises over the interpretation of the results. Of the studies surveyed very few identified the goals or the importance of a given service to the achievement of those goals.

Even more disturbing was a general lack of consideration for the total service program of a library. Most of the studies, for presumably sound reasons (although seldom spelled out), confined themselves to one or two evaluative measures applied to one or two service functions. While no single study can cover all services, some attention should be given to the way in which the functions studied or evaluated relate to the total program of the library. In general this total service concept was lacking, and since the study goals were not stated, it was difficult to determine whether the various criteria were appropriately selected and employed.

Even those few studies dealing with the full range of services failed to consider one of the most basic of all library functions, conservation.

168

Dissemination, the library's best-known function, has been carefully considered; however, conservation for later dissemination has been consistently ignored. None of the studies examined concerned itself with the question of conservation. While it may be true that only the large teaching-research-regional medical library must be greatly concerned with conservation, all libraries need to consider the question to some extent. Many methods of evaluation place a high premium on the performance of a service (circulation) that is or may be detrimental to the conservation of materials—an equally important library function. When evaluating library effectiveness, the total programe of library services and functions must be taken into account.

In the discussion that follows, we will analyze the literature on library evaluation in terms of the six criterion concepts we have delineated and will summarize the problems and ways of dealing with them. Although citations to individual studies are not included in the text, those studies we consider to be particularly significant are listed in the bibliography.

**Evaluation criteria**
I *Accessibility*
Accessibility to the library and its contents is without a doubt one of the most difficult criterion concepts to measure. Of the studies discussed, accessibility factors are seldom considered. There are at least two aspects to the question of access: a) physical access to the library and its materials, that is, the ease with which one may determine if a particular document is in a collection and where it is located, and b) user access, that is, to what class of user a given service is available. In order to measure physical accessibility in a quantitative manner, it becomes necessary to consider one of the other evaluation criterion concepts, response time, but many studies fail to take both aspects into account. Even in this circumscribed area of library performance evaluation there seems to be a failure to consider all aspects of the service function.

There is no question about the need to consider accessibility in evaluating any library performance. Rapid response time, low cost, may *not* be a reflection of ideal library performance. Ninety-nine percent of existing libraries could probably achieve the above performance goal, without a budget increase, if they were to concentrate only on known user needs. Libraries could achieve rapid response time, for example, at the expense of cutting back on services to 'marginal' users and on 'marginal' materials. Any system of performance evaluation that ignores the question of accessibility, or at least availability, of a range of materials to a multiplicity of users, will only compound the library's problem by encouraging a concentration on improved performance for the known factors, and thus in fact hamper the total system performance.

For example, several studies have shown that a few active users account for most of the total use of a library, while most patrons are infrequent users who make few demands for service. If the library focuses on the heavy users and their known demands and needs, it can achieve an outstanding performance record in terms of almost everything except accessibility of materials and services to the larger user population. Accessibility measures are essentially ratios of service to users. The rating can be improved by increasing services or by decreasing the number of users. The first alternative is, of course, the necessary one.

## II  *Costs*

There has always been a concern with cost control in libraries. Yet throughout most of the history of library development, libraries have approached the problem of cost analysis in a most elementary and timid manner. The reluctance to analyze costs can in part be attributed to lack of training. Also, library trustees and the general public have not been cost conscious due to the low level of library expenditures. Not until recently, when the level of expenditure rose sharply, did anyone demonstrate real concern about unit costs and cost control. While cost figures alone should not be used to evaluate a library, they are useful in determining the efficiency of some operations, and, when used in combination with other criteria, cost figures can begin to provide insights into library performance.

Although material processing costs have been studied, there seems to be a great reluctance to put a 'price tag' or unit cost figure on public service activities. Admittedly, the 'value' of a service is difficult to measure, and a high unit cost figure may create problems in demonstrating the desirability of such services. Nevertheless, efforts to assess the costs of public service activities must be continued in order to develop a complete picture of library performance.

As an example of the problem, most reference departments keep some 'statistics' on the number of reference questions asked. Dividing the total number of questions asked by the total cost of maintaining the reference department, including overhead, one can compute a unit cost figure. But what does this tell us about performance? A high or low figure may or may or may not reflect a 'good' performance. A large number of simple questions being answered by staff members from sources the users could consult without assistance would produce a low unit cost but would not necessarily

170

mean a good total library performance. Everyone can think of several other examples. The point here is simply to note that while cost is an important criterion in evaluation, it must be considered in conjunction with other factors.

Personnel costs are also often oversimplified. Many articles have been published in the number of staff required and the qualifications, special training, or skills needed to perform certain services adequately. It is generally recognized that an arbitrary number of staff members cannot be set but must depend on the kind and scope of service provided, the content of the collection, and the size of the organization served. The ALA College Library Standards prescribe a minimum number of professional librarians with additional hiring determined by size of population served, type of library organization, size and character of the collection, prevailing community interests, number of hours the library is open, and the physical layout of the building. In 1964 the Special Libraries Association suggested a ratio of 2-3 nonprofessionals to every professional library staff member. However, very little thorough research has been conducted on the number and kind of personnel needed to perform a particular library service, nor on the type of skills and knowledge that lead to better performance. Decisions are still being based on educated guesses and not on empirical studies.

One must simultaneously consider both the personnel requirements and the costs of performing various services when evaluating performance. These are interactive! One should have some method of evaluating performance to determine what the personnel requirements ought to be, and one should know what abilities are represented in the personnel performing the work being evaluated. That is, if one wishes to justify a new position or service to be performed by a certain category of personnel, one should have some method of analyzing the task and relating the performance measures to the personnel skills required for its successful accomplishment.

To expect clerical personnel to perform at a professional level is unrealistic. Yet in many instances of gathering cost figures, no record has been made of who performed the task involved. If one calculates costs without considering efficiency of the operation or the personnel skills required, the cost figures could be meaningless or even misleading. The important factor is to be sure the costs are included and that they are valid or at least clearly defined costs in terms of the service being evaluated. The measures we have listed under II *Costs* are representative of the techniques that have been used in evaluating the costs of library services.

### III  *User satisfaction*

Within the broad heading of user satisfaction, there are two distinct sub-groups to be considered: (1) user satisfaction with existing services and materials, and (2) user needs for services and materials not presently available.

Determining user requirements is most important as an aid to the evaluation, selection, and weeding of materials. One common technique utilizes an examination of user attitudes and methods of gathering information. Another technique surveys patrons' use of the library. Such studies are oriented towards basing a collection on demonstrated user needs. An equally valid procedure is to concentrate on the needs which are not being met.

User satisfaction and goal achievement are measures of effectiveness of the service performed. The degree of services provided by the library and the extent of these services should be selected because they effectively achieve a given goal or level of user satisfaction. The users of special libraries will need more bibliographic services (such as literature searches, preparation of abstracts, bibliographies, and translations) than will the much larger and more general clientele of a public or college library.

Employment of the user satisfaction criterion to measure library performance creates certain fundamental problems that need to be recognized:

a) A strong subjective element is always present. Each person has his own expectations with regard to a service. The ideas of various users may be similar, but they vary in detail. This variation can and does cause differences in the users' sense of satisfaction. In addition, there are degrees of satisfaction, and these are extremely difficult, if not impossible, to differentiate and quantify.

b) Comparative studies of user satisfaction criteria must be preceded by expensive testing of the measuring instrument and training of subjects to insure that different individuals interpret the questions in the same manner. The development and extensive validation testing of a measuring instrument which could be widely used for determining use attitudes would begin to solve part of this problem.

c) Providing a universally accepted definition of the term 'relevant' is very difficult. This is an important problem, because in order to determine user satisfaction with documents received, or with services rendered, one cannot avoid the question of relevancy. When users judge relevance by different standards, interpretation of results becomes complicated.

d) A generally low response rate to survey questionnaires precludes obtaining a representative sample of actual and potential users without a great deal of expensive preparation and effort. Even if the other problems are overcome, survey results will still not be useful unless the sample is shown to be representative of actual and potential users.

Nevertheless, user satisfaction must be considered one of the primary measures of library effectiveness. It is, however, an adequate criterion of effectiveness only when employed with a full understanding of its limitations and in conjunction with other criteria.

## IV *Response time*

The use of response time as a measure of library performance is a relatively recent development. Its use is increasing, since many investigators view this as one of the more objective measures, subject to easy quantification. It is possible to measure response time in a number of ways by varying the stopping and starting points and employing either real, elapsed, or some 'average' time for different situations. As with the other criteria it is also possible to use this measure for different purposes, eg

a) To measure the time required to secure a copy of a specific document.

b) To measure the time required to secure a specific piece of information or have a given service performed.

While response time is a quantitative criterion of library performance and has a high degree of objectivity when certain parameters are agreed upon, it tends to be used too often as the sole measure of performance. It may take longer to retrieve a document from a large library collection than from a small one, but no librarian would want to limit his collection for the sole purpose of making books easier to locate in the stacks.

There are other factors that must be considered. User satisfaction may fall off even if response time is improved should too many errors result and should costs increase.

Is a system which is excellent with regard to response time necessarily satisfying to all users for all needs? It seems unlikely because of the cost and the overloading that would occur due to high demand. As with the other criteria, response time is best considered as part of the total system of evaluation, with a weight assigned to the time factor commensurate with its value in achieving a specific goal or service objective. Such a test is difficult to develop, and so other factors are frequently omitted while response time alone is measured.

The following is an example of the problem involved in using response time as the measure of performance in the evaluation of medical libraries. All medical libraries, in theory at least, have access to national medical resources; however, *not all* medical library users have an opportunity to make use of such facilities. Medical students and others are sometimes not allowed to request interlibrary loan materials, and this limits the accessibility of library materials to them. Nevertheless, one study included interlibrary loan time as one factor in the response time and ranked performance on this basis. It seems questionable whether anything more than response time for a certain class of materials and for a limited number of users was in fact measured. The total library function and services to all classes of users were not adequately considered.

## V *Cost/benefit ratio*

Only a very few studies have been completed which apply cost/benefit analysis and use the methods developed by business and government for measuring cost/benefit in a total system. There have, however, been a number of library studies that measure cost/benefit analysis primarily in terms of services provided.

Generally, a library cost/benefit analysis uses a ratio of total expenditures to users and services in order to determine cost effectiveness. Another method of analysis is to divide the calculated costs of all services into fixed and variable groups. Performance budgeting concentrates on the character of the work performed by each unit and may have more merit than simply listing costs under categories of services and materials purchased. This method of budgeting requires a thorough knowledge of the services to be performed and the amount of use each service receives as well as accurate cost figures.

One significant feature of performance budgeting is the burden it places in the administrator to justify, on the basis of performance, budget requests for additional funds. This is extremely difficult; however, if this method of budgeting is increasingly applied to educational institutions, including libraries, perhaps significant progress in evaluating performance of all service oriented nonprofit organizations will be forthcoming. Reliable methods of evaluation are not yet available.

Cost/benefit analysis could be considered, at least in theory, as the sole criterion of library performance. In practice, this would be possible only if a large number of different benefits were considered (for example, cost/accessibility, cost/use, cost/user satisfaction, cost/response time). In order to evaluate total library performance each broad division would have to be subdivided for analysis (for example, cost/medical student/accessibility, cost/house staff/accessibility, etc). While cost/benefit seems to have a great deal of promise, it is at present subjective, imprecise, and inconsistent, and thus involves more measurement problems than most of the other criteria that have been discussed. A 'benefit' can be almost anything, and 'costs' can be computed in many ways. As a result there are many variations and slight modifications which make comparisons difficult if not impossible. Terms and procedures need to be operationally defined. In spite of the difficulties, cost/benefit seems to be a very important potential criterion for measuring library performance.

## VI *Use*

Although library use has been employed as a measure of performance for some time, the units measured have not been very precise or meaningful. Normally the unit employed is the number of documents circulated. Occasionally the number of registered borrowers has been used as a measure of library use. As the number of items circulated or the number of borrowers increased, the level of performance was assumed to rise. Recently, attempts have been made to predict through circulation figures the amount of use a library will receive. These newer approaches represent an improvement in measurement techniques and should provide a better basis for evaluating and improving library services.

Some of the newer techniques have been designed to improve the utility of the library collection. Studies of this type may lead in some cases to reduction in size of collection to make it easier to find materials and, therefore, to reduce the response time, thus generating greater user satisfaction. It is conceivable that use studies, employing probability statistics and involving the characteristics of used and unused materials could isolate some basic factors that could be employed to improve the selection of material. If that were to happen, a more efficient expenditure of funds could result.

Some attempts have been made to determine the relevance of the collection to user needs by gathering data on the actual use of the collection. This in turn is considered a measure of the library's performance capability. Another approach to partially evaluating the collection and the library on the basis of use is to analyze reference questions asked, whether answered or unanswered. Such an approach will clearly define the active user's needs and can be a partial guide for collection development. However, one would need to be extremely cautious about applying these data for evaluating the library's total performance since only the needs of active users would be apparent, and even such users do not ask all of their questions at the library.

There are a number of problems that arise when the use criterion is employed to measure library performance:

175

a) It fails to differentiate between types of use (significant and insignificant).

b) It seldom includes 'in-house' use. (Such data can only be gathered with expensive data collection methods.)

c) It is susceptible to radical variations if the very active users (a small percentage of the total user population) change their use patterns.

d) It fails to reflect the needs of those potential users who have either not attempted to use the library or have given up as a result of repeated failure.

Evaluating performance on the basis of use is difficult; however, this is a necessary criterion which, if carefully employed, would begin to provide an objective measure of the total library effectiveness. Measures of use are basic; they encompass all library functions, and they are not subject to misinterpretation. Costs are also objective, but performance cost figures often do not relate to user satisfaction. Cost/benefit analysis appears to be reasonable, but actually subjective definitions of benefit are often involved. Response time is also an objective measure, but it does not measure the relevance of the information provided. Thus use, while not completely satisfactory, can be considered a partial index of relevance and of a library's ability to provide needed services to some portion of the total potential user population. Use as a criterion concept is basic to all performance evaluations, but the techniques employed to measure use must be made more reliable and meaningful.

## Summary

Our literature search indicates that in measuring library performance a great many variations of a few basic approaches have been tried. Most of the studies concentrate on one or two services. The literature in general reflects the lack of consideration of (a) the total service program, and (b) the importance of using multiple criteria for evaluating service functions. Without such considerations it seems to be impossible to arrive at any valid measures of library performance.

As a further complication, one must consider whether all the measures, even the six 'basic' criterion concepts, are equally important for measuring all services. If not, these should be weighted to reflect their relative importance both for the evaluation of a specific service and for the total library program. Research that would provide an empirical basis for deciding these issues would seem to be of primary importance. Libraries perform mutliple services, and therefore it seems unlikely that any single criterion can be considered as the sole valid measure of library performance. When it is possible to apply several different criteria, the question of weighting each one becomes critical. In order to determine what the weighting factor should be, one needs to know the relative importance of each element in achieving a specific library function.

In light of these considerations, it is suggested that research should be directed to the development of a technique to aid in establishing for each individual library a list of its services, ascribing to each service its relative importance to the total library program. A second phase of this problem would be to determine which criteria were appropriate to measure the performance of these services and the weight that should be assigned to each. For example, does it seem valid to give the same weight to response time for two such different services as translation and information-reference? While response time would be a valid criterion in both cases it seems likely that most people would rather see a slower response time (less weight) and more accessibility (more weight) when evaluating a translation service. However, these differentiations have not yet been made.

Considering total library performance, conservation is another area that needs to be investigated. No studies were encountered in the literature search that even discussed conservation as an aspect of library performance. A library may incur conservation losses when user services are increased, and some techniques should be developed for counterbalancing these functions. From an overall point of view, it would seem that less effort should be devoted to developing modifications of existing measures of performance evaluation and more effort should be directed toward developing precise operational procedures for

a) defining the variables involved in the measurement of each criterion concept;

b) specifying the statistical data and formulas needed to calculate the criterion measures;

c) suggesting a procedure that will enable one to combine these individual criterion measures so as to evaluate total library performance;

d) developing a procedure to weight the individual criterion measures in accordance with each library's estimation of the importance of services being provided; and

e) eventually arriving at a procedure whereby meaningful comparisons can be made of libraries.

*Note*
* The study was conducted from August 1969 to April 1970 under a grant (1G04 LM 0078 18-01) from the National Library of Medicine and the Pacific Southwest Regional Medical Library (University of California, Los Angeles, Biomedical Library).

## References

Andersen, Arthur, & Co: Research study of criteria and procedures for evaluating scientific information retrieval systems. Washington, National Science Foundation, Office of Science Information Service, 1962. NSF-C218 (AD-273 115).

Anderson, A A: Multi-level file structure as a frame of reference for measuring user interest. Presented at the International Advanced Study Institute on the Evaluation of Information Systems at the Hague, Netherlands, 1965. (AD-636 832).

Aro, Barbara, Judith Gripton and Carol Strashem, eds: Cost analysis study: technical services division, University of Denver Library. Studies in librarianship, no 4, Denver, University of Denver, 1965.

Bach, Harry: Scientific literature use: a survey. Special libraries 48: 466, 1957.

Bare, Carole E: Conducting user requirement studies in special libraries. Special libraries 57: 103-106, 1966.

Bedsole, Danny T: Formulating a weeding policy for books in a special library. Special libraries 49: 205-209, 1958.

Bernal, J D: Scientific information and its users. Aslib proceedings 12: 432-438, 1960.

Bornstein, Harry A: A paradigm for a retrieval effectiveness experiment. American documentation 12: 254-259, 1961.

Bouman, G P: Cost analysis in company libraries. Bibliotheekleven 36: 281-290, 1951.

Bourne, C P, and others: Requirements, criteria and measures of performance of information storage and retrieval systems. Washington, National Science Foundation, 1961.

Budington, William S: Cost of information service. In: The library as a community information center. Champaign, University of Illinois, 1959, p 51-66.

Bush, G C, H P Galliher and P M Morse: Attendance and use of the science library at MIT. Am doc 8: 87-109, 1956.

Carnovsky, L: Evaluation of library services. UNESCO bulletin for libraries 13: 221-225, 1959.

Clapp, Verner W and Robert T Jordan: Quantitative criteria for adequacy of academic library collections. Coll res libr 26: 371-380, 1965.

Cleverdon, Cyril W: The evaluation of systems used in information retrieval. In: International Conference on Scientific Information, Washington, DC, 1958. Proceedings. Washington, National Academy of Science, 1959, p 687-698.

Cleverdon, Cyril W: An investigation into the comparative efficiency of information retrieval systems. UNESCO bulletin for libraries 12: 267-270, 1958.

Cuadra, Carlos A: On the utility of the relevance concept. Santa Monica, System Development Corporation, 1964.

Fisher, Eva Lou: Checklist for organization, operation and evaluation of a company library. New York, Special Libraries Association, 1966.

Fussler, Herman A: The problems of physical accessibility. In: Shera, Jesse H and Margarte E Egan, eds: Bibliographic organization. Chicago, University of Chicago Press, 1951, p 163-186.

Goffman, W and V A Newill: Methodology for test and evaluation of information retrieval systems. Comparative Systems Laboratory Technical Report No 2. Cleveland, Western Reserve University, Center for Documentation and Communication Research, 1964.

Hirsch, Rudolph: Evaluation of book collections. In: Yenawine, Wayne S: Library evaluation (Frontiers of librarianship, no 2). Syracuse, Syracuse University, 1959, p 7-20.

Hodgson, James G: The literature of library standards. Third Military Librarians' Workshop. Monterey, US Navy Postgraduate School, 1959.

Kopkin, T J: Circulating the table of contents of magazines. Special libraries 46: 211-212, 1955.

Lehigh University. Center for the Information Sciences: Studies in the man-system interface in libraries. Report no 2. The application of psychometric techniques to determine the attitudes of individuals toward information seeking, by Victor Rosenberg. Bethlehem, Pa, Lehigh University, 1966.

Logsdon, Richard H: Time and motion studies in libraries. Library trends 2: 401-409, 1954.

Maizell, R E: Standards for measuring effectiveness of technical library performance. IRE transactions on engineering management. EM-7 (2): 69-72, 1960.

Maybury, Catherine: Performance budgeting for the library. ALA bulletin 55: 46-55, 1961.

Meier, R L: Efficiency criteria for the operation of large libraries. Library Quarterly 31: 215-234, 1961.

Monroe, M E: Standards—criteria for service or goals for the future? ALA bull 56: 818-820, 1962.

Morse, Philip M: Probabilistic models for library operations. Presented at annual meeting of Association of Research Libraries, Jan 1964.

Mueller, Max W: Time, cost and value factors in information retrieval. General information manual (IBM Information Retrieval Systems Conference). Poughkeepsie, 1959.

Ohlman, Herbert: The activity spectrum: a tool for analyzing information systems. In: Heilprin, Lawrence B, Barbara E Markuson, and Fredrick L Goodman, eds: Proceedings of the Symposium on Education for Information Services. (American Documentation Institute). Washington, Spartan Books, 1965, p 155-166.

Orr, R H, V M Pings, E E Olson, and I H Pizer: Development of methodologic tools for planning and managing library services, I Project goals and approach. Bulletin of the Medical Library Association 56: 235-240, July 1968.

Idem: Development of methodologic tools for planning and managing library services, II Measuring a library's capability for providing documents. Bulletin of the Medical Library Association 56: 241-267, July 1968.

Idem: Development of methodologic tools for planning and managing library services, III Standardized inventories of library services. Bulletin of the Medical Library Association 56: 380-403, Oct 1968.

Pundsack, Fred L: What the user expects from a library. Special libraries 46: 163-166, 1955.

Randall, Gordon E: Journal routing: greater efficiency at lower cost. Special libraries 45: 371-373, 1954.

Randall, G E: Special library standards, statistics, and performance evaluation. Special libraries 56: 379-386, 1965.

Randall, G E Who uses a technical library? Special libraries 47: 195-199, 1956.

Risk, J M S: Information services: measuring the cost. Aslib proceedings 8: 269-287, 1956.

Rubenstein, Albert H: Setting criteria for R&D. Harvard business review 35: 95-104, 1957.

Schutze, G: Measure of library service—statistics. Special libraries 43: 263-265, 1952.

Shank, Russell: Library service to research laboratories of a large university. American documentation 10: 221-223, 1959.

Slater, Margaret: Types of use and user in industrial libraries: some impressions. Journal of documentation 19: 12-18, 1963.

Taube, Mortimer: An evaluation of use studies of scientific information. In: Emerging solutions for mechanizing the storage and retrieval of information. Washington, Documentation, Inc, 1959, p 46-71.

Taylor, L: Cost research on a library service. Aslib proceedings 13: 238-248, 1961.

Tomlinson, Helen: Defining technical information needs for a research library. Lackland AFB, Texas, Personnel Research Laboratory, 1965.

Trueswell, Richard W: A quantitative measure of user circulation requirements and its possible effect on stack thinning and multiple copy determination. American documentation 16: 20-25, 1965.

Vickery, B C and C W Hanson: Optimum use of staff: the medium library. Aslib proceedings 3: 225-234, 1951.

Wallace, Everett M: User requirements, personal indexes and computer support. Santa Monica, System Development Corporation, 1966.

Weber, David: Criteria for evaluating a college library. Association of American Colleges bulletin 43: 629-633, 1957.

Wessel, C J: Criteria for evaluating the effectiveness of library operations and services. Phase I (Atlis Report no 10). Washington, DC, John I Thompson and Company, 1967.

Idem: Criteria for evaluating the effectiveness of library operations and services. Phase II (Atlis Report no 10). Washington, DC, John I Thompson and Company, 1967.

Idem: Criteria for evaluating the effectiveness of library operations and services. Phase II (Atlis Report no 19). Washington, DC, John I Thompson and Company, 1968.

Idem: Criteria for evaluating the effectiveness of library operations and services. Phase III (Atlis Report no 21). Washington, DC, John I Thompson and Company, 1969.

# MANAGEMENT TECHNIQUES APPLIED TO THE OPERATION OF INFORMATION SERVICES

*D Mason*

Confucius, that ancient Chinese sage who has been held responsible for so many pseudo-philosophical statements, was asked by one of his disciples what was the first thing he would do if he were appointed head of government. 'I would rectify the use of terms' replied Confucius. The disciple then enquired what such an action had to do with government, and received the answer 'If words are not used correctly then speech becomes tied in knots, and business comes to a standstill'. Confucius may have been stating the extreme case but nevertheless it is perhaps as well to define terms, so let us begin with the verb 'to manage'. The Oxford English Dictionary states that it derives from the Latin *manus* (a hand) and it can mean 'to train a horse in its paces; to make an object serve one's purpose; to control the course of affairs by one's own actions; to administer; to husband; to treat a person with indulgence; to cause persons to submit to one's control; to bring about one's wishes by artifice and flattery; and to contrive to get along or pull through'.

A manager is defined as one skilled in managing affairs, money etc, and one who manages a business or institution. While management is the action or manner of managing; the use of contrivance for effecting some purpose; and, rather interestingly in view of certain styles of management, the manuring of land.

Most of these meanings have some relevance, but for most purposes today I prefer to define management as the art, or science, of controlling enterprises and organizations through people. So when we come to examine techniques of management we are concerned with the relationships between the manager and other persons, some of whom are in some way subject to his control, some are his bosses, while others who are not directly involved can nevertheless influence his actions, or be influenced in their actions by him.

We can represent a company as a triangle of forces with a group of people at each of the points. There are the shareholders who provide the capital to operate the company, the staff who provide the know-how, and the customers who purchase the products. And I refer to it as a triangle of forces because it is necessary to keep the system in balance. Undue preference for any one or two groups and consequent down-grading of the remainder will bring about a state of imbalance that can lead a company into difficulties.

A service department can also be represented in the same way. Here the three groups consist of the top management who allocate the resources, the staff who convert those resources into services, and the customers who use the services (some of whom will also, of course, be top management). Again it is necessary to keep the forces, or demands, in balance. Sufficient resources must be obtained to provide adequate services for customers and job satisfaction for staff; and sufficient information must be made available to demonstrate to top management that the resources are being used effectively. Thus management becomes, in effect, a continuing compromise between what is desirable in terms of service and satisfaction, and one or more of a range of feasibilities which depend on the availability of resources.

In addition it is essential to be aware of the objectives of the enterprise, to know why something is being done as well as how it is being done. In a service context this means that the job objectives of individual members of staff must be compatible with the departmental objectives, and these in turn must match the company's objectives. All activities need to be examined in this light, bearing particularly in mind the old saying 'Never do a thing well if it needn't be done at all'.

The usefulness, or otherwise, of any management technique has to be judged within this framework. A company usually has an overall style of management which has to be modified to fit the service environment. It also usually has at any one time some particular management fad to which all managers are expected to pay at least lip-service. However, it does not require many years of experience to teach the Information Manager to recognize and use those fads which can help him in his job; and to circumvent, while apparently using, those that do not.

The range of management techniques available for use is wide, and the manager must make his own selection to match his own needs. Some techniques are useful because they provide the manager with information which enables him to plan and control his systems, services and staff; and also to provide information to higher management in order to influence the allocation of resources. Other techniques can be used, as required, to provide optimized solutions to particular problems. In examining a selection of these techniques I intend to categorize them into those relating to, first, systems, then services, then staff, and last, but not least, finance.

*Systems analysis*
The totality of activities within an Information Unit forms a system which exists to provide information, and access to information, to a group of users. The technique of systems analysis can be used to study this system and its sub-systems in order to demonstrate the inter-relationships of the component parts, their effectiveness or otherwise, and whether there is a need for any modification or replacement. It is also of use in design and implementation of new systems. Because of the complexity of information systems, and because information staff usually cannot down tools in order to carry out a full analysis, most systems investigations have been made into particular activities and technical processes. Some studies have been made of the relationship between two or three sub-systems, but there is a lot of work still to be done in this field.

A systems analysis must always start from the objectives of the system, and then look at the functions of the system and how these are carried out (1). The relationship of the system to other systems must be determined so that any necessary constraints are observed. A useful approach is the 'critical examination' of each activity within the system. This is nothing new, it forms a part of what used to be called 'method study', but nevertheless it is effective. Each activity is defined, then examined by asking the following questions:

1  Why is this done, need it be continued, can the need for it be avoided?
2  How is it done, why this way, can a better way be found?
3  When is it done, why then, can a better way be found?
4  Where is it done, why there, can a better place be found?
5  Who does it, why is it done by him/them, would another person/ group be better?

At the same time performance data can be collected, eg time spent on each operation, volume of work, rates of pay, etc.

In the next stage the system is analysed. This can be done by drawing up such things as organization diagrams and flow charts. Process flow charts can demonstrate the physical movement of materials, and logical flow charts can show where decisions are made, and their effect on the subsequent parts of the process (2). From the times of the activities staff costs are determined, material and other costs are added to obtain a total cost. Costs of any alternative methods can also be estimated for comparison.

If and when decisions are made to modify the system, or introduce a new system, the stage of system design is carried out, although the major part of the thinking out of the design will usually have been done during the analysis stage. Finally, there is the implementation and evaluation of the new or modified system. This needs to be controlled carefully because, however good the design is, there will always be unexpected factors arising, usually at the interface between the new system and other existing systems.

In designing new or modified systems one must be aware that the system is not intended to operate in a vacuum. It will have effects on the people who operate it, and the people who derive service from it. Therefore in looking at a particular system, one not only examines the *technical* needs, possibilities and constraints to draw up a list of possible improved methods; but also one identifies the *social* needs, possibilities and constraints, listing alternative systems and eliminating those which do not improve on or maintain the present position. The two lists of alternatives can then be compared, and the elimination of incompatible solutions will lead to a list of those that are acceptable on both technical and sociological grounds (3).

*Operations research*

It has been pointed out that libraries and information services do not lend themselves easily to experimentation. Yet there are many occasions when it would be useful to compare different methods in order to get some idea of which is the most effective. Operations research techniques are useful for such an investigation, particularly in the development of mathematical models of systems, and in computer simulation.

Leimkuhler, in reporting work carried out at Purdue University Library, says 'A higher level of elegance and sophistication can be reached with mathematical models at the cost of greater precision in the statement of assumptions and some loss in the ease of enumeration. As with literary language, mathematics can be made to convey an enormous amount of meaning in a very concise way to those who are prepared to understand the fullness of the language. On the other hand, admittedly, it can be a prohibitive barrier to the layman; it can be used to disguise the true facts in a study, and can lead to sterile working of old ideas. But when properly used, quantitative models can provide the most general insights into the behaviour of a system, allowing for experimental validation and meaningful comparison with other systems' (4).

The important point to note is that mathematical models are not intended to be other than guides to decision making. Because they present a simplified version of a *real* system, they enable managers to understand the nature of the system; and in using this understanding, together with other factors of which they are aware, they should arrive at better management decisions.

The use of operations research techniques within a library environment is well demonstrated by the work of the University of Lancaster Library Research Unit (5). Analyses have been made of technical processes and library usage. Their study of a variable loan and duplication policy included the comparison of the loan period and the number of copies of a book, with the popularity rating of the book, and the satisfaction level of the user. The proportion of books at various levels of demand was estimated from loan records, and the effect on the satisfaction level was computed for any given combination of length of loan, amount of in-library use, number of copies, and the probability that a user would ask for a book to be reserved or recalled if he could not find it on the shelves. The borrowing process was then simulated on the computer so that the effect of different policies could be ascertained. Other calculations were made in order to assess the costs of the various policies. As a result of this work a variable loan policy was introduced which led to a sudden increase in library use. The increase in borrowing from the shelves was 200 percent over two years. An increase of this size had not been expected so this led to further work on the development of models of user behaviour (6).

Another interesting outcome of the work at Lancaster has been the Library Management Game, which uses a computerized simulation technique to predict the likely consequences of any set of decisions that the participants make (7). The game has been developed for use in library management education. The student is faced with a problem involving allocation of resources in a certain year and has to make a series of decisions. These are input to the computer using a remote access terminal, and the effects of his decisions are almost immediately printed out. Decisions can then be made for the next year and the cycle repeated. This enables the student to see within a very short time the likely outcome over a period of years of his particular policies. The importance of this game in library education lies particularly in the way it helps to develop the understanding of the decision making process, and also to give an appreciation of the multitude of variable factors involved.

*Market research*
In any decision to make changes to systems and services, one of the major factors to be considered is the likely effect of the changes on the people

who operate the systems or use the services. Management decisions that are based on hunches about what will give satisfaction to service users can turn out to be very expensive if the hunches are wrong. To ensure that the changes are both effective and acceptable, information on users' needs and attitudes is needed; and this information is usually obtained by means of a survey.

A survey can take many forms, from a circulated questionnaire to the collection of data from the Information Unit's own records. Most Information Managers, however, do not usually have the time to design and implement a survey that will produce a good level of information, and in any case they might not get the willing cooperation of their customers in such matters as the completion of questionnaires. I can recall an Organization and Method survey, made many years ago, into the content of the research worker's day. It was organized on a random observation basis, and the method used required each worker to put a tick on a form against the category of activity in which he was occupied on each occasion that a bell was rung. An O&M man hidden somewhere in the middle of his web, rang the bell at times which were derived from random number tables. A good statistical approach, as I am sure you would agree. There was, however, a major snag. The research workers soon got fed up with being summoned by bells, and there was a conspiracy, the results of which demonstrated to the astonished O&M investigator that scientists spent 80 percent of their time in the loo.

There is no doubt that a properly designed survey can yield valuable results, but with the limited resources he has at his command, the Information Manager can rarely afford such a survey. However, if he is a good manager (and I am sure that you all come into this category) he and his staff will have such a wide range of contacts with their customers that they will be able to ask on a personal basis for guidance in the improvement of the services; and if the services are badly in need of improvement they won't have to ask, they will be told in no uncertain terms.

However it is always as well to check opinions against facts. It has, for instance, been found that scientists' *recollections* of what they have done, correlate poorly with *facts* obtained by observation. In at least one survey, many of the scientists spoke of the importance of abstracts, the use they made of them, and the need for better coverage of the literature; whereas observations of their activities showed that they made very little use at all of abstracting journals.

If the information required can be obtained by observation or by analysis of records it will usually be more accurate than opinion sampling.

186

Some years ago I was faced with the problem of deciding whether or not to purchase Chemical abstracts in microform. There was pressure on me to make this purchase because of the resultant saving in space, and also because of the other advantages that were being extolled for microform at that time. Although I have always been a believer in these advantages, I was not convinced that there would be any in this case. To make a correct decision I needed information on the use made of Chemical abstracts in our library, but I felt that it would not be useful to ask the research workers for their 'best guesses'. So we decided to obtain the details by observation, using a member of staff who was working in the abstracts area and was therefore ignored by the customers. Each period of observation was half-an-hour, the days were selected randomly and the observations were continued until we had a reasonably accurate picture of an average day's usage. The results demonstrated that to match the usage of one bound set of Chemical abstracts we would need two microfilm sets and twelve microfilm readers. We concluded therefore that we were better off as we were, even though we were losing the advantage of easy production of hard copy.

Although one can obtain factual information in this way, obviously it is the interpretation of these facts that is important in the making of management decisions. For example a study of the use of periodical literature within a particular information and library service may well be biased because of the availability to the users of the titles actually held. In such a case it is best to check the findings against those in one of the more general surveys that have been made, in the same subject area if one exists for that subject (8).

In evaluating both systems and services, we need to have various measures of effectiveness. Over the last few years work has been carried out in the field of what is now known as 'bibliometrics', and for library operations several measures are becoming reasonably well established. However, there is a need for more research to be done on measures of effectiveness in the supply and use of information. Perhaps before long we shall have a science of 'infometrics', and be able to calculate the value of the information which we supply.

*Network analysis*
In examining and evaluating systems and services, and particularly in planning the implementation of new services, there is a group of techniques available to guide the manager in his decision making. The general term to describe them is 'network analysis', and the individual techniques include PERT (Program evaluation and review), PEP (Program evaluation procedure),

SCANS (Scheduling and control by automated network), and CPM (Critical path method). Some of these methods are used to analyse very large networks. For example, it has been estimated that the completion time of the Polaris missile system was reduced from 7 years to 5 years by this type of planning. For our purposes the critical path method, which is not difficult to apply, can prove a useful technique.

A project consists of a series of activities which are interrelated, and these can be represented diagrammatically as a network. The critical path through this network is the one which links those activities which are critical in the sense that if any one of them is not completed on time, then the completion of the whole project will be delayed. The elementary form of critical path analysis is concerned only with the time of the activities. A more advanced form also takes into consideration the relationship between time and costs. The technique can be used to plan and control a project, and is also useful when a deadline has to be met, because it will show those activities which will require increased manpower in order to be completed within the required time. I have used CPM to plan the implementation of large computerized information storage and retrieval systems, and more recently to analyse the interrelationships of the activities involved in the final examination of students.

*Personnel management*
Let us turn now to techniques used in the management of personnel. As I indicated in my introductory remarks, because we operate our services through people and for people, this is the most important area of management with which we are involved. The 'motivation' of staff has been investigated fairly thoroughly and it is generally accepted that the factors involved in motivation fall into two groups. There are the 'dissatisfiers' which deal with conditions relating to the work situation, such as pay, working conditions, company organization and policy. These can and do lead to various levels of dissatisfaction, but rarely lead to positive feelings about the job. On the other hand, the 'satisfiers' which are characteristics associated with a specific task, such as achievement, recognition, advancement, value of the work, produce favourable reactions to the job. The Information Manager can often only indirectly influence the negative dissatisfying factors; and if he wants to have a staff who are competent, capable and happy in their work then he must see that the 'satisfiers' are all present and correct (9).

One of the techniques which appears to offer this state of affairs is management by objectives, usually referred to as MbO. Now I have heard a certain amount of cynical comment on MbO; some managers have said they prefer MbM—management by management, and others that they go for MbBO—management by being objectionable. However I think we should look at what MbO has to offer and see whether any of it is of value in a service environment.

MbO has been defined as a dynamic system which seeks to integrate the company's need to achieve its goals of profit and growth, with the manager's need to contribute and develop himself (10). If the technique is to be successful there has to be whole-hearted company commitment.

The first stage consists of strategic planning. The company's performance, strengths and limitations have to be assessed, together with the external environment and the expectations of the shareholders. This assessment leads to the clarification of company objectives, and to the evaluation of alternative courses of action. The next stage is tactical planning. This covers a whole range of activities including the planning of the organization itself, planning for product and market development, resource development, and actual operations. From this stage the detailed plans emerge and unit objectives can be agreed with individual managers.

The manager himself is informed of the main purpose of his job, his position in the organization and the limits of his authority. He is also concerned with the preparation of an analysis of key tasks within his unit. This analysis shows for each key task the performance standard by which the progress of the work is to be measured. This can be qualitative, in the sense of a judgement on how well it is done; but is usually quantitative in the sense of how much work is done, can it be completed more quickly?, can the costs be reduced? The analysis also gives the control data by which the performance standards can be metered, and any suggestions for improvement. Plans can then be drawn up for the improvement of these jobs and obviously must be agreed with the people who are doing them. In fact the best results can come from this if staff are given a fairly free hand to devise their own improved standards, although, like Father O'Flynn, the manager must always be

> 'Checking de crazy ones
> Coaxing unaisy ones
> Lifting de lazy ones
> On wid de stick.'

Each member of staff, and this includes the manager, has certain needs in order to do a better job. The first is agreement on what is expected from him. This is met by clarifying unit and personal objectives, and by drawing up job improvement plans. The second need is to be given the opportunity

189

to carry out his work effectively and this is met by proper organizational planning so that each person knows the range of his activities and authority, and that there is no overlap or underlap. The third need is to be informed of how he is getting on. This is done by agreeing with him performance standards and time schedule, and by a regular series of performance review meetings. The fourth need is for guidance in achieving improvement and this is met by training.

Training is of vital importance in staff development. It is no use the manager looking for improved standards if the staff are, through lack of knowledge, not capable of reaching these levels. For each member of staff it is necessary to compare the required performance with present abilities, identify the training needs, and then ensure that training is given. It may be on-the-job training that is needed, or perhaps one or more short courses will provide the necessary knowledge. One must also look beyond the present job and identify training needs for the future, both for the person whose job is changing because of different requirements or new systems, and for the person who is being considered for promotion to a higher level job.

The main points that emerge from an examination of MbO are the formulation of objectives, the involvement of staff at all levels in the effective furtherance of those objectives, and the continuous need for staff training. Now most information units are small. The 2-3 man band is fairly common; and, probably because most of us operate in these small groups, we have long been aware of the fact that good service is given by efficient team work. All our staff tend to be deeply involved in the operation of the information unit, simply because we cannot carry passengers and so we learn to either recognize them before we appoint them, or, if we have made a mistake in the appointment, to move that mistake smartly on to somewhere else. When it comes to objectives, we have perhaps been a bit slow in putting them down on paper, but the sense of purpose and dedication that is found in most information units shows that staff are fully aware of what the unit is trying to do. John Humble, the leading authority on MbO, has said 'The best managers have always practised Management by Objectives', and I think we can go along with that statement.

However, the sort of thing that can happen which leads to cynicism about MbO, is the introduction of the system by a company and the insistence of higher management that all increased performance shall be measured quantitatively. In most service environments this leads to difficulty, but for suppliers of information it is a real problem. What is the

190

value of the information we gave to Dr Bloggs? He doesn't really know and neither do we. How can we increase this value? If we usually put about 200 abstracts in our weekly bulletin, will stepping it up to 300 be an increase in performance? Well it may be in one sense but it is likely to be counter-productive in that the smaller bulletin may have been scanned regularly whereas the larger will be put to one side to be read later—which means never.

The important factor in an information service is its quality and this can only be assessed by judgement; and the Information Manager has to have the confidence and ability to make these judgements and be able to justify them. If we must show performance improvements then let us demonstrate our effectiveness by having a rapid response time to requests for service, and by supplying only the information required, not too little and not too much.

I have heard of a certain company that introduced a partial MbO scheme in which all members of staff were to hold meetings in their units and departments to prepare task analyses and work improvement targets. They were also to discuss with members of other departments the effect of any proposed changes on those departments. The carrot was a rise all round for each department as soon as it had produced and had accepted by higher management, its improvement plan, together with a quantification of the money saved annually by the plan; this latter being the stick that went with the carrot.

The first effect of this scheme was that most communication within the company ceased overnight. Nobody could contact anybody else because everybody was in a meeting. What this cost the company I shudder to think, but I am certain that it would have had to save a lot of money through the improvement plans before it even began to balance the cost. The second effect was that, particularly in the service departments, there was an insistence on reduction of overheads which could often only be achieved by cutting down on staff, which in turn led to failure of services. Often the enforced cancellation of a service led to the work being done at a greater cost within those departments who had previously received, what was to them, an essential service. It is not surprising that one of the end products of this exercise was an increase in staff union activity. The moral of this cautionary tale is that if the MbO system has to be implemented, it must be remembered that an essential part of the scheme, when properly applied, is that benefits accrue to the staff as well as to the company. And this is only right and proper, for what is one without the other?

## Job evaluation and staff assessment

In implementing a personnel policy, the manager has constantly to be aware of the value of the individual jobs in his department, and the worth of the person in each job. The former is dealt with by the technique of job evaluation and the latter by staff assessment. Although distinct, the two are obviously interrelated, because the remuneration of staff, even when dependent on ability, will still lie within a particular scale based on the estimated value of the work done.

There are many different methods for assessing job values but most of them concentrate on the characteristics of the work being done and the mental and physical attributes needed to do the job to an acceptable level. A typical scheme might award points on a scale for the degree of responsibility required in, for example, such matters as number of staff controlled, number of communications (ie the disruption factor) and level of decision making. The total of the points awarded to the various factors determines the pay scale. Information Managers obviously have to operate the particular scheme used in their company, and do so with fairness. It is often difficult to slot information activities into schemes designed for less specialized activities, and information staff can suffer because of this. The remedy is to obtain special interpretations of the information jobs in relation to the scheme, and also for the manager to be constantly aware of the salaries for similar jobs being offered on the open market. It is true that many job advertisements do not specify salaries, but if an information manager needs comparative figures he can ask Aslib for help. Also the Library Association, who keep a close watch on salaries in special libraries and information units, can often provide the information needed.

Staff assessment fills two roles. It used to decide such matters as the annual increment (or annual insult, if you prefer to look at it that way); and also the personal maximum within a job grade. Assessment is usually against certain performance criteria (here, of course, there is a link with MbO) and certain personal factors. I am sure that many of us have met the problem of making an assessment of a person who is capable and efficient in performance, but personally gets up the backs of both information staff and customers.

The assessment is usually made by the person's immediate supervisor, and should be followed by an interview (which can be with the supervisor concerned or with the supervisor's boss) at which the assessment is discussed, and the person involved can agree or disagree, giving reasons for the latter. His views are then recorded on the assessment form and signed by both people present as an agreed accurate record.

192

I have tried various ways of making assessments but this was the only one that worked. On one occasion I suggested to the staff that, using a standard form, they should assess themselves. This turned out to be just one more time when democracy did not appeal. I was told in no uncertain terms that I was the one who was paid to manage the department, that they were not going to do my work for me, and that I could get on and do the assessment myself, otherwise I knew what I could do with it.

## Finance

It was St Paul who said that the love of money is the root of all evils. This may be true but it does not prevent us having to face up to the problems of financial management, which in our terms means obtaining adequate resources to operate our services, and using those resources effectively and efficiently. Within any organization there is only a certain amount of money available for internal services, and it is the information manager's job to see that he gets a fair share of the cake. If he can get better than a fair share then more power to his elbow but he had better keep a sharp lookout for Nemesis.

How do we go about getting our fair share? The traditional approach requires an annual estimate for expenditure under the usual headings of staff, stock, stationery, etc, and this is usually done by taking last year's figures and adding certain percentages for inflation, plus additional amounts for planned new activities. The estimates, or more usually the modified and reduced estimates are accepted and become the annual expenditure budget; and, if your accounting department is good, every month you will be told what you have spent under each heading. But none of this really helps you answer the top-managerial question which is usually framed in the form 'Good heavens—80 percent of your budget on staff—you'd better justify that—or else!'

The Planning-Programming-Budgeting System, PPBS for short, is a useful technique for showing the cost of each of your activities (11, 12). Once again we have to start from the unit's objectives. If you operate MbO in any form, then the unit objectives will have been defined and can be used for PPBS. The next stage is to list the activities of the information unit and ensure that each of them is justified in terms of the objectives. This can be a useful stage at which to review your activities to see whether any of them are now no longer necessary, or need modification to fit changed requirements.

There are several ways in which a manager could analyse and list the activities of his department. When I carried out this exercise I divided them into two main categories—operational and service. The former consists of four main groups or programmes, namely acquisition of materials; preparation of indexes; stock control and maintenance; and evaluation of services and systems. The latter has five programmes—current awareness; information retrieval; reference and loan; supply and distribution; and training and advisory. Each of these programmes has a number of elements: SDI, abstract bulletins, periodical circulation. For each of these elements cost of the activity is derived. As I was particularly interested in the full cost of the various information services provided I went a stage beyond this and found out the proportion of operational costs which supported each service. These were then transferred to the service elements thus giving the complete costs. In some cases it turned out to be surprisingly lower than I would have guessed, and the converse was true as well.

When all the activities have been costed in this way, the manager, having checked to see that the total of all the costs equals his traditional budget total, is in a position to do several things. First he can cost alternative and/or modified methods for providing the same service. This would demonstrate whether what he is doing is cost-effective or not, because another method which is cheaper, but still preserves the quality of the service, may emerge from his analysis. This could of course be an external commercial service as an alternative to in-house service. Secondly by adding to each factor in the costing the appropriate percentage increase for each of, say, the next five years, he can see if unacceptable increases in costs are likely to occur for any particular service, and also estimate his future budgets with a higher degree of accuracy.

All this derives from PPBS. There is however a further stage beyond PPBS which can help the manager when he is called upon to justify a particular service, or his costs for a particular activity. It is not an easy stage because the information required is often difficult to obtain. The manager looks at the use made of each of his information services, and then calculates what it would cost the users to obtain the information for themselves *if the service did not exist.* The difference between the cost of supplying the service and the costs when no service exists can be regarded as the cost-benefit accruing to the service. The total of all the differences will give the cost-benefits which arise from the information unit as a whole. As I said earlier we still do not have any accurate way of measuring the value of information supplied to a customer, but the cost-benefit of the service is the next-best-thing, and the value of the information, whatever it is, should be a bonus on top. But when it is suggested to an Information Manager that he could stop a particular service, he has figures to show what it will cost to do without the service.

## Conclusion

There are many other management techniques that can be used in the operation of information services. If I had attempted to cover them all, this paper would have read like a catalogue. If I missed out your favourite technique, I apologize; but naturally I preferred to discuss those of which I have made use myself. Also, although I have spoken separately about techniques relating to systems, services, staff and finance, I would not wish to give the impression that they operate independently. PPBS, for example, although concerned with costs, covers all the other categories to which I have referred. And it is possible to build up your own package of interrelated techniques. Maurice Magson has recently written about the linked use of MbO, work measurement, activity sampling, critical examination and programmed budgeting (13).

Finally in evaluating or implementing any technique for use in your unit please do bear in mind that the quality of a service is more important than any quantitative measurement, and that staff morale and their trust in you as their manager, are fragile things, which once broken take a long time to recover.

## References

1 Burns, R W: 'A generalised methodology for library systems analysis , College and research libraries, 32 (4), July 1971, 295-303.

2 Gull, C D: 'Logical flow charts and other new techniques for the administration of libraries and information centers', Library resources and technical services, 12 (1), Winter 1968, 47-66.

3 Mumford, E: Systems design for people. National Computing Centre Ltd, 1971.

4 Leimkuhler, F: Mathematical models for library systems analysis. School of Industrial Engineering, Purdue University, 1967. PB176113.

5 Buckland, M K, et al: Systems analysis of a university library. University of Lancaster Library, 1970.

6 Buckland, M K: 'An operations research study of a variable loan and duplication policy at the University of Lancaster', Library quarterly, 42 (1), January 1972, 97-106.

7 Brophy, P: A library management game. University of Lancaster Library, 1972.

8 Brittain, J M: Information and its users. Bath University Press, 1970. (Chapters 1 and 2).

9 Mason, D: 'Problems of getting—and keeping—staff', Aslib proceedings, 18 (1) January 1966, 6-15.

10 Humble, J: Improving business results. McGraw-Hill, 1968.

11 Mason, D: 'PPBS: application to an industrial information and library service, Journal of librarianship, 4 (2), April 1972, 91-105.

12 Mason, D: 'Programmed budgeting and cost-effectiveness', Aslib proceedings, 25 (3) March 1973, 100-110.

13 Magson, M S: 'Techniques for the measurement of cost-benefit in information centres', Aslib proceedings, 25 (5) May 1973, 164-185.

# BIBLIOTHECONOMICS: OR
# LIBRARY SCIENCE REVISITED

*A Graham Mackenzie*

Since I became a librarian, more years ago than I care to remember, I have never been ehtirely happy to use the phrase 'library science' as a description of what I do from day to day, or even of the theoretical basis which under-lies all my practical work. I was brought up in a scientific environment, and 'library science' in its present sense does not meet the criteria which have been accepted as the basis of scientific method since the time of the Renaissance. A true science proceeds in a fairly standard way: observation, measurement, hypothesis, and testing the hypothesis by conducting a re-peatable experiment—and this, I think, must be true even in the less quanti-tative social sciences, among which librarianship must be included if it is to be called a science at all, rather than an art or mere set of techniques.

As a social science it is subject to the same drawbacks as the others: a library is a complicated ecosystem; like a human being it is an individual, and no two are exactly alike. Hence it is difficult to observe a library in detail, and even more difficult to carry out experiments on it, for two reasons: first there is the Hawthorne effect (which says, basically, that the mere fact that you are carrying out an experiment tends to affect the results—a sort of sociological equivalent of Heisenberg's Uncertainty Prin-ciple); and secondly, perhaps more important to the practising librarian, since libraries are one-off, unique, it is very difficult to establish a con-trolled and repeatable experiment. In addition, any experiment must have some effect on standards of service—there is some parallel here with the doctor who claimed to have a cure for the disease which had always been fatal until then; he was cross-examined on this matter of some importance, and defended his claim vigorously, adducing all kinds of facts. Finally his inquisitors were almost convinced, but as final proof wished to interrogate the patients; 'You can't do that,' replied the doctor, 'I cured the disease, but unfortunately the patients all died!'

I think the librarian-experimenter runs something of the same risk as the mythical doctor: he has an obligation to his university, or college, or town, or county council, to provide as good a service as his means allow, and it would be very difficult to justify providing a different level of service for two otherwise similar groups of users, which is the normal way of doing a controlled experiment. (You could not, for example, deny some students access to the shelves for a year to see how this affected their examination results.)

We are, then, in some difficulty with 'library science'. This is not to deny that there is a flourishing library *technology*; the distinction corresponds to that generally accepted to lie between pure and applied science. We have largely in the past concentrated on the applied side; understandably, perhaps, since the librarian as manager inevitably needs answers to the pressing problems of the day—how best to reproduce his catalogue cards, to record issues, to classify, even to design sophisticated computer systems which will do everything except brew the tea! To my mind, however, this does not constitute science—it does not go to the root of the matter as 'pure' research should. Our profession is rapidly approaching a crossroads: we have held—for many years—the belief that we instinctively *know* what a library should be like; and indeed there may well be something in this belief.

On the other hand, it may be that some of our accepted ideas have little foundation on fact: if we take, for example, the question of size, it has never been *proved* that the biggest library is necessarily the best—there is some evidence to the contrary, at least enough to make us want to examine this axiom critically. Size is only one of the matters we need to ask about if we are to construct a valid theoretical substructive on which to base our professional lives, and if we are to raise ourselves from the somewhat doubtful position we sometimes occupy in the eyes of outsiders (I was once told by the head of an ancient university—and he was quite serious—that his librarian's only task was to buy what he was told to buy and put it on a shelf!). Thank goodness, most of us have progressed beyond this stage; but we have not in the main achieved the same kind of standing as, say, the physicist or the philosopher—and we will not do so until we can meet the criteria of the scientist I mentioned before.

I have probably said enough to convince you that the term 'library science' as we know it, is an overstatement; yet I am sure you would agree that librarianship is potentially something more than an art and a collection of miscellaneous techniques (although I would not deny that these are important as well).

The major question facing us today may sound simple; but to my knowledge nobody has ever answered it satisfactorily: 'What is the job of the librarian?' We all think we know, or we wouldn't hold our present posts; the traditional answer is to provide for our readers more books and better access to the information contained in them. And up to a point this is true in theory; but we are in a real-life situation—show me the librarian who claims he has enough money and I will show you a liar! We can, perhaps, develop our hypothesis about the librarian's job slightly—tentatively we can now say that it has become 'to provide a service to his readers at the optimum combination of high success rate and low cost.' This, of course, is only a first approximation, and indeed the word 'optimum' begs a great many questions; but with the introduction of the vital factor, cost, I think you will now see the relevance of the title of this paper—Bibliotheconomics: this I defined as managing a library economically and rationally, in the light of all relevant circumstances. (Like Humpty-Dumpty, I can make it mean what I like, since I invented it!)

Now I am sure that every librarian *tries* to manage his library economically—we are, in the main, conscientious public servants—and some of them do it very successfully; nevertheless, even those who succeed are, so to speak, flying by the seat of their pants. Their decisions are constantly influenced by their psychology, their previous training and experience, by local or university politics, sometimes even by whether they have a hangover from last night's party! It is the aim of bibliotheconomics to give the librarian a tool to aid him to use reason, or science, rather than intuition, in performing his management function; if you like, to justify the 'science' in 'library science'.

To become a science as I have defined it we must do four things: observe, measure, hypothesize, experiment. We can certainly do the first three: we observe (say) reader behaviour; we measure by making surveys or 'instant diaries' (in passing, this is a vastly over-rated and dangerous procedure: in 30 months' work at Lancaster we are very proud that we only administered two questionnaires to our readers, and one of these was done for an outside body!); we can hypothesize up to a point—but can we experiment in a scientific way?

My belief is that we can, in spite of what I said earlier. It requires great self-confidence (some of my colleagues have called it brashness) to experiment *in vivo*, with all the possible consequences to the library system and its users; it is certainly very difficult to control such experiments satisfactorily. However, when an aircraft designer has a new idea he doesn't just commandeer a factory and spend £20m building the thing—he makes a model and tests it in a wind tunnel to make sure it won't crash, that it will do the job he wants it to do, and that it is better than the planes built by existing methods. The key concept here is the *model;* and there are in existence techniques by which we can build models of even quite complex abstract systems such as large organisations—in fact, many of our industrial giants, such as Shell and ICI, maintain quite large staffs doing exactly this.

Of course, the models they build don't fly; they don't even exist in a physical sense, but they perform the same function as those in the wind tunnel—they allow various decisions to be followed through, and all the consequences to be examined in detail to see how other parts of the organisation may be affected. It is this kind of technique which I believe should be applied to libraries.

Almost 30 years ago a group of mathematicians was created in the Royal Air Force with a specific task: to analyse the results of raids on Germany and to devise methods of making Bomber Command more effective in destroying the Nazi war machine. This was the origin of what was known, for obvious reasons at the time, as Operational Research. The name has stuck, for although the techniques have advanced beyond all recognition and the purposes behind them have changed, it is still basically the same thing—the use of scientific method (especially mathematics and statistics) to guide decision making in the managerial process. It doesn't matter whether you are managing Bomber Command, ICI, or Puddleton College of Education Library, OR is still potentially a very valuable tool: it won't provide all the answers, even given perfect information input; value judgements must still be made by experienced managers; but OR can tell them the probable results of any particular course of action.

Standard OR procedure can be broken down into four parts: define the objectives of the organisation (perhaps, for a firm, maximum profit over 20 years, subject to certain constraints such as the law of the land and the maintenance of good working conditions); flow-chart all processes, both manufacturing and managerial, in whatever detail may be necessary; construct a mathematical model, using the appropriate equations to describe each process or operation; lastly, use the model to optimise the whole operation so that the highest possible proportion of each of the given objectives is attained. The whole procedure is fairly well understood, and in the case of industry there is no doubt that it works; when we come to look at libraries, however, there is one fundamental difference: their objectives are not to make a profit and therefore cannot be so easily defined; this is the crucial phase of any OR study. We know too little about how people use libraries, and more important, how they *should* use them to get the best results. Until a great deal of work has been done in this area (the 'library/user interface') a full OR study is not practicable.

Nevertheless, some of the techniques can be used without necessarily having full information about every aspect of a library's operations; and to illustrate this I should like to talk about some work we have been doing at Lancaster for the past three and a half years. We are lucky there on many counts, but especially on two: we have extremely active and cooperative departments of Operational Research, Systems Engineering and Educational Research, as well as a Vice-Chancellor interested in library problems; and secondly we obtained a grant from OSTI which supported one and one-half research workers for 30 months. The project was entitled 'Systems analysis of a university library'; although it did not fully achieve its stated end (from the beginning it was clear that a complete analysis would be quite beyond our resources) it did teach us a lot about methodology in an almost virgin territory, and brought in its train some significant improvements in the library services to the university.

The first step in any OR study is to define the objectives of the organisation being studied; and not in any vague manner—since most OR techniques depend on mathematics the objectives themselves must be expressed in quantitative terms. With a library service, as I said earlier, this is far from easy; in fact, I must confess here and now that for three and a half years we have found it quite impossible, with present knowledge. It is comparatively easy to do for certain sub-systems: for example, if we take the technical processes between the time a book is recommended for purchase and the time it first reaches the shelves, we can say that the objective is to see that these processes are carried out as cheaply as possible, subject to the constraints that the backlog at any one stage is never more than x days' work, and that the standard of processing (eg cataloguing) should not drop below a defined level. Of course this level, and the value of x, depend on a value judgment of the library manager; but by adopting various values we can construct our model and play with it to our hearts' content.

This approach, however, is not entirely satisfactory: the danger is that if we optimise a number of sub-systems it may become impossible to optimise the system as a whole, since each sub-system may add a new set of constraints which taken together are self-contradictory. As an hypothetical example, in technical processing it might seem desirable to adopt (as indeed many libraries have done) a 'non-conflict' rule for main entry headings in the catalogue; this will clearly save considerable time in cataloguing and thus achieve cost savings; but if we suppose that another

201

section of the library operates a bibliographical service which requires full forenames, then it may well be worth spending extra money to establish these originally as a routine process in spite of the increased cost.

It was precisely this difficulty at Lancaster which led to our abandoning the modelling of technical processes and concentrating rather on library use: until we know more about the interaction with users and their demands we felt it would be a waste of effort to spend a lot of time on subsystems; nevertheless we have a model available which can, at some future date, be 'plugged in' and used to allocate our manpower resources in the best way.

One of the major problems in an academic library is the provision for undergraduates of required or recommended reading on a big enough scale: when there are, say, 200 students needing the same group of 20 titles for an essay in the space of one month the librarian has to take action of some kind. I want now to illustrate the OR approach by describing our investigations in this area: they are not perhaps earth-shaking in their novelty, but they do show the attitude of mind which we have tried to adopt.

From the very earliest days of the university we had recognised the problem of required reading: we had, and still have, a Short Loan Collection of about 3,000 volumes (perhaps 1,800–2,000 titles) at any given time; these are kept on closed access, and, as the name implies, lent only for 4 hours or overnight. We therefore had a rare situation in an open-access library—a heavily-used collection whose total use could be measured, but in addition one for which we could accurately observe the *demand* in addition to the actual use. We felt that this offered an opportunity to learn more about reader habits; perhaps any relationships discovered could then be extended to the more usual open-access situation.

Four factors seemed to be important in analysing this particular type of library use: number of requests for a given title; loan period (4 hours); number of copies; and standard of service, defined as the percentage of total demands which were immediately satisfied. By recording demands and actual use, and by assuming that the demands arrive according to the Poisson distribution (later investigation showed that this was almost certainly true) it is fairly easy to construct a table showing the number of copies of a title which will achieve any given standard of service for a given request rate: thus if one can expect 7 requests per day for a title, 1 copy will give a satisfaction level of 47 percent, 2 copies gives 77 percent, 3 gives 92 percent, and 4 only 97 percent. It is therefore probably *not* economic to buy the 4th copy, since it will improve the service on only 5 occasions out of every 100 requests.

From this investigation, which is probably of theoretical rather than practical value (for it is difficult to predict the request-rate for any individual title) we turned to a study of the more general case of the open-access library, and how availability of books in it would be affected by changing loan policies or other parameters.

Every library has a loan policy, even if it reads 'No books will be lent'; in an academic library, university staff traditionally have the benefit of a more generous policy than students either in length of loan or number of volumes out at a time, and there will probably be several different loan policies hidden in the regulations of the library.

It is axiomatic that one of the main objectives of a university library is to provide required reading for students; yet it cannot afford massive duplication for this purpose (at least with grants at a British, as opposed to an American, level) if it is to perform its other main function to acquire and store other materials on a scale which will satisfy the research worker. There is a straight conflict of interest here, and since books are scarce one of two approaches must be adopted: you can ration the student either by time or by the number of books he can have in his possession; conceivably you can do both, but this is expensive in staff time, and is probably not necessary. This factor, staff time, has led a number of libraries in the past ten years to adopt a single-slip issue system, with which it is difficult to enforce return after a stated period, since there is no date-file of issues.

At first sight this is an attractive idea: all books are lent, say, until the end of the term; students are limited to 3 or 6 on loan at one time, and by a combination of this and an efficient recall and reservation system it seems that all reasonable student needs will be met. In fact, this was the system which I originally adopted at Lancaster, based on previous experience elsewhere: I had no doubt that it was an economical system—only one issue file to maintain instead of two (or even three, as some universities have), plus an absence of renewals at most periods of the year, enabled me to keep the service desk staff to a minimum, and hence I believed that the library was running efficiently and economically.

Unfortunately there is a flaw in this reasoning, which became apparent when we were examining our objectives and levels of performance: we found that in our Short Loan Collection (books on 4-hour loan) that the availability rate was about 90 percent, or, in other words, that 9 out of 10 requests were being met immediatley. This made us think about standards of service generally, and examine what was happening with the open-access collections: it seemed that availability was only about 60 percent, which was judged to be too low. This situation had not been apparent: we were not getting complaints about the service, and the number of reservations was not high; we therefore had no reason to expect that all was not well.

When we had measured availability we started to wonder *why* there were few complaints and reservations in a situation where one might expect them: there are no definite answers to this, but we suspect that 4 factors are involved: 1) new students generally have no standards of comparison—they accept what they find as normal; 2) they tend on the whole to go straight to the shelves rather than use the catalogue (especially the classified catalogue) and hence only choose from the books on the shelves; 3) they do not like using the reservation procedures, even though these work well—perhaps because when they need a specific book they do not wish to wait even 2 or 3 days for it; 4) the mere expectation that in 4 cases out of 10 they will *not* get the book they want immediately is in itself a disincentive to looking for it—they will seek other sources of information or reading material, and overall use of the library service will decrease.

In passing, note that this situation is a good example of the difficulty of defining objectives: the service was, to our knowledge, running economically, in that few staff were engaged in it; it was running efficiently, in that we were doing what we were being asked to do. From a cost effectiveness point of view, therefore, things were all right, since effectiveness was being achieved cheaply, at a low unit cost per loan; but taking the cost-benefit point of view, we were doing very badly, since the library as a whole was only meeting at most 60 percent of its potential demand.

We had, then, a classic OR situation: we had a sub-system of the library, with defined objectives—to maximise book availability at minimum cost; we could measure both sides of the equation, and proceeded to do so, and to construct a mathematical model of demand and supply, using a computer programme to simulate the library service and the demands on it (this in itself was an interesting technical exercise in logic and flow-charting). Once we had the model (which we tested by using real data), we could apply various differing sets of borrowing regulations and find out which seemed to be likely to give the best results.

Analysis of the problem gave two parameters which seemed to be crucial: Satisfaction Level, which is for any given period of time the proportion of demands which can be satisfied immediately; and Collection Bias, which is the proportion of the most-popular 10 percent of the collection absent from the shelves at any given time (a high collection bias means that the enquirer finds a collection on the shelves which systematically tends towards the least popular—and hence the least useful—books). Sampling of the existing situation gave a figure of 60 percent for Satisfaction Level and 45 percent for Collection Bias: these were deemed to be unacceptable, and I, as librarian, made the value judgment that we should aim at increasing S to 80 percent and reducing B to 20 percent. These figures were fed into the model, and three methods of achieving them were proposed.

The first was the relatively simple one of massive duplication; this would have cost perhaps £15,000 initially and £2,000 a year thereafter. The second was to change the loan regulations so that students would have a 2-week loan period, instead of a term; the cost of this would have been perhaps £1,500 pa in junior staff. The third method—the one which we finally implemented—was calculated to give the highest S (86 percent) and the lowest B (8 percent) of the three, and to cost about £2,000 pa in junior staff to handle the increased work load. This set of loan policies is non-traditional: it allots different loan periods not on the basis of the status of the borrower, but according to the popularity of the individual book, irrespective of whether the borrower is the Vice-Chancellor, a first year student, or Joe Soap, the cleaner. Such a principle is, of course, not new for sub-sets of a library's holdings—most academics are used to some variant of a reserved-book collection with a short loan period; but so far as I know it has never been adopted for a total collection.

It rests on the assumption that in general it is possible to predict, from part use as recorded on a date label, how a given title will be used in future. This has been demonstrated quite often, notably by Fussler & Simon at Chicago*; and it seemed to us that it was a hypothesis worth testing in detail. Our model indicated that 10 percent of the book-stock generated 70 percent of all loans; and it seemed that by restricting this 10 percent of books to 7-day loan the S level would be about 86 percent. The remainder of the stock could then stay on term-loan, with all the convenience to the reader that such a system brings.

Possible objections were, of course, considered: the number of renewals might defeat the system, and make extra work at the service desk; 7 days is not enough time to keep a book; the work of identifying the 10 percent of popular books would be too great, and possibly accurate prediction is not feasible. However, it appeared from our investigation that readers tend to return books at the due date, rather than before it, no matter how long the official loan period is, and that the length of loan makes little difference to the number of renewals; and we were confident that we could identify popular books quite readily. Accordingly the regulations were changed in October, 1969.

What has happened? First of all—and this to my mind makes the whole exercise worth while—the number of books borrowed has more than doubled, although the student body has increased by only 25 percent;

since the bulk of the increase is in single borrowings, rather than renewals, it is clear that the slight personal inconvenience of having to return books after only 7 days is more than counter-balanced by the general gain to the university of much greater library use—in other words, our productivity or cost-benefit index has soared.

Secondly, we shall in due course be able to test the Fussler hypothesis that past use is a good indicator of future use.

Thirdly, we have demonstrated that OR work of this type is feasible in a library situation, even although it is not yet possible to model a total system; as a result of this the university has set up a permanent Library Research Unit, staffed at least partly from UGC funds, which can undertake research and development work within the library, or for outside bodies under normal contract research procedures.

It is clear that we do not yet understand enough about libraries and how they interact with thier users to lay down a firm set of optimum procedures; my guess is that such understanding is at least 10 years in the future, depending as it does on many man-years of research in many relevant disciplines. Nevertheless, even now a methodology is slowly beginning to emerge by which the librarian can investigate his own procedures, and base his management on such investigations and techniques rather than on the traditional contemplation of his navel.

*Note*
\* Fussler, H H, and J L Simon: Patterns in the use of books in large research libraries, 2nd edition. University of Chicago Press, 1969.

# Conclusion

In this reader we have been dealing with the management of organizations called libraries.

Management is not a skill which is exercised only by the senior professionals. It must be appreciated and exercised at all levels. Everyone has to take decisions which have a bearing on the efficiency and the effectiveness of the library. A generalization might be that staff with less responsibility are concerned with decisions about efficiency, and that, as staff gain more responsibility they take decisions about the effectiveness of the library. Top decision-making is (or should be) primarily about benefits, or the value of the service. We do not pretend that everyone can be as competent as a fully trained manager in the application of the techniques of management. Some of these techniques require specialist knowledge and experience which is not often in the possession of readers of this book. On the other hand, it is very important that staff in libraries are able to identify and define the problems that really matter, and that they are able to discuss these problems intelligibly with management experts. The often quoted 'interest in books and people' is obviously a central requirement for anyone working in a library, but this statement leaves out an equally important phrase: a desire to bring the two together. In a soft area like the library service, this is not as easy as it looks.

To help you, some of the many management theories referred to in this book offer various paradigms of the situation: classical/human relations, theory X/theory Y, hard/soft, mechanistic/organic, systems/action. None of these provide a total explanation. Some are more useful than others and there are no prizes for guessing which ones we prefer. You probably realise by now, even if you did not before, that an interest in 'books and people' and an involvement in the management of an organization called a library which aims to bring the two together requires some appreciation of scientific method, sociology and psychology.

The essence of management is a conscious and systematic attempt to organize the resources available to achieve the goals desired. In a library, as in any organization, the goals are not always what they seem to be. They conflict. Some are accepted by one part of the organization and not by the remainder. Management decisions in a library have to take into account all the people involved and their value systems in an attempt to produce the services which are possible within the real (not imagined) constraints. These services must be demonstrably of value to the users and potential users, and it must be judged cost-effective for the particular library to supply these services.

# Bibliography

[Bains report. 1972.] Great Britain. Department of the Environment: The new local authorities management and structure. HMSO, 1972.

Baker, R J S (1975): 'Systems theory and local government', Local government studies 1(1) New series Jan 1975, 21-36.

Beer, Stafford (1966): Decision and control. The meaning of operational research and management cybernetics. John Wiley & Sons, 1966.

Beer, Stafford (1967): Management science. The business use of operations research. Aldus Books, 1967.

Beer, Stafford (1975): Platform for change. John Wiley & Sons, 1975.

Beishon, J, and G Peters, eds (1972): Systems behaviour. Open University Press, 1972.

Bellomy, F L (1968): 'The systems approach solves library problems', ALA bulletin 62, 1968, 1121-5.

Bertalanffy, L von (1971): General systems theory. Allen Lane: The Penguin Press, 1971.

Blasingame, R, and M J Lynch (1974): 'Design for diversity: alternatives to standards for public libraries', PLA newsletter 13(2), June 1974, 4-22.

Bone, L E (1975): 'The public library goals and objectives movement', Library journal 100(3), July 1975, 1283-6.

Brookes, B C (1970): 'The viability of branch libraries', Journal of librarianship 2(1), Jan 1970, 14-21.

Brown, R, and R Surridge, eds (1974): Output measurement. Public Libraries Research Group, 1974.

Buckland, M K, A Hindle, A G Mackenzie, and I Woodburn (1970): Systems analysis of a university library. University of Lancaster Library, 1970. (University of Lancaster Library Occasional papers no 4.)

Burns, T, and G M Stalker (1968): The management of innovation, 2nd edition. Tavistock, 1968.

Cooper, M D (1973): 'The economics of information' in: Cuadra, C A, ed: Annual review of information science and technology, Vol 8. American Society for Information Science, 1973, 5-40.

De Prospo, E, E Altman and K Beasley (1973): Performance measures for public libraries. ALA, PLA, 1973.

Elton, M, and B Vickery (1973): 'The scope for operational research in the library and information field', Aslib proceedings 25(8), Aug 1973, 305-19.

Etzioni, A (1959): 'Authority structure and organisational effectiveness', Administration science q 4(8), June 1959, 43-67. Reprinted in Wasserman, P, and M L Bundy: Reader in library administration. NCR Microcard Editions, 1968, 193-205.

Flowerdew, A D J, and C M E Whitehead (1974): Cost-effectiveness and cost/benefit analysis in information science. London School of Economics and Political Science, 1974. (Report on OSTI project S1/97/03.)

Fothergill, R, ed (1971): A challenge for libraries. National Council for Educational Technology in association with Aslib, Audio Visual Group, 1971. (Working paper no 4.)

Fothergill, R, ed (1973): Resource centres in colleges of education. National Council for Educational Technology, 1973. (Working paper no 10.)

Gilchrist, A (1973): 'Objectively speaking', Information scientist 7(2), June 1973, 37-42.

Great Britain. Department of Education and Science (1973): Aspects of public library management. HMSO, 1973.

Green, Daniel M (1964): 'The structure and functions of management', Special libraries 55(8), Oct 1964, 550-4.

Hall, R H (1972): 'Professionalization and bureaucratization', American sociological review 33(1), Feb 1968, 92-104.

Hamburg, M, and others (1974): Library planning and decision-making systems. MIT Press, 1974.

Hamburg, M, L E Ramist and M R W Bommer (1972): 'Library objectives and performance measures and their use in decision-making', Library quarterly 42(1), Jan 1972, 107-28.

Humble, J (1973): Management by objectives, rev ed. British Institute of Management, 1973.

Hunter, N (1974): A management decision bibliography: library management. MCB (Management Decision) Ltd, 1974.

Johnson, R A and others (1970): Theory and management of systems, 2nd ed. McGraw-Hill, 1970.

Jones, K H (1972): 'Staff deployment', New library world 73(864), June 1972, 320-23.

Likert, R (1961): New patterns of management. McGraw-Hill, 1961.

Line, M (1974): 'Draft definitions: information and library needs, wants, demands and uses', Aslib proceedings 26(2), Feb 1974, 87.

Lumsdon, C A (1975): 'Communication within the organisation: organisational development, team making and informal meetings', Aslib proceedings 27(8), Aug 1975, 327-38.

Lynch, B (1972): 'Participative management in relation to library effectiveness', [with Marchant, M P: 'And a response'], College and research libs 33(5), Sept 1972, 382-97.

McGregor, D (1960): The human side of enterprise. McGraw-Hill, 1960.

Mackenzie, A G (1973): 'Systems analysis as a decision-making tool for the library manager', Library trends 21(4), April 1973, 493-504.

Magson, M S (1973): 'Techniques for the management of cost-benefit in information centres', Aslib proceedings 25(5), May 1973, 164-85.

Mangham, I L, D Shaw and B Wilson (1971): Managing change: a practical guide to organisation development. British Institute of Management, 1971. (Management guide no 3.)

Marchant, M P (1971): 'Participative management as related to personnel development', Library trends 20(1), July 1971, 48-59.

Merton, Robert K (1957): 'Bureaucratic structure and personality', in Etzioni, A: A sociological reader on complex organizations, 2nd ed. Holt, Rinehart and Winston, 1969, 47-59.

Messenger, M (1975): 'Professional staff assessment: the Shropshire pattern', Library Association record 77(1), Jan 1975, 2-4.

Morse, P M (1968): Library effectiveness: a systems approach. MIT Press, 1968.

Noble, P, and P L Ward (1976): Performance measures and criteria for libraries: a survey and bibliography. Public Libraries Research Group, 1976.

Orr, R H (1973): 'Measuring the goodness of library services: a general framework for considering quantitative measures', Journal of documentation 29(3), Sept 1973, 315-32.

Overington, M A (1969): The subject departmentalised public library. Library Association, 1969.

Peele, M R (1972): 'Some aspects of staff appraisal in the UK and the USA', Library Association record 74(4), April 1972, 69-71.

Pugh, D S (1971): Organization theory. Penguin, 1971.

Raffel, J A, and R Shishko (1969): Systematic analysis of university libraries. MIT Press, 1969.

Rayward, W Boyd (1970): 'Bureaucratic organization of libraries', Australian library journal 19(7), August 1970, 245-53.

Reynolds, R (1970): A selective bibliography on measurement in library and information services. Aslib, 1970.

Roberts, N (1973): 'Graduates in academic libraries: a survey of past students of the Post-Graduate School of Librarianship and Information Studies, Sheffield University, 1964/5- 1970/71', Journal of librarianship 5(2), April 1973, 97-115.

Rodwell, John (1975): A review of the recent literature on the assessment of library effectiveness. University of New South Wales School of Librarianship, 1975. (Occasional paper no 1.)

Salten, G (1973): 'Proposals for a dynamic library', Information Pt 2 2(3), 1973, 3-27.

Schein, Edgar H (1970): Organizational psychology, 2nd ed. Prentice Hall, 1970.

Scrivener, J E (1974): 'Subject specialisation in academic libraries— some British practices', Australian academic and research libraries 5(3), Sept 1974, 113-22.

Shera, J H (1972): The foundations of education for librarianship. Becker and Hayes, 1972.

Silverman, David (1970): The theory of organisations. Heinemann, 1970.

Simpson, D J (1968): 'Before the machines come', Aslib proceedings 20(1), Jan 1968, 21-33.

Smith, G C K (1973): 'A general survey of senior and intermediate staff deployment in university libraries', Journal of librarianship 5(2), April 1973, 79-96.

Smith, G C K, and J L Schofield (1971): 'Administrative effectiveness: times and costs of library operations', Journal of librarianship 3(5), Oct 1971, 245-66.

Stecher, G (1975): 'Library evaluation: a brief survey of studies in quantification', Australian academic and research libraries 6(1), March 1975, 1-18.

Thompson, V A (1968): 'The organizational dimension', Wilson Library bulletin 42(7), March 1968, 696.

Unesco Public Library Manifesto (1972): Unesco bulletin for libraries 26(3), May-June 1972, 129-31.

University of Durham (1969): Project for evaluating the benefits from university libraries. Final report. University of Durham, 1969.

Vickery, B C (1972): 'Research by Aslib into costing of information services', Aslib proceedings 24(6), June 1972, 337-341.

Vroom, W H, and E L Deci (1970): Management and motivation. Penguin, 1970.

Wessel, C J (1968): 'Criteria for evaluating technical library effectiveness', Aslib proceedings 20(11), Nov 1968, 455-81.

Whyte, W H (1957): Organization man. Cape, 1957.

Williams, M R (1972): Performance appraisal in management. Heinemann, 1972.

Wilson, T D, and W A J Marsterson (1974): Local library cooperation. Sheffield University, 1974.

Woodburn, I (1969): 'A mathematical model of a hierarchical library system', in Mackenzie, A G, and I M Stuart: Planning library services: proceedings of a seminar held at the University of Lancaster 9-11 July 1969. University of Lancaster Library, 1969. (University of Lancaster Occasional papers no 3.) Or see chapter 4 of Buckland, Hindle, Mackenzie and Woodburn (1970).

Woodhead, P (1974): 'Subject specialisation in three British university libraries', Libri 24(1), 1974, 30-60.